Directing the Story

Directing the Story

Professional Storytelling and Storyboarding Techniques for Live Action and Animation

Francis Glebas

Routledge
Taylor & Francis Group

LONDON AND NEW YORK

First published 2009 by Focal Press

Published 2018 by Routledge
2 Park Square, Milton Park, Abingdon, Oxon OX14 4RN
52 Vanderbilt Avenue, New York, NY 10017, USA

Routledge is an imprint of the Taylor & Francis Group, an informa business

Library of Congress Cataloging-in-Publication Data
Glebas, Francis.
   Directing the story : professional storytelling and storyboarding
techniques for live action and animation / by Francis Glebas.
        p. cm.
   Includes bibliographical references and index.
   ISBN 978-0-240-81076-8 (pbk. : alk. paper) 1. Motion pictures—Production
and direction. 2. Storyboards. I. Title.
   PN1995.9.P7G448 2008
   791.4302′3--dc22

                            2008026270

ISBN-13: 978-1-138-41803-5 (hbk)
ISBN-13: 978-0-240-81076-8 (pbk)
ISBN-13: 978-0-080-92809-8 (ebk)

Printed in Canada

Contents

PART TWO

Preface

Welcome all who wish to learn the secrets of making movies. This book is really the documentation of my trying to learn the real secrets of what makes movies great. When I began teaching, my students gave me feedback that they had never heard of a lot of the things I taught. This surprised me and I decided it was necessary to get the word out. Beware though that once you open these pages, watching movies will never be the same again.

> The classical Hollywood style ... asks that form be rendered invisible; that the viewer see only the presence of actors in an unfolding story that seems to be existing on its own; that the audience be embraced by the story, identify with it and its participants. Unlike montage and the long take, the continuity style was neither theorized nor analyzed (not by people who developed and used it, at least); its rules were developed intuitively and pragmatically through the early years of filmmaking. The continuity style developed because it worked, and its working was measured by the fact that it allowed filmmakers to make stories that audiences responded to with ease and with desire. They liked what they saw and wanted more.[1]

In my review of the literature, the classical Hollywood style was never fully analyzed, until now. So what is unique about my teaching? I began by asking myself what it is that the audience is doing when they watch a film. I then proceeded to create strategies to address this when making a film. Here's what the viewers do:

1. First, they pay attention to the screen.
2. They perceive what is being shown and identify what things are.
3. Then they read the signs as characters are performing actions. They are following the story and starting to identify with the characters they like.
4. Then they start to make connections as to what it all means.
5. Then they guess what will happen next and where it is leading.
6. Then they worry about the characters and the outcome, continually adjusting their hypothesis according to new information provided.
7. Finally, when the film ends, they should feel the emotional closure of surprise and vindication that it ended the way they thought but not in the way they expected.

What is very interesting is number four. Once the audience starts to connect the pieces of what the story events mean, they start to feel emotions. This was an amazing discovery: *Meaning automatically evokes emotions!*

Francis Glebas
Phd. in Fantasy

Reference

1. Hill, J. and P. Gibson. *Film Studies*. New York: Oxford University Press, 2000.

Acknowledgments

I could not have created this book without the generous help of my many mentors and guides. I would like to thank Dr. Alwyn Scott, Dr. Felisha Kaplan, Dr. Marlene Kasman, Dr. Elena Bonn, Dr. Milton Erikson, Anthony Robbins, Gregory Bateson, Jacques Lacan, Slavoj Zizek, and George Lakoff for teaching me how to think. My fellow artists Ed Gombert, Bill Perkins, Dan Cooper, Fred Warter, Vance Gerry, Walt Stanchfield, Sterling Sheehy, Jean Gillmore, Larry Scholl, and Dante Barbetta for teaching me to paint and draw. I would like to thank all my students who have taught me while I was engaged in teaching them. I wish to thank all those who gave me opportunities in the film business: Michelle Pappalardo Robinson, Donovan Cook, Norton Virgien, Mike Gabriel, Eric Goldberg, Kirk Wise, Gary Trousdale, Roger Allers, Rob Minkoff, Kathleen Gavin, Tom Schumacher, Sharon Morill, Roy Disney, Jeffrey Katzenberg, Charlie Fink, and Tom Ruzicka. I would especially like to thank Ron Clemens and John Musker for believing in me when I was just starting out. The following people gave me opportunities to teach and develop the material for this book: Jack Bossom, Tenny Chonin, Alex Topeti, Ed Oboza, Pam Hogarth, Kristin Bierschbach, Alegria Castro, Peggy Van Pelt, and Toni Pace.

In making this book a reality, I wish to thank my editor, Georgia Kennedy, and the crew at Focal Press, Chris Simpson, Lianne Hong, and Dennis Schaefer. Nancy Beiman read the material with a fine-tooth comb and helped me clarify concepts and take out the "fluff." She would probably tell me to cut this part. Toni Vain helped give the book a vision in its very early stages. My film editor, Ivan Balanciano, worked with me as I experimented with learning different editing approaches. I would like to thank the students who helped clean up some the illustrations: Jessica Dru, Aernout Van Pallandt, Karen Yan, Rajbir Singh, and Joan LaPallo.

Finally, I especially wish to thank my friends and family for believing in me and teaching me how to live and love: Doug, Joan, Toni, Tatty, and my parents. A great thanks and love for my wife, Carolyn, and son, Ryan, for going on this journey with me.

Part One

The Goal: Why Do We Watch?

Why Do We Watch Movies?

This is the first question I ask my film students: "Why do we watch movies?" Most of them have never thought to ask this question. They think about it, raise their hands, and start suggesting answers.

There are many reasons why we all watch movies, and as my students comment, I write their answers on the chalkboard. There is the wish to share experiences with the characters and our friends. We watch to learn all kinds of things. We watch to see spectacles. We get to see other worlds that we'll never go to. We want to hear a good story. Someone suggests we watch to escape. Escape what? "Boredom!" comes the answer, and the students laugh. But why do they laugh? Maybe there's a clue there.

The most interesting answer to this question that I always get, without fail, is, "We watch to be entertained." To this I always answer, "Yes, that's true." Okay, now we know that we watch movies to be entertained. Then, I challenge them, "Can knowing that we watch movies to be entertained help us become better filmmakers?" They unanimously agree that it doesn't help. It really doesn't tell us anything useful except to point out a direction. But we don't have a map. We have to dig deeper and chart out the territory ourselves, and that's what we'll do in this book. We're going to dig deeper until we get some answers that provide us with specific tools and techniques to "entertain" our audience. So our question is: What is entertainment? Well that reminds me of a story. ...

1001 Nights of Entertainment

We're going to take a trip in our imagination. I'd like you to read this paragraph, and then take a slow deep breath and close your eyes. I wonder if you can imagine that you have been invited to a wonderful paradise. If you're a skier, then it could be high up in the Alps. Can you feel the cold, brisk wind blowing the fresh snow powder in your face? If you love beaches, it's your own private beach with a perfect surf break mixing in with the ocean roar and the seagull cries overhead. Maybe you prefer a jungle with the smells of exotic flowers and interesting animals crawling around. Take a moment to imagine how it feels. What do you see? What sounds do you hear? How does it feel, such as the temperature? Take a moment to entertain the fantasy. After you do this, hit the "pause" button on your imagination and come back.

It feels wonderful, doesn't it? But do we have a story? No, so far we merely have a fun fantasy. How long would you be willing to watch this onscreen? A minute? Five minutes? My guess is not that long before you're wondering when something is going to happen.

Let's go back to the fantasy now, and I'll give you some more information. The powerful ruler has summoned you—just you—to this paradise and magnificent palace. Hit "pause" again. Any story yet? Well now we have some questions. Why did she summon you? What does she want? Still no story yet, but we're getting warm.

Hit "play" and go back to your imagination. There's something I forgot to mention. It's kind of important, and I just thought you should know: The ruler who summoned you is crazy. Yes, you heard right, he is planning to kill you in the morning. Quick, hit "pause" again.

Do we have a story now? Almost—we certainly have some tension and conflict. These introduce the beginnings of a story.

Hit "play." What do you do? Your mind races as you search for solutions. Escape is impossible—guards are everywhere. What if you tried to explain to the ruler that killing is wrong? She's crazy, remember? Explanations won't change a crazy person. Unfortunately, logic and facts don't even persuade normal people. If you've ever tried to change someone's religious or political beliefs, you'll know how totally useless logic is. What else could you do? Maybe you could try to seduce the ruler, make her fall in love with you. But, alas, you discover that she was once betrayed in love and that's exactly why she has gone crazy. Got any more ideas?

You're faced with a crazy ruler who's going to kill you in the morning. What do you do? Hit the "pause" button on your imagination? Pray tomorrow never comes? No, simply take a deep breath and begin with the magic words, "Once upon a time...." Yes, you tell a story. This is exactly what Scheherazade did in *One Thousand and One Arabian Nights*.

The story goes something like this: In a mythical land there once was a powerful sultan king whose wife betrayed him. This broke his heart, so in order never to suffer this pain of betrayal again, each night he would take a new bride and then have her killed at dawn. He was a powerful ruler, but not the best problem solver.

The king's madness was destroying his kingdom, so Scheherazade decided to put a stop to it. She would become the sultan's next bride. Her father was very dismayed at hearing this, but trusted his daughter and agreed to the proposal.

The night that Scheherazade met the king, she had a secret plot with her sister Dunyazade. As the wedding night grew late, according to their prior arranged plan, Dunyazade was to ask the king a favor. Since this would be the last night that she would ever see her sister, Dunyazade asked the sultan king if she could hear one of Scheherazade's wondrous stories. Seeing no harm in this innocent request, the sultan agreed. Scheherazade began to weave her magic using words that described great adventures. As she told her tale to Dunyazade, the sultan listened too, and without realizing, he became captivated by Scheherazade's spell.

But this isn't the end of Scheherazade's story, for she still had to face the coming dawn. What would she do? She left her imaginary hero and heroine hanging from the edge of a cliff and pronounced that it was getting late. You see, Scheherazade knew the magical secrets of storytelling—they're driven by questions. Her secret is ... wait, I can't tell you yet. Let's continue to discover what happened to Scheherazade.

Scheherazade knew that the sultan king was burning to know what happened to the hero and heroine who were left hanging on a cliff. Instead of having her killed the following morning, the sultan waited until the next night to hear the continuation of the tale. He wanted to find out what would happen next. Her secret plot had worked. Scheherazade's storytelling continued for 1001 nights, during which the sultan was transformed. He and Scheherazade lived happily ever after, and the kingdom was saved.

How did the sultan king change? Well, Scheherazade knew that a storyteller is kind of like a ventriloquist. It appears that the ventriloquist dummy has a life of its own—just like a story. A dummy can say outrageous things, and, since it appears that it's the dummy speaking, can get away with it. A story functions in the same way: It appears to unfold all by itself while actually developing through the storyteller's art. Scheherazade knew exactly what she wanted to say to the sultan and she knew how to say it to him. She used the form of a story, and like a great weaver, she wove ideas about morals seamlessly into her tales of high adventure. She chose themes about right and wrong and being able to trust people and embedded these concepts into her tales. She wasn't telling the sultan that killing was wrong; her stories were demonstrating it right before his eyes. If she had just told the sultan that killing was wrong, she would have been killed. If she said "trust me," she'd have been killed even sooner. Instead, in the guise of telling her sister the tales of great adventure, she was able to convey her real message. When the sultan lived the experience of the story, over 1001 nights' time, it transformed him. She was a master ventriloquist. Her stories appeared to tell themselves, and the sultan got lost in them, and in them he found himself.

When I'm nervous about pitching a story, I always remember Scheherazade. She's an incredible inspiration. That's why I chose to use her story to demonstrate the principles and techniques that we're going to learn here. Luckily, if you or I don't tell a good story, we won't be killed. Sometimes it feels like we will be though. But, that's what is at stake in storytelling—nothing less than life and death.

But wait, you ask, what about the secret of storytelling? I told you already that you have to wait. Read on and you will learn Scheherazade's secrets of storytelling—storyboarding, the magic of visual storytelling.

What follows in these pages is the true account of what happened on those mythical nights, "once upon a time." It is presented just as Scheherazade offered it to the sultan king with all of the learning, doubts, obstacles, and fears that it took her to become a storyteller—a transformer of lives. A few liberties were taken with the story so that events of the tale can better demonstrate Scheherazade's storytelling secrets. The Scheherazade story is presented in storyboard form with commentary on how the boards demonstrate the principles in the text.

When you watch a movie, you have to watch it twice before you can really analyze it. This is because if the filmmakers have done their job correctly, you get "lost in the story," just as the sultan did. You can't be paying attention to how it's constructed because you're involved in following the story. We'll soon see what an active process following the story actually is. You need to watch a movie a second time, when you already know what's going to happen, so you can begin to analyze how it is put together. Ironically, it's easier to learn about visual storytelling from bad movies than great classics. With a classic film, the story appears seamless. It's designed to be that way, and later we'll learn why. With a bad movie, mistakes are obvious and the seams show, making it easier to see what not to do. With this is mind, I recommend that you read Scheherazade's story more than once in order to clearly see the principles and techniques at work in the visual storytelling.

Scheherazade knew she had to grab the sultan's interest and never let it go. But she also had to keep him excited about the story. Where did she get ideas? Was she a naturally gifted storyteller? Did she know some esoteric or obscure secrets? No, she simply asked questions. That almost sounds too easy, but it's true. She asked, "What if …?" What if the character tied this or that? What could happen next, and so on? What would happen if …? She learned that her unconscious mind would answer her questions, automatically. Asking a question sets off an unconscious search (we'll learn about this later). It's our brains' job to answer it. All she had to do was set up a character in a quest, throw obstacles in the way, and ask herself what she would do. Then all she needed to do was relax and let her mind play with it. No forcing, interfering, or judging. She just had to listen and the answers would come; the answers might be disguised or in need of some refining, but they would come. They will come for you too. It just takes some practice.

As a storyteller she had to make an implicit pledge that if the sultan followed along on the journey, he would be rewarded. She needed to present a character with whom he could identify with on his quest. He could imagine that he himself was on the journey. To keep the sultan's continued interest she would have to keep topping herself and keep the sultan guessing as to whether each character would succeed or fail in his or her quest. Another one of her tricks was to sometimes allow the sultan more knowledge than the characters knew themselves. When he knew more than the characters did, he was led to anticipate horrible things that might happen to them.

What's at Stake Is Nothing Less Than Life and Death

The most important thing about making a movie is that it *must* be about something big, important, and significant. Otherwise, why should we care? Even if it's about the friendship of two little frogs, it has to say something important and timeless about friendship. It has to speak to something that we can all relate to, perhaps how taking their friendship for granted led to the loss of their friendship. Something has to be at stake. It doesn't have to be a big story. It does have to have big issues, such as family, fatherhood, motherhood, honor, the law, crime and punishment, prejudice, wealth and poverty, freedom, understanding, pleasure, spirit and body, guilt, war, sickness and health, and love and hate. Stories answer the big questions in life. How can we find love? Can love conquer fear? Where did we come from? What does it all mean? You need to find the universal in the particulars of your story.

Once you know what your story is, you have to show your audience what's at stake. Don't tell your audience. You have to show them what's at stake if the mission fails. According to psychological research, "studies suggest that three days after an event, people retain 10% of what they heard from an oral presentation, 35% from a visual presentation, and 65% from a visual and oral presentation."[1] We also remember things better when we are emotionally involved.[2] Show the audience why your characters are absolutely driven to do what they do. Characters drive stories, like characters who go after a goal and face obstacles, make decisions, and then take actions of life-changing consequences. If they don't, you better create new characters that do. We follow their actions emotionally through the ups and down of the plot.

You have to promise your audience that it will be worth it for them to follow the journey and the emotions of the characters. In order to make the journey worthwhile it must be difficult for the characters. No, make it impossible for them. Create obstacles in the way of the character's goal. This is how the characters grow and how stories become interesting. Remember how our fantasy changed when you found out that what appeared to be paradise was a living nightmare? We're going to see how the audience is going to go along on this journey as active participants.

Dramatization through Questions

Drama involves exaggeration. It takes ordinary events and brings out qualities to show how significant they are. While it might not literally be about life or death, at least it has to feel that way to the characters. A story about a little boy with a crush on a girl is not a matter of life or death. But that is exactly how it feels to the boy. Anyone who has ever watched teenagers knows that many things qualify to signify the end of their worlds.

A simple dramatic form would be the classic three-part case of boy meets girl, boy loses girl, and boy gets girl back—happy ending. What makes this dramatic form work? We have a situation about a character, the boy. He meets a girl. Then we create a problem or conflict—he loses the girl. This can happen in any number of ways. Then we have a solution to the problem—through his actions, he gets the girl back. All of these actions are interrelated as a series of causes and effects. One character acts and that causes other actions, which in turn causes more reactions. Achieving any goal often involves a trial-and-error process of learning what works and what does not. The unique aspect that makes this story worthy is that it all has to be interconnected as a sequence of cause-and-effect actions.

Tell stories about characters we care about going through intensely challenging experiences that we can vicariously live through, wanting to know what will happen to them. We have a vested interest. The characters have to act in ways that get themselves into trouble and then have to act to get themselves out of it, like the boy going after the girl. We present this to our audience in the form of questions and then provide imaginative answers.

Storyboarding is a tool for the visual planning of a movie. It is the rewriting of a written script into a visual plan. It's telling a story through a series of pictures. Directing is the process of magically turning pages of script into exciting sequences of action that "entertain" an audience. People in the film business often say that a film is made in the editing process. Storyboarding is the first pass at directing and editing a film. It's the most important step and should be created before one frame of film is shot.

The storyboards presented in this book are just as they would be in the actual making of a movie. Artists first work out ideas in a rough form, and then, once the story is working, the drawings are polished. You'll see drawings in all stages of finish throughout this book.

1001 Nights Entertainment Revisited

As you read, think about what you're expecting to happen in the story. Were the expectations met? If not, how did the story differ? Were your expectations met, but not how to develop your storytelling muscles?

A long time ago, in a far off place, there was a sultan king who each day would marry a new bride, and on each following morning as the sun rose, she would mysteriously disappear. On this particular day a girl would come who would change the sultan's life forever. That girl was called Scheherazade.

Lightning flashes.

A door opens …

Light spills out.

A nervous figure comes out.

He motions to those inside.

A girl comes out …

And quickly descends the stairs.

Her family follows.

They join others leaving the city.

The mass exodus encounters two figures …

Going the opposite way.

The girl approaches them.

She looks …

And intently watches.

Scheherazade meets her gaze.

She smiles at the girl.

GIRL: "Mother, that was Scheherazade."

MOTHER: "Maybe there is hope after all."

Scheherazade and Dunazade, her sister, continue toward the palace.

Dunazade tries to persuade her sister to stop her insane quest.

DUNAZADE: "What makes you think the sultan will listen to you?"

DUNAZADE: "They say he's gone crazy!"

SCHEHERAZADE: "What if the sultan chose that girl as his next bride? Or even you?"

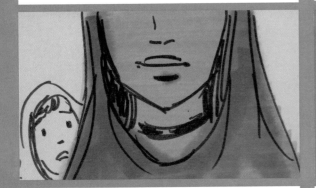

SCHEHERAZADE: "Just stick to our plan."

Dunazade races to catch up.

The palace beckons them.

They stop to stare at the palace.

[Music swells.]

The palace looms overhead.

BEGGAR: "Beware! Beware!"

The sisters are startled.

BEGGAR: "Do not dare to enter the palace. It's a place of death."

BEGGAR: "Turn around and return from whence you came."

BEGGAR: "He's raving mad!"

SCHEHERAZADE: "Be gone."

BEGGAR: "Beware of the voices. They'll haunt you too."

They ignore this warning and continue on.

They climb the palace steps.

They arrive at the gates …

As they open for them.

Now in storyboard form, we are going to see how one girl, Scheherazade, goes through this process of intensely challenging experiences, while at the same time struggling to tell a good story—she better, her life depends on it.

The descriptions under the panels are what the storyboard artist might say when he or she pitches the storyboard sequence. Normally only the dialogue is written under the drawings on separate slips of paper. This allows the dialogue to be easily repositioned.

Critique: Is It Too Late to Turn Back?

Scheherazade has taken on the task of providing the sultan with emotionally satisfying experiences with her stories. What do we know so far? What narrative questions have been raised? What have you been led to expect?

We know Scheherazade is going against the tide in her determination to stop the sultan from having any more disappearances. This is her want. If she fails she will disappear. This is what's at stake. Scheherazade faces overwhelming obstacles symbolized by the magnificent scale of the palace of the sultan king. In this way she is already the underdog. We can root for her and admire her determination, but is she too self-confident?

Let's look at some of the things we're visualizing in the storyboards.

While Scheherazade and her sister Dunyazade walk through the dungy marketplace to the magnificent palace of the sultan, Dunyazade tries to persuade her sister using logic to give up the crazy plan. Scheherazade's emotional quest to save any more of her friends from disappearing is stronger than any logic that her sister can summon forth. She has to become the sultan's next bride to stop his madness. This is what is at stake. She tells her sister just to keep to the plan. Dunyazade continues to protest until Scheherazade asks what if the sultan chose her, Dunyazade, to be his doomed bride. Now it hits home emotionally for Dunyazade and she agrees to continue the plan.

In this scene the blocking and camera work visually tell the story. The camera continually pulls back tracking the sisters' progress through the marketplace. Scheherazade walks directly toward the camera, representing that she has a clearly defined goal. Her sister zigzags in and out trying to stop her. The camera allows us to identify with Scheherazade's action and quest. Her quest has become our quest.

The people are fleeing through the crowded marketplace. This shows the audience the location and sets the mood, but it also starts right in with action. Always start right in the middle of the dramatic action. Don't make the audience wait to see if something is going to happen. Why are they leaving? Present any backstory information dramatically. Backstory is information the audience needs in order to make sense of the story. When we see Scheherazade fighting her way against the crowd, we know something is different about this girl. We don't know what yet, but we want to find out. Is she determined or just crazy? Already in a few shots we have intriguing questions.

We create a dramatic reveal of the palace and almost immediately interrupt it with the warnings from the beggar. This suggests that the palace is not what it seems. It also ramps up the stakes: Scheherazade's life is on the line.

Entertainment Explained

So once again we return to our question: Why do we watch? Before we answer, let's look at why anyone does anything. In Tony Robbins' CD series, *Personal Power II*, he explains, "Ultimately, everything we do in our lives is driven by our fundamental need to avoid pain and our desire to gain pleasure; both are biologically driven and constitute a controlling force in our lives."[3]

But wait, didn't we just learn that film is about tension and conflict? Tension and conflict are painful and we want to avoid them. We want to avoid pain and gain pleasure in that order. Why would anybody go to the movies? Well a character learning to avoid pain is a learning experience. In watching them we can learn what not to do. Learning how to avoid pain itself is pleasurable.

Have you ever had the experience of really having to work hard for something that you really wanted? When you finally got it you cherished it all the more. Why is that? It's because you appreciated it because you knew what went into getting it. You wanted something, lived with the tension of wanting it, and then finally got it and it felt even better. This is known as delayed gratification. Movies provide this kind of gratification. At the end all of the questions are answered, and our characters get what they wanted and it feels good.

Let's look at some of the other reasons we watch. Why do we want to see other worlds? Because it feels good. Why do we want to share our experiences with others? Because it feels good. Why do we like to watch characters struggle? Because it feels good. So the bottom line is that we watch movies to feel good. In more formal language, we watch to have an emotionally satisfying and meaningful experience. But as we'll learn, there are other pleasures along the way that the audience gets to experience.

The audience is your customer—give them what they want. First we lead them into what to expect. But what would happen if you just gave them what they expected? They'd get bored, because it would be predictable. You have to give them what they want, but not in the way they expected it. There have to be surprises along the way.

How do you make the audience feel good? How do you make a film emotional? You can't just put raw emotions on the screen. It doesn't work that way. If you do, your audience might experience the wrong emotion.

Let's say you show a bunch of people crying. That won't necessarily make the audience feel sad; in fact, it might provoke laughter. In my story class we watched a movie about an ogre who was ridiculed. She was very sad and began to cry. The student had set up the scene well and the audience was touched. But then the ogre kept on crying and crying and this went on for a long time. Slowly the class started to laugh. Even though it was probably only 30 seconds, it went on for too long.

You can't put raw emotions directly on the screen and expect the audience to feel the same feeling.

You can show people laughing but that won't necessarily make an audience think it's funny. They might laugh contagiously for a while. If it goes on too long they might get angry. Why? The audience will feel left out, like they're not in on the joke. That's the key: The audience has to be brought to the place where they can understand why someone is crying, or clue them in so they can get the joke when everyone is laughing. Bringing an audience to that place is the journey of the story.

So far we've learned that we watch movies to feel good. How do you make your audience feel good? Since we can't put emotions directly on screen, what can we do? As a director, David Mamet points out, "All you can do is take pictures."[4] So how do we meet the spectator's goal? Dr. Alwyn Scott gave his students great advice when he told them to aim for the heart by working at a structural level.[5] That's the path we're going to take. We're going to take it one step at a time, with each step building on the previous step to develop an easily remembered structure that will help you give your audience an emotionally satisfying experience. We'll do this by structuring the elements of film thematically using the only thing we have: images made of light and shadow, words, and sounds. It's taken me years to fully understand how to do this and there's still more to learn.

Opportunity from Criticism

I was working as a storyboard artist at Walt Disney Feature Animation and wanted to get feedback about my work. I went and asked my boss how I was doing. His response was that I was doing fine, however, sometimes my storyboards were "emotionally cool." This cut me to the quick. The heart and soul of filmmaking is emotions, and here I was being told mine were unemotional.

The meeting ended and I felt hurt. Then I felt angry. Then I made a decision. I could shrug it off, but instead I used it as a learning opportunity. He was right, and I would correct it. It became my challenge. I was working on *Pocahontas* at the time. The end was very flat like the ending of a summer camp movie, "See you next summer." *Pocahontas* was to be Disney's first ending not to be "happy ever after." How could I still give the audience an emotionally satisfying experience? His criticism had given me the seeds of opportunity.

The next time that I saw him in the hall I made a promise to him: "I won't be satisfied until I make you cry." I'll continue this story in a while, but before I do, we know that the audience wants to feel good. But what are they doing while waiting to feel good?

What Is the Audience Doing?

I used to watch Jeffrey Katzenberg (at the time, head of Disney Animation) watch story reels.* His comments were like a laser beam, always right on target. Other people's comments were all over the map. I often wondered how he did it. From little things that he said I pieced together the following fantasy of what he was doing. He sat and watched the movie imagining that his kids were sitting next to him, and he would take notice whether they were glued to the screen or were fidgeting around needing to go the bathroom or get popcorn. In other words, he was thinking about the film, *not* from the filmmaker's point of view, but rather that of the audience's. He was asking if he was bored or confused, and these, of course as we shall learn, are the two enemies of good design. He was also well acquainted with the story being thoroughly versed in every stage of the script process.

This became my point of view to study film. "What is the audience doing?" became my second most important question. "Why do we watch?" and "What is the audience doing?" are the two questions that shaped this book.

Reverse-Engineering Approach

What's going on in the mind, body, heart, and soul of the audience every 1/24 of a second? We're going to learn about how the mind works, about how we see, and how the mind processes information and how it creates emotions. Once we know what the mind is doing watching movies, we'll work backward to know how to utilize that information as a way to structure our movies for maximum impact because we'll know what to aim for. This is known as a reverse-engineering approach, working backward by carefully examining the relationship of all the parts.

Let's take a closer look as what the audience is doing. The common assumption is that they're sitting in the dark, eating popcorn, just watching the movie. Nothing could be further from the truth. The audience is not passive. Even before they get to the theater or turn on the TV they are creating a set of expectations about what they will see.

James Elkins describes the "just looking" part of the process in his book, *The Object Stares Back*. "When I say, 'Just looking,' I mean I am searching, I have my 'eye out' for something. Looking is hoping, desiring, never just taking in light, never merely collecting patterns and data. Looking is possessing or the desire to possess—we eat food, we own objects, we "possess" bodies; there is no looking without thoughts of using, possessing, repossessing, owning, fixing, appropriating, keeping, remembering, commemorating, cherishing, borrowing, and stealing. I cannot look at anything—any object, any person—without the shadow of the thought of possessing that thing. Those appetites don't just accompany looking; they are looking itself."[6]

Why Do We Watch and More …

What we need to know is not only why we watch but also what the audience is doing when they watch. What's going on in their minds? The answers to these questions will serve to guide us. Let's imagine a man watching a movie about a man and a dog. We're going to get inside his head and see what happens when he watches the movie. Let's go to the movies; but we're not going to watch the screen, we're going to watch the audience.

---

* A story reel is a version of a movie using just storyboard drawings complete with dialogue and musical score.

VIEWER: *"When's this gonna start?"* Your audience is not just sitting there eating popcorn. In a mode of anxious expectation, they're looking forward to an exciting story.

VIEWER: *"It's starting. Shhhh."* The lights go down and the screen comes alive with images. The first thing that the audience does is focus their attention on the screen.

VIEWER: *"Hey. Focus. Focus!"* Secondly, they visually hunt for information. Hunting is a very appropriate metaphor for what they are doing. They have to be able to find and clearly see the images.

VIEWER: *"What is that? It looks like a man with a sack."* Once we can see the images, we identify the things we see on the screen. We read these images one at a time just like a string of words.

VIEWER: *"Now, the man's climbing the tree."* We narrate to ourselves what we see, translating the pictures into words and constructing a story in our heads. Guessing what might happen.

VIEWER: *[Offscreen dog bark] "There's the dog. I bet the dog chased him up the tree."* Even without all the facts, we're trying to put what we see together into a meaningful story. Like solving a puzzle, we test our "theories" to see if all the pieces fit.

VIEWER: *[Train horn] "What's that sound?"* The audience continues visually hunting, now searching for clues to the answers to their questions.

VIEWER: *"It's a train coming right at us!"* We participate "as if" we were there, just as if we were experiencing it, kind of like we're dreaming it.

VIEWER: *"Duck!!!"*

VIEWER: "What's that man doing now?" We're given just enough information to hold us in suspense. We're engaged with trying to discover what we don't yet know, and fearing what might happen.

VIEWER: "Oh no! He must have put the dog in the sack and he's putting it on the train track." We fear that the worst might happen, and yet we hope for the best. We continually swing back and forth between hope and fear.

VIEWER: "He must have hated that dog." We attribute motivation to characters. We decide whether we like or dislike the characters and decide for ourselves if they're good or bad.

VIEWER: "That poor dog, what did he ever do?" We feel for the characters and worry about them as if they were our friends.

VIEWER: "Oh no! Here comes the train! I can't watch!" We're led to expect certain things, in other words, it begins to mean something for us.

VIEWER: "Is it over?" When we learn what something means, we feel emotions. It happens automatically.

VIEWER: [Sound of train] "He's laughing. How cruel. I wish he would get hit by the train!" Justice is a powerful driving force in storytelling. We all have an internal sense of justice and want revenge for those who do bad things.

VIEWER: "What's that man doing now? Oh, he's eating the pieces. That's horrible." Dog barks!

VIEWER: "Wait, there's the dog!" When the worst doesn't happen, we experience relief. We keep watching to see what's going to happen next.

17

VIEWER: "Then what was in the bag? It's apples. He was making applesauce! Now everything makes sense."   The new pieces of the story change the meaning of what we've seen. This new version replaces the story that we thought was happening.

VIEWER [Laughing]: We experience tremendous relief, when what we feared, didn't happen. In other words, it feels good. The goal is met.

VIEWER: "Did you see that? I knew that was going to happen."   We want to share our experience with others.

VIEWER: "When I see a film, I want it to end the way I want, but in a way that I never would have guessed."   We want stories that fulfill our expectations and fantasies and at the same time surprise us in ways we could have never have dreamed of.

VIEWER: "I can't wait to see another one."   Once all the questions that were raised in the story are answered, the story is over and we feel closure.

Remember the storytelling advice of the March Hare: "Start at the beginning, and when you get to the end, stop." Source: Walt Disney's Alice in Wonderland, 1951.

As you have just seen, the audience isn't just sitting there passively watching. They're actively engaged in the story, creating it for themselves in their head, and we've gotten a glimpse of what they do when they watch. Based on this information, we're going to construct our map of what we need to know to tell clear dramatic stories.

The first thing the audience does is bring their expectations, and pay attention hoping to have their expectations met by the story. We have to tell and show them the story in a way that meets their expectations and more.

Second, they have to see the images clearly. This is the realm of design, composition, perspective, and lighting. They have to be able to see what is happening or they won't be able to follow the story.

Third, the audience reads the images. They see characters, things, and signs in movement and action. We have to choose what to show them and to show how it's significant. This is the domain of the science of signs, which studies how signs signify meaning for us.

Fourth, the audience constructs the story in their head assigning meaning to what they see. We have to help them follow the story. This is the realm of editing and cause-and-effect sequencing to maintain suspense. Here we'll also look at the larger structures of storytelling such as the three-act structure or the hero's journey.

Next, meaning evokes emotions. When the audience is led to expect certain outcomes, they automatically feel things. This is the area of identifying with the characters and the point of view of the story. We'll also look at specific genres of emotion to see what makes them tick. Finally, with closure of all the narrative questions, they feel validation, closure, and relief.

Now all of these processes don't happen one after another; many of them overlap and affect each other. We're not even aware of most of it going on; it happens outside of our awareness. We're "lost in the events of the story" and wondering what's going to happen next.

Promise to the Reader: Intuition Illuminated!

There's a problem with the first time you try anything. Since you haven't done it, you don't have any experience to draw upon, so it becomes a process of trial and error. Unfortunately, most people who I have encountered who teach film-making or storyboarding use an intuitive approach. This is great if you have experience. But if you don't, then you have to use trial and error and make lots of mistakes. Wait, let's call them "learning opportunities." I do believe that the way to learn directing and storyboarding is to make storyboards and make movies. There is no substitute for that experience. But there are tactics and techniques you can use to help your chances of making your audience feel good. Now that you know the goal, you're off to a great start.

I believe that you can and will learn many skills by working through this book. You'll have Scheherazade as your companion along the way. In the beginning it will be like learning to walk. There is so much to pay attention to all at once that you'll probably fall a few times. But eventually you did learn how to walk and now you can do it without thinking about it. Once you have mastered these skills you can forget them because you will have the experience to intuitively make movies that are emotionally powerful. Then you can use these techniques as analytic tools to polish what your heart brings forth.

Scheherazade knew the secret of storytelling. Remember that I told you that you have to wait? *That is the secret: You have to wait.*

The Secret of Storytelling Is Story-Delaying

Scheherazade used exciting cliffhangers to prolong her life from one night to the next. There's a whole repertoire of story-delaying techniques based on the control of the flow of information of who gets to know what, when, and how. Scheherazade would tell a story about a character who would tell a story and then that character would tell a story—she'd embed one story within another, within another, within another, and so on. Once I counted story levels six deep.

Getting back to my boss's comment, the result of the *Pocahontas* screening was that there was not a dry eye in the house. I felt vindicated and learned a valuable lesson. You have to put your heart into your work, whether it is comedy, drama, horror, action, or romance. That's our goal.

Remember the class comment that we watch movies to escape boredom and everyone laughed? That was a great clue. We want to avoid boredom. We want excitement in our lives. We watch movies to feel alive, and yes, that feels good.

Join Scheherazade's journey and learn how to make powerfully emotional stories with specific tools, techniques, and tactics, just as you will promise your audience that if they follow the threads of your story, then they will have an emotionally satisfying experience that makes them feel alive!

Scheherazade knew another profound secret about why we watch: *We're made of stories.* Dan P. McAdams believes that we create ourselves through narrative: "If you want to know me, then you must know my story."[7]

POINTS TO REMEMBER

- We watch movies to feel good. Meet that need in your audience.
- Make sure your story is about something that matters.
- Aim at providing an emotionally satisfying experience for your audience, but work at the structural level.
- The secret of storytelling is story-delaying. Learn the different tactics to tease your audience by making them wait.
- The next time you're at a movie pay attention to what experiences you are going through as you watch. Notice what triggers your emotions.

References

1. Occupational Safety and Health Administration. "Presenting Effective Presentations with Visual Aids." OSHA, U.S. Department of Labor, Washington, DC: May 1996.
2. Dryden, G., and J. Vos. *The Learning Revolution*. Jalmar Press, 1999.
3. Robbin, Tony. *Personal Power II*. Robbins Research International Inc., 1996.
4. Mamet, D. *On Directing Film*. Penguin Books, New York: 1992.
5. Scott, A. *Vocabulary of the Media Critic Class*. Institute of Technology, New York, 1992.
6. Elkins, J. *The Object Stares Back*. Simon & Schuster, New York: 1996.
7. McAdams D. *The Stories We Live By: Personal Myths and the Making of the Self*. Guilford Press, 1997.

Common Beginner Problems

Where Do You Begin?

We need images that can clearly tell a story. Most beginners do not think in story terms when they draw. Common drawing problems do arise. For example, drawing a high-angle look into box viewpoints doesn't invite your viewer to identify with the characters, but many beginning artists will choose this viewpoint. When I started drawing I did this too. Why do people draw this view looking down into the room? Do they wish they were a bird?

Don't we normally see things like this second view? Why don't most people draw like this?

It is easy to learn how to fix these types of problems. However, telling the story using pictures is the harder part of the job.

How do we learn to tell stories? We tell stories from life experiences. I went here and we did this, then we did that. We've been doing it all of our lives since we learned to speak. We tell many stories every day throughout our lives. Over time we've fine-tuned our storytelling so that we can make ourselves understood by others. The story form is how we organize our experiences.

Most of us, however, have not had the same amount of experience or need to tell visual stories in everyday life. Verbal communication is much more efficient and quicker. Although we don't remember it, we did have to learn how to tell verbal stories. *The skills involved in how*

Why do we draw from a bird's point of view?

This is the way we normally view people. (Credit: Art by Jessica Dru.)

to present a story visually also have to be learned. Daily life doesn't teach this skill. Drawing itself is usually seen as a skill you're either born with or not.

Movies are consciously designed to appear seamless. This makes it harder to analyze how they're put together. We have also learned that you have to watch a movie at least twice before you can really analyze it, because on first viewing, people are "lost" in the story. It's often easier to learn what not to do by watching bad movies because the flaws are visible. Where can you learn how to put together visual stories?

The Catch-22 of the Character-Driven Intuitive Approach

When I was learning about storyboarding I always heard the phrase that the story has to be "character driven." I still hear it all the time. What is a character-driven story? A character-driven story is one in which the desires of the characters drive them to take actions and these actions are what drives the story. Is there any other kind of story you may ask? The opposite of a character-driven story is one that is plot driven. This is where the sequence of actions is decided independent of characters. In actuality, most stories are a mixture of the two.

What do your characters want? This question is what drives the character-driven story. When we "identify" with a character, we're really identifying with the process of him or her wanting something. In this way we can identify with characters who are in many ways unlike us physically or emotionally. They may be a lion, an alien, or a mermaid but we all have the same desires.

Characters have to take action to get what they desire. It's these actions that lead characters into trouble based on their personalities. Most characters are presented as not knowing how to deal with their desires. That's why we can relate to them. They have to use their own skills and learn new ones to solve their problems. This is very powerful. Plot and characters are interconnected but the characters have to be active. In a sense, they are the ones driving the story.

According to Harold Innis, author of *The Bias of Communication*,[1] each medium has it's own strengths and weaknesses. It has aspects it can represent well and other aspects that get lost in translation. Novels excel at depicting what people think. Plays are really good at portraying dialogue. Movies don't deal with people's internal dialogue the way a novel can. They also don't represent people speaking with the depth that they do in plays. What can movies do well? Movies, like the name implies, move! Lights, camera, action! Movies show people in action. We watch movies to see what people do. Specifically, we watch to see what they do under pressure—extreme pressure—and why they do it.

So character-driven stories are about characters taking action to get what they want. So what's the problem? The problem is that while the drives of characters are crucial, it doesn't help you structure the visual telling of your story. There are literally thousands of ways to show an action. How do you know which to choose? Besides, often it will be the job of the writers to make sure the story is character driven. They will write what each character does. The director's job is to figure out how to visually structure the story.

The problem with learning about a character-driven approach to storytelling is the same problem with intuition. How can you use your intuition if you don't have any experience to base it on? You have to learn how to visualize a story into a series of pictures.

What Can Possibly Go Wrong?

We've all learned to tell stories, so telling a story in pictures should be easy, right? Well, when I was directing *Piglet's BIG Movie* I realized that even professional storyboard artists sometimes have trouble telling a story in pictures. Each of my storyboard artists had different problems with his or her storyboards. I was the director, so it was my responsibility to make sure the whole film worked. How would I be able to help them? What was wrong? Was it just bad storyboarding or was some principle being overlooked?

Speaking Problems

There are several problems that can arise when we speak. We can talk on and on trying to say too much until we run out of breath, yet we keep talking, possibly trying to make sure there's no silence. We can leave a thought unfinished—What was I saying? We can confuse the sentence with unnecessary tangents about red herrings and other exotic fish. We can mix up the tenses tomorrow. We can speak talk verbalize without pausing for punctuation. We can speak—no transitions between ideas. Worst of all is that we can speak when we have nothing to say. The result of all of these is that we don't communicate what we had intended.

Humpty Dumpty in *Through the Looking Glass* had some great advice.

"When I use a word," Humpty Dumpty said, in a rather scornful tone, "it means just what I choose it to mean—neither more nor less."

"The question is," said Alice, "whether you can make words mean so many different things."

"The question is," said Humpty Dumpty, "which is to be master—that's all."[2]

This is wise advice from an overconfident egg, but what does this have to do with visual storytelling? It's been said that a picture is worth a 1001 words, give or take a few. This is their strength and it is also a weakness. Why should this be a problem? If we're trying to tell a story with pictures, the problem comes because of the fact that pictures can say too much. We need to be able to control our pictures so they say exactly what we want them to, just like Humpty Dumpty. We need to master our images.

The most common types of speaking problems have a filmic equivalent when we tell a story using images. When we speak, we talk about one thing at a time. Very often without realizing it, beginner's pictures say two things at once.

This conflicts with attention theory that states that we can only pay attention to one thing at a time. When the film is racing by, which one will your viewers look at? Suppose they see the wrong one, and thus miss the thread of your storytelling?

Let's look at some visual examples of these types of problems. This first one says too much. The focus is split between multiple things of interest.

With the focus split you don't know where to look first.

Filmmakers have developed techniques to solve these types of problems. For example, instead of showing two things at a time, you can pan from one to the other, you can cut from one to the other thing, or you could rack focus from one to the other. All of these solutions present one thing at a time, simplifying what to look at for the viewer's sake.

Here the camera pans from one thing to another.

Cutting from one shot to another shows us one thing at a time.

Racking the focus shifts our view from one thing to another.

Understanding these common problems can fix a lot of film problems and most importantly, help ensure that the film says what you think it says. As a quick illustration of that, when I storyboarded on *Pocahontas*, the farewell ending scene was very flat. It had no emotion. This was a major problem, for here were two impassioned lovers who wanted to be together but they knew they had to part for noble reasons. The problem was that this tragic scene played like the ending of a summer camp movie— "See you next summer." I realized that the images were not telling the audience what the filmmakers thought they were saying. Pocahontas was supposed to be feeling alone. Yet, the script called for her to be surrounded continually by a group of people. The images telling the story never showed Pocahontas alone, which is exactly how she felt. The images didn't say what the filmmakers thought they were saying and the audience wouldn't have gotten the message they wanted to convey.

When she is surrounded, it's hard to see that she feels alone.

Here the visual impact is much more dramatic, and it is clear that she feels alone.

So what were the problems with my storyboard artists on *Piglet's BIG Movie*? I realized that they were speaking problems, and once my artists became aware of them, they easily fixed them. There are always problems in making a movie, but the result is what counts. I think they did an awesome job.

Let's discuss some of these problems. I had one artist who suffered from run-on sentences. His sequences just went on and on. It was almost like he gave me coverage. Coverage is extra footage shot to cover potential problems in the editing room. But this wasn't live action, it was animation! Unfortunately, I ended up having to cut most of his charming drawings.

Lack of punctuation was the drawback of another one of my storyboard artists. When a standup comic tells a joke, he or she sets up the joke, pauses, then delivers the punch line; waits for the laughter to die down; then continues on with the routine. If you don't wait for the laughter to recede, the audience will miss the beginning of the next joke. In the case with pictures, you can miss the punch line. My storyboard artist would have the drawing of the punch line, which was well drawn, but rather than holding that drawing for a beat, he added a character coming into the shot on that very same drawing. The result was that the viewer's eye went right to the new character coming into frame, instead of seeing the punch line. It spoiled the joke.

Here's the setup.

Here's the action.

Where does your eye go?

And here's the punch line—wait, who's that entering? They're stepping on the punch line, thus ruining the joke. It was like creating a sentence without a period. Punctuation is crucial for us to determine the meaning of things, whether it is the pause of a comma, the full stop of a period, or the excitement of an exclamation point.

Wikipedia describes: "A shaggy-dog story is an extremely long-winded tale featuring extensive narration of typically irrelevant incidents, usually resulting in a pointless or absurd punch line."[3] This can be a real danger to any kind of storyteller and sure enough one of my storyboard artists suffered from this malady too. The problem is that the tangents don't drive the story along and you chance losing your audience because they've lost what the story is about.

Incorrect grammar is comparable to poor sequencing of visual images. This breaks the flow of time or cause-and-effect relationships. Another related problem is not using connectives to connect different ideas. When we speak we use words like "and" and "so" to make sentences flow. We'll learn more about creating flow when we talk about editing.

The worst speaking problem of all is a lack of something important to say. This occurs visually when there is nothing happening in the frame, or worse yet, at the story level.

Catch-22 Revisited

When I was a teenager I got my first movie camera. It was a Super-8 color without sound. Film with processing was about $9. It took about a week to process the film, and it gave my friends and I only three minutes of film. Editing was accomplished on a small hand-cranked movie editor with invisible tape. This experience taught me a number of things. One, that I was very impatient—it was really hard to wait a week to see the results of a shoot. Second, I learned that making movies was a lot of work involving a lot of preplanning, but that it was also a lot of fun. Third, we had to be very careful with the shots because the film was expensive. We needed to be concise in our shots, but more importantly, because there was no sound, we had to tell our story visually.

We learned the value of that old proverb, "Necessity is the mother of invention." We learned to improvise. As an example, my first camera didn't have a single frame release. This is required to shoot animation, which is shot one frame at a time. Therefore, I invented what we needed. I put the camera on a tripod and made a little lever next to the record button. I tied a string to the lever, and with a short tug, the camera fired off one frame.

Special effects was another area where we needed to be inventive. Digital effects didn't exist back then. You either had to shoot the effects live or use an optical printer. We chose to shoot them live. We made our own homage to the TV show *Star Trek*. We shot a model of the Enterprise spaceship against a black cloth for the space shots. Halloween masks came in handy when we needed monsters, but we also learned mold making, makeup, and costume design. Pajama shirts with cardboard badges covered in glitter looked just like Star Trek uniforms on film. Painted cardboard boxes formed the consoles for the ship's bridge and the Super-8 movie screen made for a great bridge monitor for spotting Klingon spacecraft.

So how did a bunch of kids make movies without any instruction? Actually, that's a trick question. We did have instruction, only it just wasn't formal instruction. We had limited life experiences but we had some understanding as to how things worked. We also knew how to speak and tell stories verbally. Everyone learns this growing up. But how did we know how to tell stories visually? We learned by watching TV. This gave us the basic skills, but not enough to avoid being boring or confusing. Sometimes our films suffered from both problems. But we got better.

Things are very different today. Most families have camcorders, and you can buy two or three DV (digital video) tapes for about $9. Some camcorders have built-in hard drives that store hours of video. No more three-minute limits—they each last an hour and with full stereo sound. You can even mix surround sound at home. Armed with a video camera and a computer loaded with Apple's iMovie® editing software or it's equivalent, you can literally shoot a feature-length film, create digital special effects, add your own score and sound effects, and deliver it on DVD or post it on the Internet. The filmmaking process can still be just as much fun as your imagination allows.

Before we continue, let's see how Scheherazade is doing. As you last remember, she had just arrived at the gates of the sultan's palace determined to stop the sultan's madness and find out what happened to his missing brides.

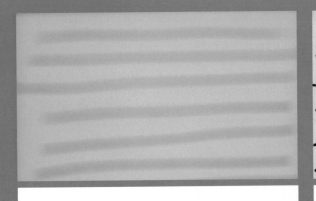

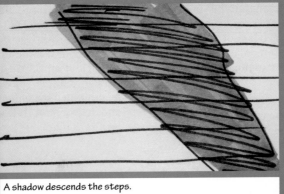

A shadow descends the steps.

Scheherazade and Dunazade await anxiously.

The king's vizier greets them.

They bow to the vizier.

VIZIER: "This way."

They climb the majestic steps in silence.

They follow the vizier along endless hallways.

DUNAZADE: "What's in there?"

VIZIER: "That is not your concern."

VIZIER [Voiceover]: "You are not to leave your room."

VIZIER: "Follow me."

VIZIER: "You will wait here until the Sultan calls for you."

They enter and wait.

What Do Directors Direct?

Another question that I ask my class is, "What does a director direct?" Most of them have not thought about it. Their answers cover a wide range of possibilities. The director directs the story, the actors, the crew, the camera, the lighting. Once again, all the answers to this question are true. Then I ask, "Does knowing that the director directs all of these things help tell you how to become a better director?" The answer that comes back is no.

When I get an answer that doesn't specifically help me know how to make better movies usually that means that I haven't dug deep enough. Remember the goal we're after? We want to give our audience an emotionally satisfying experience. Maybe a better question would be, "Who do directors direct?" Yes, the actors and crew, but they are also directing the emotions of the audience. We're getting warmer.

But we can't directly affect their emotions; we have to do it by structuring the film. So what do we direct? We direct their attention while telling the story.

How does one direct someone's attention? For now, let's just say we point things out to them. Later, we're going to go into great detail about how to direct attention, but for now we need to know what to avoid.

Enemies of Good Design

When we're directing the audience's attention, boredom and confusion are two enemies of good design that we need to be continually on the look out for. Knowing about these problems will help us in our goal of giving the audience an emotionally satisfying experience. Let's see how this works.

Here is an image. Nothing's going on. Look at it for a while. How do you feel? With so little going on, it feels boring. This doesn't help our audience to feel good.

When nothing happens visually, we get bored.

Let's look at another image. This one is the opposite of the first—there's too much going on. We don't know what we're looking at or where to look. How do you feel? We show the first image and then state that it's boring because nothing is happening.

When there is too much happening visually we get confused.

Most people seeing an image like this will feel confused. If your audience is confused, they won't be able to follow your story.

So we have two extremes: boredom and confusion—the enemies of good design. They are both unemotional, one from a lack of emotion and the other from a sensory bombardment of too much information. We need to find a middle path.

A Fine Mess

My first professional experience of storyboarding was on Disney's *Aladdin*. I had storyboarded before, but this was different—this was the big time! I was given the scene where Aladdin is supposed to distract a merchant while his accomplice, Abu, his monkey, steals some food. I had the script, paper, and pencils. I was all set—so I thought, until I realized that storyboarding is really the first pass at directing! My reaction: Total panic! I had tons of questions and no place to get answers. How many drawings do I use? What are story beats? How much detail do I put in? Where do I put the camera? Why? When do I cut? What will make it creative? What are the writers looking for? What's my goal?

What did I do? What could I do? Well, other storyboard artists made lots of drawings, so I just started making lots of drawings. Then it came time to pitch the sequence. It was a giant mess. No one knew where the characters were. The pacing was all off. Worst of all it wasn't "entertaining." In fact, it was boring and confusing. Then came even worse news. The director, John Musker, suggested that maybe I couldn't storyboard. "NOOO!" I screamed (in my head of course).

Codirector, Ron Clements, and John had liked my visual development ideas and character designs. They took me off storyboarding and put me back in visual development. I was given a new task of developing the magic carpet ride. I had to prove myself, but how?

Once again, I had the script, paper, and pencils and I started drawing. No, it's probably more correct to say that this time I started creating images. I found the key beats of the scene. I started to see a connection between images and put them in sequential order. I added drawings to connect ideas and make it flow.

The sequence was "A Whole New World," and it became a whole new world for me. They put me back in storyboarding and the sequence went on to win the Academy Award for best song.

A story is like a giant knot that we have to unravel and show the audience how all the pieces connect in a linear way and then tie it all back up for them at the end. It's not about creating the drawings as much as deciding which images should be shown and when.

Clear and Dramatic Fights Confusion and Boredom

Often beginner's work can be boring and confusing. It helps to remember the old acronym, KISS—Keep It Simple, Stupid! We are going to fight confusion with learning how to be clear. In other words, we are going to fight confusion with clarity! And, we are going to fight boredom with drama and careful editing!

Boredom results from a lack of dramatic questions. You must arouse the interests of your audience, and make them want to know what's going to happen next. Direct emotions indirectly by directing attention as you tell your story.

The Speaking Metaphor

The discovery of speaking problems led me to create a technique that I call the "speaking metaphor" of storytelling. It's simply this: *We tell a story with pictures just as if we were speaking it with words.*

We put the noun and verbs into a series of pictures. Each time we have a new idea, we add a new image. Just remember, present one idea at a time. It is really that simple. "Speak" clearly with your images. Don't let them get confusing. If we forget this cardinal rule, then we can run into speaking problems.

Let's see how this works. The script describes a squirrel that sits on a branch in the forest, above a cat. We can portray this with a camera move. Let's verbalize the story by drawing it and then draw boxes that frame the action. Basically, we're deciding the framing for each part of the sentence.

Pictures show actions.

Some verbs have an inherent dramatic quality to them. For example, flirting, making pacts, betray, fight, challenge, lie, cheat, promise, and steal all seem to suggest stories. Nondramatic verbs might include to walk, celebrate, chop wood, read, and sleep. The difference is that dramatic verbs have unknown answers to narrative questions. Nondramatic ones have known outcomes. Since we know or can easily guess what will happen we lose interest. The squirrel "sitting" isn't a dramatic verb, but the cat sitting below adds dramatic interest to the image.

Show and Tell

How do you tell a story with pictures? Let's start with a simple action and put it into a series of pictures. Here's our action: Someone picked up something.

This first image shows someone holding something. We didn't see that he picked it up. He could have taken it out of his pocket.

All we really know is that he's holding something and looking at it.

We need to show a series of drawings, each showing one stage of the action. Most actions have at least three stages: the anticipation of the action, the action itself, and the aftermath or follow through. We need to show the anticipation of picking up the object, the actual picking it up, and finally showing it already picked up.

Anticipation

Action

Aftermath

We said our action described someone who *picked up* something. It was past tense. The drawings show someone picking up something but as if it's happening right now. Film always shows the present tense. Film scripts are written in present tense. They're happening now! Even flashbacks are experienced by the audience as happening now, in the present.

What does this drawing say? Yes, someone's stealing something. It's the same action as before picking it up, but how do we know that it's a theft. The answer is we really don't know, but we're guessing that what's happening. We guess that it's a theft because of the behavior of the person we're watching. He is hunched over and looking around to see if anyone is around watching him. The object is on a pedestal that could suggest it's valuable. The context and the body language tell the audience important information about the story.

In this next image, it is the same structure of events, but now we have a different action—robbing a safe. Again, how do we know? This time the environment shows a safe inside a room. But is he robbing it? We really don't know, because he could be opening his own safe. We most likely assume that he is robbing the object because we are in a mindset of theft from the previous drawing. This is an example of how context can affect how we create stories from the images we see.

Remember: Draw attention to one idea at a time, just like when speaking, and you need to make sure your drawings say what you think they're saying.

Every Shot Is a Close-Up

If a picture is worth 1001 words, how do we keep from overwhelming the audience and get them to see what we want them to? It's simple: *We point the camera at our subject and choose what goes in the frame*. In effect, every shot is a close-up. But wait, what about all those charts in film books that show wide shots, medium shots, close-ups, and extreme close-ups? The description of shot sizes is useful for a director to communicate their vision to their crew, for instance a shot list will call for a long shot, over-the-shoulder medium shot, or extreme close-up.

Close-ups are the only shots that show just what you want to say. They say, "Look at this…. I'm pointing the camera at this for a reason." We're using the speaking metaphor of film to tell the story with pictures, one idea at a time. In writing we use grammar and composition to structure what we want to say. With film we use sequencing and visual composition. We want to show exactly what we want to say in the context of a series of shots.

Let's say we wanted to tell a story about a princess looking out her castle tower window, pining for her love.

Well, there's the princess. Can you see her? We're too wide or far away. This is a close-up of a mountaintop. Let's go closer.

Can you see her yet? We've moved closer, and now we've got a close-up of a mountaintop town. Let's go closer still.

Now we've got a nice close-up of a castle. No sign of the princess yet.

Here is a close-up of her castle tower. Getting warmer ...

Ah, there she is. But as you can see we're still *too* wide to be telling the story about the princess pining away. We can't see her expressions.

Each of these shots says something very specific. Each framing is a close-up that shows different things.

Now that we've begun to look at how we tell a story with pictures, let's return to Scheherazade. Then we'll look at what a story is.

Night arrives at the palace.

DUNAZADE: "We've been waiting forever."

SCHEHERAZADE: "Patience is a virtue you have not mastered."

SCHEHERAZADE: "The rain's getting ..."

The rays of the setting sun break through the clouds.

The light glints off the executioner's axe.

DUNAZADE [Voiceover]: "Getting ready to what?"

The gravity of her situation sinks in.

DUNAZADE: "Scheherazade, what's wrong?"

DUNAZADE: "Why don't you say something?"

Scheherazade tries to speak but nothing comes out.

DUNAZADE: "You can't speak. What are we going to do?"

DUNAZADE [Startled]: "I don't think we're alone."

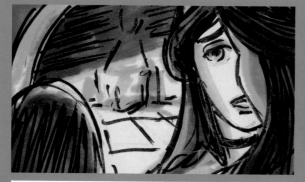

A figure in the shadows watches them.

The vizier enters.

VIZIER: "It is time for you to go."

Not knowing what to do, Dunazade looks back at her sister.

Scheherazade motions for her to go on with the plan.

DUNAZADE: "I have a last request, that may I hear one of my sister's wondrous stories?"

VIZIER: "This is out of the question."

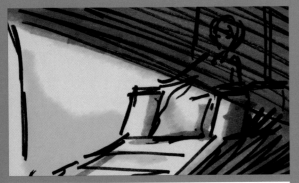

VOICE [Offscreen]: "What is it she requests?"

The vizier approaches the shadowy figure.

VIZIER: "Your highness, she requests a story from her sister."

Scheherazade's shocked that they have been in the presence of the sultan without knowing it.

VIZIER: "I don't think that this is a wise course of action."

The sultan takes water from a bowl …

And washes his face.

He stares from the shadows.

VIZIER: "I believe they are up to trickery. She can't even speak let alone tell a story."

SULTAN: "I see no harm in it, if she can't speak …"

SULTAN: "It will not be a long story. Please begin."

In the mirror, Scheherazade sees a mural.

Scheherazade brightens seeing the image.

VIZIER [Offscreen]: "What does she wait for?"

Scheherazade walks toward the sultan.

Is the story over for Scheherazade before it begins? Scheherazade's plan is to tell stories to entertain the sultan and thus stay alive. How can she possibly do this when she has lost her voice? Stories have to be about something important—no less than life-or-death stakes. In this case, they have to be about something important enough to capture the sultan's attention and retain his attention. Once Scheherazade has something at stake, then she can begin.

Scheherazade approaches the sultan.

She bows before the sultan.

Scheherazade lights an oil lamp.

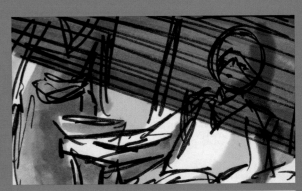

VIZIER: "Sire, I tell you, it's a trick."

VIZIER: "She's mocking you."

The sultan motions for him to be still.

To everyone's surprise, Scheherazade begins to draw.

Scheherazade holds the drawing up for her sister to see.

Dunazade looks at the drawing with delight.

It shows cupid.

DUNAZADE: "It's one of your romance stories. I love those."

Scheherazade quickly draws another drawing …

And holds it up for view.

A couple kisses.

Dunazade smiles.

The lovers part leaving a trail of saliva.

DUNAZADE: "Yuck!"

DUNAZADE: "You never know what's going to happen in your stories."

Dunazade begins to narrate the tale: "The couple stands on a narrow rope bridge."

Arrows begin flying from both sides.

The lovers run to opposite sides.

The sultan listens eagerly …

Scheherazade has caught the sultan's attention. He leans in to hear more.

The lover looks back to see her beloved …

… as he trips …

… and falls off the bridge.

She's heartbroken—speechless.

Scheherazade keeps drawing as Dunazade continues the narration.

Since the opposite sides destroyed her love with their hate, she wove a spell.

She put a curse on the two towns. "Who soever would mock love would fall …

... into the mouth of ...

... a great dragon.

And if anyone dared raise even a stone in battle against the other side ...

... the dragon would rise up and destroy them all."

Dunazade watches as her sister draws more.

DUNAZADE: "This is your best story yet."

The sultan watches Scheherazade draw.

He comes out from the shadows.

Could it be that he's hooked into her story?

What Is a Story?

I think that there are as many definitions of a story as there are stories. In fact it reminds me of a joke told by anthropologist Gregory Bateson: "A man wanted to know about mind, not in nature, but in his private, large computer. He asked it (no doubt in his best Fortran), 'Do you compute that you will ever think like a human being?' The machine then set to work to analyze its own computational habits. Finally, the machine printed its answer on a piece of paper, as such machines do. The man ran to get the answer and found, neatly typed, the words: 'That reminds me of a story.'"[4]

In its simplest form, a story is the telling of a series of events about a character who wants something. But, the character doesn't know how to go about getting what he or she wants, so he or she has to face obstacles and the complications that ensue. The story builds to a crisis until the character gets not what he or she wants, but what he or she needs. This is the basic structure that most stories follow.

There can be many models that can be used to create exciting movies. A story could be like a rubber band. Pick it up, stretch it, aim it at the goal, stretch it some more, relax, stretch it further, and release all the energy until it hits the target and comes to rest.

War is another great model for stories. Stories are structured like human conflicts best symbolized by war. You need opposite sides. Opposition is what gives it contrast and creates meaning. The story has to feel that important even if it's about something seemingly small.

In war there are casualties. Something has to die. These can be old beliefs, ways of thinking often embodied in villains. A new way of being emerges out of this fight to the death. We want to bring the audience along for the ride. Storytellers have helped us become aware of the consequences of conflict and have helped lessen human suffering.

A story is a type of play hypothesis. It's a quest in the form of a question. It's a chase of questions and answers. It's like a seduction in the shape of a war. It's how characters are revealed and change under conflict. Characters reveal their desires and the audience, by linking with these desires, get the experience that life's struggles are worth it and that their lives have significance to others.

Great stories have a character with an internal conflict that is played out as an external war. It is because these heroes solve their inner conflicts that they can win the external conflicts. The audience gets reborn along with the heroes. This message has all the more power because they receive it in the trancelike state of movie going, and there is also the safety of distance between them and the characters; for example, "Even though I'm feeling what I think they're feeling, this is not about me, so I can feel safe."

A story is a seduction that hooks the viewer's attention with a "What if …" hypothesis about human emotions, ending with a race to the finish that gives the audience the experience that life's struggles are worth it when we identify with the story. I say identify with "the story" rather than a specific character because I believe that we identify with the desires of multiple characters during a film. We may be nothing like the characters in the story. The movie *Romancing the Stone* opens with an exciting Western action scene starring a cowgirl heroine. At the conclusion of the sequence, we reveal that this scene has just been written by Joan Wilden, a romance writer. She's sobbing over what she wrote. Joan's real life is nothing like that of her fictional star, yet her exploits have moved her to tears. During the course of *Romancing the Stone*, Joan will grow to become like her heroine. Yes, I believe that we identify with the story. What is a character if not the sum of his or her stories? As Scheherazade knew, we're made of stories.

Once we have our story in mind, the next skill set is to be able to visualize it, in the sense of being able to communicate our ideas pictorially. The second skill is being able to tell/show the story so it engages our audience. We're going to look at these two skill sets from the point of view of what a film director does.

What does a film director do? We learned earlier in this chapter that directors direct the audience's attention. The first skill set involves being able to tell a story clearly with pictures using various techniques of directing a viewer's attention.

Second, once you have your audience's attention, you must keep their attention. We do this through dramatization of the events of the story, again using various techniques of directing a viewer's attention.

Let's look at a way to visualize this information. First we have our story to tell, about characters involved in chasing their dreams. Their actions are the story events.

Events of the Story

In the Vocabulary of the Media Critic class at NYIT, Dr. Alwyn Scott[5] told his class to aim at the heart by working at the structural level. Unfortunately, while he taught mind-blowing information, he didn't explain explicitly how to work at the structural level. In this book, we're going to learn how to work at the structural level to give your audience an emotionally satisfying experience.

Several film writers have used a simple graph to show the relationship between content and form. David Bordwell uses the Russian terms *syuzhet* and *fabula*. "The *fabula*," writes Tynianov, "can only be guessed at, but is not a given."[6] "The *syuzhet* (usually translated as "plot") is the actual arrangement and presentation of the *fabula* in the film."[7] The *fabula* is the story of what happens that the audience creates in their own heads. Bob Foss relates content and form to the "plane of events" and the "plane of discourse," or as he calls them, "The *what* and *how* of film narrative."[8] Seymore Chatman articulates it even further by suggesting that form or narrative structure "communicates meaning in its own right, over and above the paraphrasable contents of its story."[9]

Events of the story	
Structure of the telling of the story	

An Experiment

Don't worry if this sounds complicated; it's really simple. To get an idea about the difference between the events and the structure of a movie, let's try an experiment. Go watch a scene from a movie that's at least five minutes long. Then continue reading.

+ + + + +

In a simple description, describe the story. I'm sure you'll find that this is easy. It probably went someth ing like, "This guy was trying to get this, but this other person got in the way, so he ...." You remember the *events* of what happened.

This next step is trickier. Now I want you to draw, in simple stick figures, the sequence of the shots that told the story. This isn't so easy. In fact, it can be very difficult. But you know the story, why should this be so difficult? We remember the story but not how the story was presented. How the story is presented is the *structure.*

All stories need to be told with words and or pictures, so we must put our story into some structure that tells the story clearly and dramatically. As you just saw from our experiment, when we watch a story for the first time, we don't pay attention to how the movie is structured. If the director has done his or her job correctly, the first time we watch a movie we get "lost" in the story. By directing attention to the flow of telling the story, the audience won't pay attention to the acting, cinematography, blocking, editing, lighting, art direction, sound effects, and musical score. Instead, the audience will be watching people struggling to achieve their dreams and facing insurmountable obstacles. In other words, they will be "lost" in the story.

If this is the director's job, what happens to all of this structural stuff? Is it invisible? Why doesn't the audience see it? The fact is that *the structure is totally visible.* We can see the editing and hear the background music. It's all there. When we watch a film for the second time, we can pay attention to it and see how the film is structured, but during the first viewing, we simply are not paying attention to it.

Many books that I have found on filmmaking say that we willingly suspend our disbelief when we watch a movie. There is no "willing suspension of disbelief."

Let's say I go to a movie. I buy a ticket—check. Buy popcorn—check. Find a seat—check. Willingly suspend my disbelief—*what*? I cannot remember ever going into a movie theater and willingly suspending my disbelief. I don't even know how. Belief is automatic. As long as the structure presents a filmic world that is seamless and doesn't break the spell by calling attention to itself, we get sucked into the world of the story.

Structuring Stories

What is structure? It is a relationship between the parts of something. What are the parts of a film story? The parts are comprised of the narrative questions and the delays and answers to those questions. The structure is simply how the movie story is presented—which shots are chosen and in what order. This structuring of the events of the story is what can make the difference between a simple plain story and one that is unforgettable and profoundly moving.

So what separates the events from the structure? Why don't we notice the structure if it's right there in front of our noses? The director tells and shows us a story. Like magic, we're distracted by the story, and don't notice how it's put together. It drops below our threshold of attention. This is an imaginary line separating what we notice and what we don't.

Any part of the structure can cross the line and come into our attention. It is the job of the director to direct the audience's attention to the events of the story by careful attention to the structure. We're going to build this chart step by step. This chart form will make it easy to remember the key ideas taught in this book.

Chart of Story Events and Structure

The **events** of the story are what happens. We're "lost" in the story.

The threshold of awareness divides what the audience pays attention to into what we notice and what we don't. We usually don't pay attention to what's below this line unless something catches our attention by being out of place.

Structure is how the story is told. Throughout the course of this book we're going to learn the tools, tactics, and strategies to work structurally.

What Is Character?

What is character? A character is a person represented on screen. A good character is one who appears believable, strongly wants something, and goes after it by taking action in his or her own unique way. Phil Connors in *Groundhog Day* goes after romance repeatedly. As he relives Groundhog Day over and over, his character slowly changes, so each time he tries his romantic pursuit, he does it differently. Phil, played by Bill Murray, goes after romance uniquely differently than say James Bond.

How do we make characters seem believable? Would they seem believable if they acted like real people? Yes and no. Most of the time real people would be too boring to watch. Story characters are crystallized into essences. Real people are often driven by unconscious motivations. They're driven to do things that may be dangerous or otherwise not under their conscious control. This can make them appear unpredictable.

I have found that a great way to look at characters is to look at what rules govern their behavior. We all have rules that determine our behavior. These are arranged in a hierarchy depending on the context. When we communicate, certain rules can override others. Let's look at a simple rule governed by character. Bugs Bunny generally approaches life with a live-and-let-live attitude. But if you push him too far, his rules shift. He then will go on the counteroffensive declaring, "Of course you know, this means war!"

To create interesting characters we need to visually show their goals and limitations. We all have various kinds of limitations that, at least temporally, constrain our behavior. We need to show characters' decisions as to which goals they will go after, the actions they take, how they deal with others during the process, and how they deal with the obstacles that get in the way of their goals. We need to show the moment they discover what they're doing wrong or inspirational moments that keep them on their quest. We need to show how they change and the events and new information that change them.

What about inanimate objects as characters? How do we give them a personality? My mentor, storyboard artist Ed Gombert, taught me to use pets as an inspiration. What would it be like if a giant acted like a big slobbery puppy? It's all up to your imagination.

Keith Johnstone describes wonderful ways to develop characters in his two books, *Impro* and *Impro for Storytellers*. He describes great games and exercises that help teach actors to interact and keep the story moving. Often beginning acting students will perform actions that block a story's forward development.

Keith makes a very important point that all stories should contain moral decisions. "All stories are trivial unless they involve a moral choice, and it can be especially thrilling to watch the hero make the wrong choice (for example, Jack the Giant-killer selling the cow for a handful of beans)."[10] Keith gives a great example of how nervous actors can block a story's progress because, "Making a moral choice alters you, makes your character experience relief, or sadness, or despair, or whatever, so moral choices are avoided."[11] They're afraid to go into the unknown so they'll play it safe by not taking any chances.

Critique: Introducing Scheherazade

Let's look at our heroine Scheherazade. Suppose we had introduced her in the following way: "Here's Scheherazade, she's smart, loves kids, pets, and is very inventive, but prone to stubbornness."

Scheherazade is going against the crowd. This shows her determination in the face of obstacles.

Scheherazade smiles as she passes the nervous young girl. This indicates her compassion. She is beautiful. The audience wants to watch idealized beautiful people; they call them "stars."

Scheherazade will not be deterred by the logical arguments of her sister. She doesn't let the beggar persuade her either. She is determined if not stubborn.

Stop! We haven't *shown* our audience who this character is. We've told them about her, but we don't feel as if we know her so we don't care about her dilemma. Let's look at how we actually introduced Scheherazade.

Scheherazade is vulnerable. She sees the executioner and loses her voice. This is a major obstacle to her goal. It was an unexpected crack in her self-confidence. She, as well as the viewers, has now seen what's at stake if she fails. Is this what happened to the other brides?

The sultan king is presented as hiding in the shadows. This visually shows his state of mind. Scheherazade has to draw him out into the light. When she begins the storytelling she starts with a simple ritual that she will repeat each time. Part of her ritual is lighting the candle, thus creating light. She will become the light of his life. Pay attention to these types of metaphors as they can enhance your storytelling. The pendulum starts with hope as Scheherazade enters the palace.

When Scheherazade saw what could happen to her, her attitude swung to the negative. She lost her voice. We fear for her safety. What did you expect she would do? Being that this is a book on directing and storyboarding, did you guess that she would draw stories for the sultan? I told you that this version of One Thousand and One Arabian Nights wasn't like the original book. We're talking movies here! Now the pendulum has swung back to hope. Be alert, there are more surprises ahead.

Notice also how we're presenting the material using the speaking metaphor. We're showing the audience a series of close-ups, one at a time, of what we want them to see so that they can follow along in our story.

Hopefully, you were "lost" in the story, telling time by the swing of the pendulum of hope and fear, and didn't notice how each shot clearly progressed the story. Go back over it now that you know the story and look at what's in each shot and how they're put together. Remember you can't analyze a story on the first viewing.

Intuition is trusting your own instincts to go into the unknown. You're risking failure but gaining the opportunity to discover something truly new. Learn these techniques so that your audience will remain, "lost" in the story.

POINTS TO REMEMBER

- Make sure your story is character driven by their desires.
- Be aware of potential speaking problems that may bump your audience out of being "lost" in the story.
- Remember the speaking metaphor: Clearly show one thing at a time.
- Fight boredom by weaving interesting narrative questions that create dramatic characters in escalating conflict.
- Fight confusion by focusing the audience's attention to one thing at a time as you tell the story.
- Treat every shot as a close-up of what you wish to show the audience.
- Make sure your images clearly show the story ideas that you intend to convey.
- Aim at the heart by working at a structural level.

References

1. Innis, H. *The Bias of Communication*. Toronto, Canada: University of Toronto Press, 1999.
2. Carrol, L. *Alice in Wonderland*. Norton, 1971.
3. Wikipedia. http://en.wikipedia.org/wiki/Shaggy_dog_story.
4. Bateson G. *Mind and Nature: A Necessary Unity*. Hampton Press, 2002.
5. Scott, A. *Vocabulary of the Media Critic Class*. NYIT, 1981.
6. Bordwell, D. *Narration in the Fiction Film*. London: Routledge, 1987.
7. Ibid.
8. Foss, B. *Filmmaking Narrative and Structural Techniques*. Silman-James Press, 1992.
9. Chatman, S. *Story and Discourse*. Ithaca, NY: Cornell University, 1980.
10. Johnstone, K. *Impro for Storytellers*. London: Routledge, 1999.
11. Ibid.

The Beginning Basics

A script is a verbal plan for a story. A storyboard is a plan for the visualization of that story. A storyboard is the inspirational heart, mind, and soul of a movie. Hitchcock knew this and is rumored to have said that once the storyboarding was completed, the movie was 95 percent done and the rest was execution.[1]

We have all seen storyboards; everyday in the newspapers there are lots of three- or four-panel storyboards showing short, usually funny, stories. The first panel sets up the situation, the second panel turns it, and finally in the third panel there is the payoff, and we laugh. Yes, the comics' pages of the newspapers are all little storyboards. Some of the best storytelling drawings that you will find are in the cartoons of *The New Yorker* magazine. It is well worth the effort to study these cartoons to see how economically they arrive at their goal: making the audience feel good.

History and Function of Storyboards

The Disney method of storyboarding evolved based on the needs of the filmmakers. There are hundreds or thousands of drawings created in the making of a feature-length film. Tracking them makes for an organizational nightmare, particularly when each scene can involve changes upon changes. Disney's artists originally would lay individual panels out on the floor and point to the drawings as the composer played the music. Eventually, they got the idea to pin them up on the wall on large sheets of cork. This provided a great way to view them and allow an easy way to incorporate changes. It also created an occupational hazard. I can't recall how many times my fingers have been punctured by pushpins while repining storyboards.

Donald Graham, a Disney drawing teacher, described this flexibility:

> Any drawing can be moved to a new position on the board, or eliminated, or replaced. The board of drawings is in a state of flux. Nothing is fixed; *nothing is unchangeable*. One drawing, because of its position on the board, may suggest a gag or a piece of business which can be added. Whole sections can be interchanged ... a new film function of the board becomes apparent: pre-film cutting. Close-ups can be planned against medium shots, long scenes against short ones. Unnecessary animation is automatically ruled out, and tremendous economies result.[2]

Cartoonist and storyboard artist Alex Toth offers an alternate history. He suggests that the pioneering, animator, and cartoonist Winsor McCay created the storyboard. He postulates that he must have in order to have gotten the job done on his movies like *Gertie the Dinosaur*.[3]

Toth describes the function of storyboards:

Alfred Hitchcock, Delmar Daves, doted on their use to solve all or most continuity problems up front, on paper, in a storyboard. "If it won't work there, it won't work on film" was, I believe, Hitchcock's quote! He boarded every film he directed, to order. Still, he was in the minority. Be it small-budgeted "10-day wonder" or mega-million-dollar epic, it is expedient, on all counts, to board the continuity—since it is where type-written script meets "picture" for the first time—and, given a seasoned and savvy pro storyboard artist to interpret that script, is where that script is wrung-out, test-flown, til it cracks/breaks or flies beautifully on its first, maiden flight—right into production's hangar![4]

Various Types of Storyboards

Each medium has evolved its own version of what is included in storyboards based on the artistic and financial needs. In animation every aspect of each scene has to be designed and created. Storyboards for animation have to provide a clear depiction of the acting for the film. In live action the storyboards do not need to depict the characters' emotions because the actors themselves provide the emotions. In live action we want to give the actors freedom to explore in their performances. The actors are not going to follow a storyboard. It is a visual guide for the director.

Cinematography and blocking accomplishes for live action what the layout department does for animated films. Camera lenses have to be chosen and camera placement and movement has to be choreographed to work in time with the movements of the actors. Actors have to hit their marks on cue for a scene to work. Storyboards for a live-action scene could be as simple as an overhead diagram or map of the action.

Live television shows are often edited from a choice of three possible cameras so storyboards aren't necessary. They are usually shot on small sets. The same kind of visual thinking is still necessary though.

Television animation due to tight deadlines and even tighter budgets must be tightly composed. The characters must be on model, with the layouts established and all the continuity worked out. Continuity refers to the seamless flow from one shot to the next.

Story reels are essential for the construction of an animated film. They are the emotional road map for the film.

Another use for storyboards is that of special effects. Often these shots will be live action with computer-generated special effects composited together. The storyboard is the bridge that allows the tight synchronization involved in creating live-action actors interacting with virtual monsters, supernatural forces, or moving through complex architectural spaces.

Production Process

Step one is preparation. But, before that, you need to have a story. Storyboard artists can work from scripts or very loose treatments. If a storyboard is a plan for the film, then a treatment is a plan for the script. The first thing a storyboard artist needs after he or she has a story to work with is inspiring images. It is kind of like food for the brain. Images feed our minds. Where do you find images? They could be found anywhere. Make a list of the kinds of things you need. This could include types of characters, costumes, architectural styles, landscapes, and props. It could also cover color and lighting schemes or composition ideas.

Go to the library or surf the Web. Have a plan because it is very easy to get lost on the Internet highway. The signs on the Internet aren't well marked so make sure you bring your shopping list of what visuals you need. I am sure along the way you will find plenty of links offering a serendipity of surprises that generate new ideas to enhance your project.

Cut out magazine pictures or shoot your own references with a digital camera. You should build your own reference library of images that you can go to when you need inspiration. And of course, watch lots of movies.

After you have collected images that inspire you, the fun begins. Visual development is the creation of the look of the world of your movie.

In designing characters, physical appearances tell a lot about what people are like. The goal is to create a fresh version of stereotypes. Stereotypes allow the viewer to quickly understand the type of character that we are dealing with. That is why they are useful. Problems arise in real life when we try and judge real people as if they are stereotypes. Problems arise in movies with stereotypes because they are predictable and thus boring. In the film *Cat Balou* the infamous hired gunslinger breaks the stereotype by showing up as a washed-out drunk. Cat Balou herself is a breaking of a stereotype—she is a female outlaw. *Blade Runner* creates a novel version of a futuristic city bathed in neon and fog.

The visual look of a film is under the domain of the art director and production designer, however, the storyboard artist can often be the first one to enter and explore the world.

The Beat Board

Before the actual storyboarding begins, artists create a beat board. These are a series of single drawings that each represents a scene of the movie. The drawings tell a more complex story in a single picture much like a children's book illustration. The beat board serves as a guide for the director to pitch the story to executives, financial investors, and the crew.

Example beatboard.

Storyboarding Overview

Read the script and analyze the key dramatic storytelling beats. You want to find the shape of the material, just like our three-panel comic strips. Where do you want to start the action? Where does the action turn to a new direction? What is the payoff for the action? What is going to capture the interest of your audience?

You need to develop appealing characters with unique personalities. How would they perform the actions? Make sure they are expressive. Figure out whose point of view to use to present the material. Try to discover the compelling theme within the story. This is ultimately the reason that viewers want to watch.

Storyboards are used to plan many aspects of movies. At this early stage strict continuity is not crucial, the story is. A refinement pass can be used to map screen geography and plan cinematography, camera angles, and blocking. Storyboards help plan complex action sequences with moving cameras. Explore and experiment because it is cheaper to try out ideas on paper before animation or live-action shooting begins. Storyboards are always a work in progress. Don't be afraid to throw drawings away.

A final note: *Number your drawings!*

Story Reels

A story reel is a version of the completed storyboards combined with voices and temporary music. It gives a great idea of how the movie is playing at a very early stage. It allows for fine-tuning the progress of the movie, at a point when changes can still be made. It is a template of the finished movie set to the actual time. Story reels need to have much more reliance on continuity, including entrances and exits of characters into the frame. This will require extra storyboard drawings to be added to create a smooth flow of images. Story reels are a great way to spot and solve story problems. When the story reel plays well, the film can only get better.

The Refinement Process

The refinement process is where ideas in the reels need to be clarified for the audience to understand. The story reel allows us to see all of the pieces in context. Ideas may be reordered to find the best way to present a gag or build suspense. Parts that slow the story down should be edited out. All writing is rewriting and this applies to storyboarding.

Pitching

Once the storyboards are completed, then comes the fun of pitching them. This was a big surprise to me. When I first started storyboarding, I thought all that I had to do was draw pictures. Boy, was I wrong.

Pitching is the process of showing someone your storyboards whereby you perform the dialogue and briefly describe the action as you sequentially point to the drawings. It should be performed in real time, that is, the pitch should take as long as the sequence will take. When completed the director and producer should have a very good sense of how the sequence will appear to the audience.

When I teach how to pitch to my storyboard class, I pitch a sequence and do everything that I can wrong. Then I ask my students what I did wrong. This makes them think and it demonstrates that if you make these kinds of errors you will lose your audience. They won't be able to follow the story. Since I can't do a terrible pitch for the reader, I will demonstrate with a series of drawings.

First of all you have to rehearse beforehand. You must know the story you are pitching inside and out. You don't want to have to think about what happens next.

That is what the audience will want to know and you better have the answers for them.

Tell your story simply and clearly with passion to keep the pitch dramatic. Don't apologize for any imperfections. Storyboards are an intermediate step where changes can be made. You need to believe in the story and project that excitement. Make eye contact with your audience. You need to engage them in the story. During the pitch you are the storyteller and you set the pace.

Be passionate about your story but don't overdo it.

Pitch your story in real time. Don't drag it out unnecessarily.

Don't hide the drawings with your body. The audience has to see the drawings in order to follow the story.

Don't explain the camera work. The drawings show that implicitly. The script doesn't contain details about camera moves it simply tells the story, so should you.

Now, let's return to see how Scheherazade is faring with pitching her story to the sultan. Will he fall for her story of Dumb Love?

Scheherazade holds up the drawing for her sister.

Dunazade looks at the drawing.

The sultan approaches. SULTAN: "What is that?"

SULTAN: "I can't see it."

Scheherazade looks at the drawing and sees …

How light it is.

Dunazade reaches into the fire and grabs a piece of charcoal.

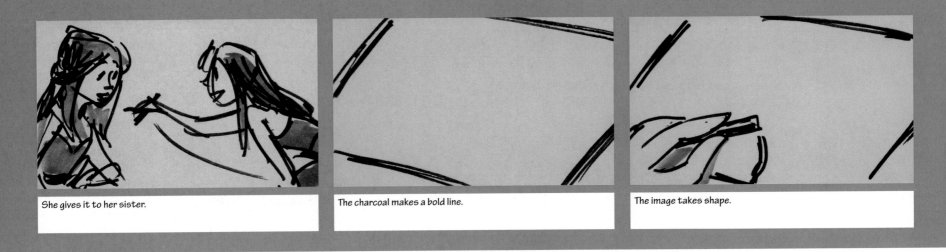

She gives it to her sister.

The charcoal makes a bold line.

The image takes shape.

Make sure that you draw **BOLD**. Use a grease pencil, marker, or 2B pencil. Don't use a hard pencil. Drawings should read from across the room. And number your drawings.

The Gong Show

In some ways Scheherazade had it easy. She didn't have to pitch her ideas at a Gong Show.

Around 1990 Walt Disney Feature Animation introduced their infamous Gong Show. This was an internal forum where employees could pitch their ideas for new animated feature ideas to the executives. When I learned about this I signed on immediately. I thought that this was an amazing opportunity that didn't happen everyday.

Unfortunately, I didn't have any ideas yet, so I worked at coming up with ideas. I created a few concepts, designed a poster to promote each of them, and went off to the Gong Show. It was a big conference room. I sat nervously waiting. All of the participants waited on pins and needles. Finally, the executives entered

and I found myself sitting across from Michael Eisner, Jeffery Katzenberg, Peter Schneider, and Roy Disney. I was nervous before, now I was terrified. To this point in my career I hadn't had much experience at pitching.

This drawing says it all. I did make it through my first Gong Show and lived to tell you about it. Learn to ignore the fear, terror, and anxiety, and relentlessly pursue your vision. Learn to create opportunities. Remember if you fail in your story, you don't risk death.

How to Tell a Story with Pictures

Tell the story in a "sequence of juxtaposed images."[5] The most important thing to remember when storyboarding is to make sure your sequence of images is telling the same story that you think you are telling. It is all too easy to assume that they are doing so, but you need to pitch the story to people and then see if they got the same story and the message you intended.

Three Little Pigs has a simple repetitive structure that even children learn how to tell easily. It begins, "Once upon a time, there were three little pigs. ..."

Our picture says, "Here are three pigs." Already we have a small problem. These pigs could be little or gigantic. We don't have a frame of reference.

Compared to the tree we can see that we have three "little" pigs. Size is always a comparison between things.

Here we have the wolf and the three pigs. But we have introduced a new problem. There is nothing happening. How do we show the pigs are afraid of the wolf?

This image says, "A wolf is chasing three scared pigs." But since this happens later in the story, we don't want to show the wolf yet. How do we show the pigs afraid of the wolf without showing the wolf?

Here is one idea. Here the drawing shows the pigs are looking at a picture of the wolf. However, since we can't see their faces, we don't know they are afraid. In this drawing their body language doesn't suggest fear, maybe more curiosity.

Here is an alternate approach. You can't literally show what is in a character's mind. This is a comic strip device. It is kind of a cheat. Search until you find just the right image that conveys the story.

At this point we don't even know that the tracks come from the wolf. It could be any large animal, but it shows the pigs are scared by what they see. We know that the *Three Little Pigs* story contains a wolf and not other large animals. So the context suggests that the prints were made by the wolf. Context indirectly conveys a lot of information.

Here is a totally different approach. This says that the pigs are mourning someone. They seem sad rather than scared. This time, the context suggests that they are mourning another pig—maybe a family member. We might have gone too far afield with this approach.

If this image was shown at the end of the story, we could assume it was the wolf's grave. Their smiles contextually reinforce the idea that it is the wolf's grave. Maybe a small statue of the wolf on top of the tombstone would reinforce the idea that it is the wolf's grave.

Keep searching till you find the right image for your particular story needs.

Drawings are interesting when they ask questions embedded within the image. In other words, when you look at them you want to know more. This is the essence of storyboarding—images that raise questions and leave you wanting to know more. You want to know what made the tracks or who the pigs are mourning.

Since she can no longer keep the pigs, their mother sends them out into the world to make their fortunes and warns them about the craftiness of the wolf. This is the theme of the story: Act wisely and carefully. This image is exactly what we don't want to do—show a "talking head." We want to demonstrate the theme by the action of the story, not having someone tell it to us.

Showing the mother teaching the pigs is about as interesting as going to school. If we have to show it in a way something like this image, we need to find ways to make it interesting.

How do we make it interesting? One way to do this is to give the pigs personalities. We could have two of the pigs act like class clowns, and they make fun of the third pig playing the part of the teacher's pet. Watching their antics makes the image interesting while the mother conveys her thematic information. There are many ways to tell your story.

Little details such as body language, gestures, and props suggest their character traits. Maybe they play different musical instruments. Perhaps the teacher's pet pig dances ballet. It is all up to your imagination. Be aware that their personalities have to fit in the context of the story. Maybe the ballet dancing pig is a little too out there for this story.

Let's move our story along. The three pigs leave home to go out into the world. We will follow their journey. But we better make sure that something happens or our audience will lose interest. Let's begin.

Okay, they are leaving home. Wait, how do we know that? They could just be going for a hike. We have to show their home. That is better, but this could be any house. How do we show it is the pig's house?

Yes, this is the pig's house. But, we want to show it with images, not rely on words. We could show their mother waving good-bye.

Okay, now we have our opening shot. This is a storytelling image that clearly shows three little pigs leaving home, and who are afraid of a wolf. Will the three little pigs be able to survive the wolf?

But that is a mouthful. When we speak we can only say one word at a time. Our image says four things at once: There are three little pigs, they are leaving home, they are afraid, and there are scary animal tracks.

The way we tell a story with pictures is to break it down into a series of images that each show one thing at a time, just like when we speak in sentences. One idea comes after another.

There is a problem with the order of the images. In this image the pigs are afraid. But we haven't shown what they are afraid of—the wolf tracks!

Let's try again.

We add this insert shot.

This works better. The pigs are afraid because of seeing the wolf's tracks. We generally show the cause before the effect.

Let's try one more rearrangement.

By adding the insert shot of the mother waving good-bye we can cut back to see the pigs are now out on the road. This creates a better flow between the images.

Any time we do not see the linear flow of time because it is interrupted by another shot, we can assume more time has passed. We don't have to show all of that walking.

Let's add one more shot. A reaction shot. The mother pig is sad that the pigs are leaving home. This shot shows how she feels.

Let's insert a bit of personality to show their characters, before the pigs see the wolf tracks.

The two pigs clown around making the other pig angry. In addition to adding something fun to watch we have reinforced the theme of our story by showing the different attitudes of our pigs.

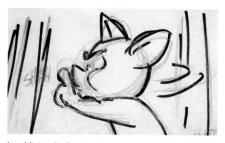

In addition, by having the serious pig remind the others that there may be a wolf around, we have also subtly reminded the audience of this potential threat. This is how we foreshadow events to come.

The pig is stepping into trouble.

We can contrast the threat with a joke. The serious pig is so busy shushing the other two that he trips. The other pigs laugh.

They laugh until they see what he has tripped over …

Wolf tracks!

Our serious pig tries to persuade the other two of the danger.

They laugh it off. We are now more concerned for the two playful pigs because we know the threat is real and they are ignoring it. The comedy has taken the pigs off guard. Contrast between comedy and horror makes the story sharper. It is scarier because we were lulled into a false sense of security.

What is next? The fairy tale starts with the first playful pig borrowing hay to make his house, then the next pig borrows sticks to make a stick house, and finally the last pig makes his house of bricks. Thematically we want to keep the contrast between the smart and clownish pigs. Let the smart one start on his house of bricks, but then we will follow the other two pigs as they continue their journey.

The problem with the story is that the pigs each repeat the same actions. Visually we would be repeating ourselves with images we have already seen three times. After we have seen something happen once it is boring to see it again, unless something happens to make it different and thus interesting.

So it is time to move on and follow the two playful pigs. We want to compress time. You don't have to show everything. We want to only show those images that move the story along, the ones where something happens.

We show the pig starting his brick house. Later when we come back to him, we show him putting on the finishing touches on the house. The audience assumes while we were watching the exploits of the two clownish pigs, the smart one was at work building his house of bricks. We have let the audience do our work for us. You do not have to show everything—only what is interesting.

The narrative question that drives the Three Little Pigs story is not, will the pigs be able to build houses? The question the audience wants answered is, will the pigs survive the big bad wolf? Building houses is the means of surviving the wolf.

A comedy version of the story could include mishaps in building houses of hay, sticks, and bricks, but for now we are going to play it straight.

The two pigs are further down the road clowning around. Their play is interrupted by a wolf howl.

How are we going to show this? We could show a shadow fleeting through the background of the frame. But we are going to do it with an expression change.

The ingredient that makes this work is cause and effect. The wolf howl is the cause, and the pigs' reactions are the effect.

They stop and their expressions change from laughter to terror. A change of expression shows what a character is feeling and thinking.

Now with the wolf near, they have to scramble to make their houses. We will stick with the one with the house made of hay.

How do we show the pig building a house? Remember we don't have to show everything.

Let's just make a patchwork of building parts of a house: picking up some hay, putting down some hay, tying it in bundles, placing support pieces. Well, you get the idea.

So how do we show it is finished?

Here is one idea, the pig is exhausted from building his house, even too tired to go inside to sleep. This can be used to create more tension. Will he get inside in time?

Finally, it is time for the wolf to show up. I think we have to go back to casting. This wolf isn't scary.

Ah, there is a sufficiently scary "big bad wolf."

But wait, we can milk more suspense out of the arrival of the wolf. What about setting the tone with a moody shot of the full moon?

Now our playful little pig is safely snuggled in his house of hay. But what if he isn't? What if we reuse the shot from before of him still sleeping outside?

Before, this image meant that the pig was tired from finishing his house. Now it means that he has rested outside too long and is exposed to danger. The very same image now has a different meaning because the context is different.

If we show the reaction of the pig as he senses the presence of the wolf we build even more tension.

The pig scrambles for the cover of his house of hay.

Now there is a scary wolf. By keeping him in the shadows he is scarier. Just by tilting the image we have raised the tension level. We feel off balance, something is amiss!

The playful pig panicked. We are working with moving pictures so let's let the pig pace back and forth not knowing what to do. The nervous motion enhances the tension.

There is the wolf but it is kind of hard to see what he is doing. Let's move the camera to get a better view of him.

The story tells us that the wolf threatens to huff and puff and blow the house down. We are not going to say it. We will show it.

What happened? It looks like the house fell down too easily. The big moment of the story was over too fast. We need to linger on the details that make up this moment. Let's break down the story beats that we will need to show this action. First, we have to show the wolf eyeing the house of hay.

What do we do next? Well, the story tells us that the wolf will "huff and puff." In our first version we left out the "huff." We didn't anticipate the action of the puff and so it appeared as if the wolf did nothing. Anticipation to an action tells the audience that something is about to happen. Let's do a big anticipation of the action by having the wolf take in air for a big puff.

Exaggerate the puff. If you are going to blow down a house, it is going to have to be a really big puff!

How can we intensify it even further? We have shown the action in a long shot showing the wolf and the house. What if we just focused on the action of the wolf? Let's just frame what is important to the action.

Our images now tell the story of the wolf huffing and puffing. But did he blow down the house? This is an added benefit of framing the action closer—it raises another narrative question. We want to know the result of the puffing.

Here is our answer. The wolf did blow down the house, and we delayed revealing what happened. When we cut to the result, it is funny! If these actions were shown all in one shot, it wouldn't have been as funny.

We always want to keep our theme in the background of our mind, so let's insert a close-up shot of the wolf stepping on the musical instrument. The wolf has destroyed the icon of the clownish attitude. That is what the image shows.

Actions take place in stages. First is the anticipation, next the action happens, then reactions happen, and finally there is the aftermath. Anticipation.

Action.

Aftermath.

For the aftermath of the puffing action, we can show the pig being eaten.

We now have a choice to make. What happens to the first pig? According to our theme, if one is foolish, you could find yourself in the belly of a wolf.

We may not want to show this gruesome detail. As an alternative, we can show the aftermath of the pig being eaten.

We have left out the gruesome action and just show the aftermath, just as we did with the pig finishing his house.

Or, we can leave it open-ended and up to the imagination of the audience to decide.

Do they think he was eaten or do they think he escaped? These questions keep the audience watching. What happened? What is going to happen?

Wipe to black. So far, the wolf has destroyed the house of hay and is traveling to the next house. The serious pig is still constructing his house of bricks. The second pig is finishing his house of sticks and maybe, if he survived, the playful pig is running seeking shelter. What do we want to show next?

The wolf going to the second house is just a traveling action and the serious pig is continuing building. There is no drama in these two actions. The drama is wondering whether the second pig completed his house in time to survive the wolf. So let's cut ahead to the second pig. He has finished his house and is on the lookout.

He sees the first pig. But wait he is running away from us.

This is better, to move the story along quicker, we cut to the second pig holding the door open for the first pig with the wolf right on his heels.

We have already shown the wolf destroy one house, so this time we can show it quicker.

We just have to show the wolf blowing down the house of sticks. We can stage it as we did before or use a variation. We might want to just vary the payoff.

You probably didn't even notice that we never showed the second pig building his house. Yet we assume that is what happened. We saw one pig build a house, then another, and what is the third going to do? Repeating something three times builds a pattern. The wolf destroys the second house and goes onto the third.

Once again we will cut ahead to the two pigs joining the serious pig, who is finishing his brick house.

How can we show they have learned their lesson? Pleading for safety? Bite marks? This is exactly how we develop stories. We keep asking questions related to the story's theme. So where are we in the story? Well, let's see what questions still remain unanswered? Will the wolf be able to blow down the house of bricks? Will the pigs learn their lesson? What will happen to the wolf? Once these questions are answered, the story is done.

The wolf moves on.

So the pigs arrive and the serious pig let's them in. They haven't learned that being wise and hard work can protect them from the wolf. How do we show this?

They are humble pigs now. They plead for help; they have learned their lesson.

It is the little details that can make stories unique and special or even add comic touches. Here we see the serious pig putting a bandage on the bite marks on the playful pig.

The serious pig has done his job well and can relax reading the paper. The other two anxiously peer out the window waiting the arrival of the wolf.

We can see from their body language how each of the pigs feel.

It is time for the final arrival of the wolf. He begins to huff and puff.

The wolf huffs ...

And puffs ...

But he can't blow down the house.

So what does he do? What do you do when you are frustrated? Of course, kick the door.

Actions lead to reactions. Causes create effects. And most of us know from experience that this doesn't work.

This time, for comedy, we could have the wolf try to blow up the house.

Now the narrative question is will the wolf succeed in blowing up the three pigs?

Of course, it doesn't work. He ends up blowing himself up!

Or maybe he does blow up the house. Is this the end of the three little pigs?

The wolf has completed his task.

He savors his success.

But something is not right.

The wolf does a double take.

The smoke clears.

The house of bricks still stands. The pigs are safe. Their hard work is rewarded. We have shown that if you build a strong house, the wolf won't get you.

The ending completes the theme and answers all the questions that were raised during the story. So, now we stop.

There are many ways to tell any story and there are equally many ways to storyboard. What if we changed the setting and made it three little penguins. They build igloos to escape from a polar bear. What if we told the story from a different point of view? What if it was the wolf's point of view? What if he was framed? What if we changed the genre and made it a romantic comedy, Western, sci-fi, or horror story? The possibilities are endless. This is the conclusion of our three little pigs story but it is just the beginning of the world of storyboarding.

Let's return to the palace of the sultan. Scheherazade has learned to draw boldly and begins telling her tale of Dumb Love.

Scheherazade continues to draw ...

And holds up her drawing for the sultan to see.

It is the two mountaintop towns of Dumb Love.

Evening on the McClod side.

Here is GOO, a self-centered but loveable monster searching for true love, but totally clueless.

Goo points, gaining the attention of the girl.

As she looks he taps her on the other shoulder.

She turns to look, as Goo moves in.

She turns back right into Goo's kiss.

She smiles. (*Credit*: This wonderful gag idea was suggested to me by story artist Andrei Svislotski.)

Meanwhile …

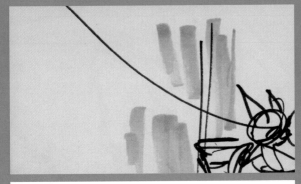

Up above connected by a string …

Sits Goo's loyal best friend …

STICKSALOT, or "Sticks" for short.

Sticks is vigilantly on the lookout.

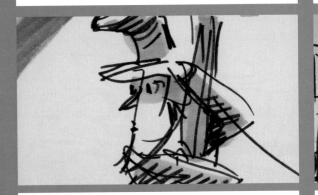

Another girl walks down the dark street.

Sticks sees her.

He pulls the string sounding the alarm.

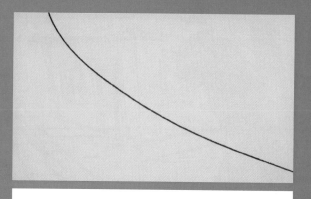

She is mad about something, we can see it in her walk.

Only *Goo* doesn't notice.

Sticks tries again.

The girl is getting closer.

He takes!*
*A *take* is an animation term designating a broad reaction usually to seeing something. The pose is usually held for a beat.

Another girl approaches from the opposite direction.

Sticks doesn't know what to do.

Girl 1 is closing in.

Sticks tugs again.

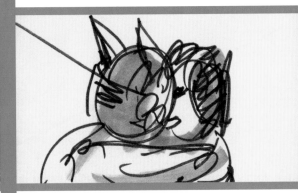

Goo still doesn't notice.

He tries hard once more and …

The string breaks.

Sticks watches helplessly.

The two girls converge on Goo.

GIRL 1: "Gasp!"

She sees Goo kissing another girl.

She is fuming.

Girl 3 nears.

She can't believe her eyes.

Girl 1 confronts Goo.

GIRL 1: "Who is this?"

The girl kissing Goo notices …

Goo looks up in surprise.

He grins sheepishly.

He tries to wiggle free.

GOO: "I can explain!"

Meanwhile Sticks slides down from his lamppost.

Like cobras, the girls are ready to strike.

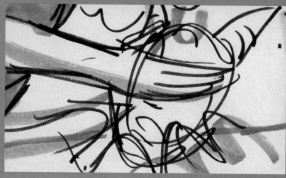

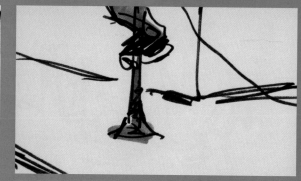

They slap Goo. One, two, three!

Sticks hits the ground.

Goo makes a run for it.

GIRLS: "After him!"

Sticks gets tangled up in the alarm string.

Goo trips, tangled in the string.

Sticks helps *Goo* up and they run for it.

They head to the edge of town.

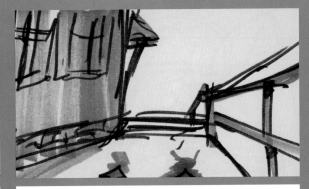

Down an old stairway.

The rotted boards give way and ...

They fall.

In the icy river below.

Scheherazade holds up the drawing for the sultan.

As he looks, Dunazade sits behind the sultan.

Scheherazade notices her sister.

She holds up another drawing while watching her sister.

Dunazade smiles.

Scheherazade smiles.

Dunazade winks, their plan is working. The sultan is totally engaged in the story.

The girls watch for any trace of life. SULTAN: "So what happened to Goo and Sticks?"

So far, Scheherazade's secret storytelling plot is working. Not having a voice has not stopped what she has to say.

Breaking Down the Script: What Are Story Beats?

Script Page

Movies usually start with a written story called a script. The character dialogue and all of the action is described as if it is happening right now. The script only describes what we will see and hear.

Let's look at a sample script page from our story (Table 3.1). This page describes how Goo tries to trick the girl into kissing him. Each story beat is represented by one or more storyboard drawings. The script is composed of scene headings, indicating the place and time, action descriptions, and character dialogue. Notice there are no instructions for the camera, just a clean simple description of action

Table 3.1

Script Format Information

INT.: SULTAN'S PALACE—EVENING	Setting is listed with time of day in capitals.
A hand draws a picture of a mountaintop town. Scheherazade holds up the picture. 　　SULTAN (VO): 　　"It's a mountaintop town."	Description describes the action in lowercase. Character indented, all capitals. Dialogue indented in a text block.
EXT.: MOUNTAINTOP TOWN—NIGHT EXT.: ALLEYWAY—NIGHT GOO, a self-centered but loveable monster, sits with a GIRL on a bench. Goo points out a star. 　　GOO 　　"Look, a shooting star."	The first time a character is introduced, the name is all capitals. Beat—Goo points.
The girl looks up. 　　GIRL 　　"Where?"	Beat—Girl looks.
Goo uses his other arm to reach behind and tap her on the shoulder. 　　GIRL 　　"Huh?"	Beat—Goo taps her.
The girl turns to look to see who is touching her.	Beat—She turns to look.
Goo leans in with lips puckered.	Beat—Goo puckers his lips.
The girl turns back right into Goo's kiss. She is surprised. 　　GIRL 　　"Mmmm."	Beat—Girl turns into Goo's kiss, surprised. Beat—She likes it.
She closes her eyes and kisses Goo back.	

INT., interior; EXT., exterior; VO, voiceover.

in the present tense as if it is happening right now. That is all we can take pictures of—something that happens in front of the camera.

A *scene* is a small unit of conflict in the story. It involves the main character trying for his or her goal, encountering the action of the opponent or other obstacles. This leads to conflicts of emotions that lead the main character to make decisions and finally take action. The action continues leading into the next scene.

A *story beat* is an idea or little action; it is the smallest unit that tells the film's story. It is the flow of these ideas that produce the questions and answer them. When a new idea is introduced, we have a new story beat. Each separate action toward the goal is a new beat. The story beats also create a sense of punctuation for sequences of actions. They allow us to follow the steps of the story by breaking the story down into chunks of actions.

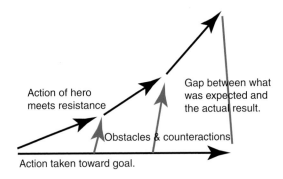

Gap between what was expected and the actual result.

Action of hero meets resistance

Obstacles & counteractions

Action taken toward goal.

Storybeats.

How to Storyboard a Scene

When you first read a script you want to break it down into main story beats. You want to look for the main narrative questions and search for the underlying theme. Everything hangs on the theme. You want to discover how each piece illuminates the theme of the story. How does each story event move the story forward? When you work on each scene you will break it down into detailed story beats. As a working process, I like to thumbnail very quick, little drawings right on the edge of the script pages.

In live action, the next step is to create a shot list. This is a list of shots of how you visualize the movie in your head. It is useful to ensure that when you storyboard a sequence you hit the important story beats.

Storyboarding is not just a translation of the script into a series of visual images. It is more like a new rewrite of the story now using the flow of images to *show* instead of words that *tell*. Movies use images, words, sounds, and music to show/tell their stories. A picture is worth 1001 words. Choose which ones your image says. Dialogue should be like icing on the cake: It is not necessary, but it makes the whole cake taste better.

Storyboarding is nothing less than the first pass at directing a film.

Staging the Action

Originally taken from the theater, *staging* refers to the physical act of placing the characters in different places on the stage to best present the story events. In film, this physical arrangement of the actors in relation to the camera is also known as *blocking*. Over time, staging has come to mean the overall method of presenting a performance. Staging is also used in film to set up each shot's composition, or what the viewer will see onscreen.

Staging should be a process of exploration by trying out different arrangements to find the best possible presentation. Best, in this case, means the clearest and most dramatic.

One of the first drawings you should ever do in planning a film is a diagram of the action—kind of like those drawings you see planning out a football play. This blocking diagram is used to establish the screen geography and the plan for movement showing where everybody is going to move to and when. It also shows where you are going to position and move the camera. These blocking diagrams also help stage the action in *z* camera axis, also known as depth.

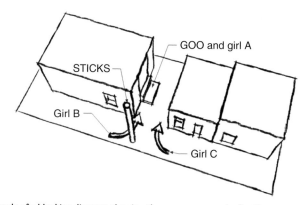

This is an example of a blocking diagram showing the screen geography for the sequence of Goo's date. Each character is labeled with an arrow when he or she moves. This is not necessary for every scene, only ones that have complex character or camera movement.

When you start storyboarding, complete your first pass quickly using thumbnail sketches. Thumbnails are postage stamp–size sketches that allow variations that can be done quickly.

Often you can't change the script but subtext is free reign. Subtext is the subtle ideas that bring a story to life beyond what is actually written in the script. How do you make decisions as to how scenes can be presented? Is it related to the theme? What is the purpose of the scene? What and where in the context of the movie are the narrative questions and answers? These give you the answers. While still in the thumbnail stage, see what would happen if you moved the pieces around?

For example, what if you kept a narrative question still unanswered while you did this? Would that help raise the story tension?

Critique: Scheherazade's Storytelling

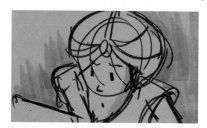

Scheherazade has a secret storytelling plot to quickly grab the sultan's interest. She does this with a trick: With great enthusiasm, she tells her sister a story. She pretends not to even care if the sultan is paying attention. Gradually the sultan gets hooked without ever knowing what hit him.

What is Scheherazade's story about? It is about the character, Goo, who is looking for love in all the wrong places. Goo doesn't really care about others and this gets him in trouble. Sound like someone we know? Yes, she has modeled her character after the sultan himself. The sultan is going along for the ride watching a character who is very much like himself. He is also watching the transformation of that character. If Scheherazade can succeed, the sultan himself will transform as well.

POINTS TO REMEMBER

- Draw **BOLD!** Make your images easy to see as a billboard.
- Number your drawings.
- Pitch clearly and passionately.
- Storyboards are always a work in process. Start out rough and don't be afraid to throw away drawings. Keep at it until you find the image that best tells the story.
- Avoid relying on "talking head" shots. Tell the story visually. Invent visual devices.
- Watch the Wallace and Gromit shorts: *A Close Shave* and *The Wrong Trousers* as an example of great visual storytelling.
- Watch old silent movies to see how they tell stories without words.

References

1. Hand, D. "Memoirs." Available at http://www.dhprod.com.
2. Canemaker, J. *Paper Dreams*. Hyperion, 1999.
3. Toth, A. *Alex Toth by Design*. Gold Medal Productions, 1996.
4. Ibid.
5. Mamet D. *On Directing Film*. Penguin Books, 1992.

How to Draw for Storyboarding: Motion and Emotion

Only 99,999 to Go...

Take a deep breath and relax, this chapter is not going to be scary. If you can remember, you once knew how to draw. Every child can draw, and as they grow, something happens and they forget how to draw, except artists.

This forgetting process usually happens when we start school. Drawing is not usually considered one of the three R's (Reading, wRiting, and aRithmetic).

Schools teach what society considers important. If drawing is to be taught as a part of an art educational program, it must be for educationally justifiable reasons. Drawing has an important place in schools because of its contribution to student's cognitive processes, to their competence and skills in the use of a valuable symbol system. School drawing should promote the acquisition of knowledge and understanding though a special visual means pervaded with feeling and aesthetic qualities.

And just what can be learned from and through drawing? Drawings and other works of art are like windows-on-the-world. Through them we see and create visions of ourselves and our universes, concerns, dreams, emotions, and sense of beauty and quality.

Although a child and artist may not set out to create fresh ideas about the world in their drawings, new and expanded worldviews are the inevitable result. The often accidental, happy by-product of drawing is the creation of insights that artists may not themselves have sought.[1]

Drawings are a great way to begin the visualization of a film.

"Drawing achievement depends upon individual abilities and traits including the desire to draw, visual memory, observational and motor skills, imagination, inventiveness and aesthetic preferences. Finally, how one draws is affected by the opportunity to learn and apply drawing skills, the amount of encouragement to draw and the type of drawing instruction one receives."[2] The legendary animation director Chuck Jones relates that his instructor at Chouinard Art Institute said, "All of you here have 100,000 bad drawings in you. The sooner that you get rid of them, the better it will be for everyone."[3] I think that this is another way of saying practice makes perfect. However, you are going to be able to storyboard without doing 100,000 drawings. You can start now.

Keep a small sketchbook with you when you go out. I like to start with a small Post-it® pad. We used to have a small theater in our town that performed melodrama parodies. I used to draw quick, little gestures while watching the show. Keep improving your drawing skills; you never know when they may be useful. I am using some of those drawings I did at the melodrama theater for gestures and costume ideas for the Dumb Love story that Scheherazade tells the sultan. It is too bad that they didn't perform *One Thousand and One Arabian Nights*.

From Stick Figures to Balloon People

Storyboarding is really about visualizing the images of the film and the sequencing of these images. Many successful directors have used stick figures to board sequences. Any one can draw stick figures. People who say they can't draw, can draw stick figures. We are going to show you how to go beyond stick figures. The more you are able to draw an image in your head to visualize a scene the better the drawing will communicate that vision to your crew, producers, and investors.

There are two things to remember about obstacles to drawing. First, the obstacles are in your head. If you think you can't draw, you are right. You won't be able to. If you think you can draw, then you will be able to. Second, the hardest part of storyboarding is not drawing, but thinking. The real work is deciding how to visualize the story into a series of shots.

Let's overcome the first obstacle to drawing. You will be able to draw what you need. Everyone can draw stick figures, right? Well then, let's begin with a stick figure.

There are several limitations to stick figures. First, it is hard to see stick figures—they are so skinny. The head is visible because it has some volume. Second, it is hard to tell which way the limbs are oriented. Third, most stick figures are stiff looking. They don't appear to be moving.

We are going to present simple solutions to fix these problems. Our first solution is to use curved lines. Watch what happens in the second image when we simply curve some of the lines. The figure immediately comes to life. The language of the body speaks. It begins to express emotions.

Balloon People

With stick figures it is still hard to tell which way the limbs are oriented so our second solution will fix that. Imagine that the stick figure is not made of sticks, but those long skinny balloons. In my storyboard class I simply teach my students to blow up the balloons. The head is already done for us. Treat each line as a balloon. Let's blow them up the rest of them.

Now that the limbs have volume they are easier to see. We can begin to see how they are oriented in space. In a while we will see how we can push the spatial illusion further. So we have started with stick figures and inflated them to balloon people.

Simple Skeleton

The next step is to add a skeleton. We just need to add two lines to our stick figure, one for the shoulders and a second for the hips.

In movement, the shoulder and hips work together by moving in opposite directions. These dynamic angles add interest and movement into drawings.

To keep the figure in balance, the head lines up over the foot supporting the main weight of the figure. In walking, the head leans because the body is actually in a controlled fall. Each step forward catches the fall and the cycle beings again.

Line of Action

Running through a figure is an imaginary line of action that represents the main thrust of forces animating the figure. The S-curved stick figure is called the line of action of the pose. It is one strong clear line that defines the pose. To create a pose based on a line of action, start by drawing the gesture line that expresses the action of the pose. If you don't get it right, draw another line. Keep at it until you find the right one. Then blow up the balloon to construct the drawing. Then clean up the lines by erasing ones you don't want or just darken the ones you wish to keep and finally add details. Many storyboard artists and animators work with a light blue pencil to rough out the pose and then use a black pencil or pen to do the clean up. So if you can draw stick figures, you are halfway there, you just need to finish the drawing.

Now let's try some poses. With poses, where the body bunches up, it is easier to work out the skeleton first. Then construct the body mass or balloon around that. Use simple figure drawings for quickly thumbnailing out your drawings. Star-shaped people are a variation of balloon people that work as well.

One exercise given to beginning animators is to animate a flour sack. The purpose of this exercise is to develop a sensitivity to getting the gesture or life into the pose. "All humans are born with a tendency to draw objects as simply as possible, to avoid overlapping, to depict things from characteristic views and to arrange lines and shapes at right angles."[4] Focusing on the gesture of the pose fights this tendency. It is not easy to do at first, but when it works, even though there is no face, you still know exactly how the flower sack feels because of the gesture.

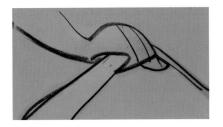

What About Drawing Hands?

Hands can be difficult to draw. Beginning art students drawing the figure will often put the hands behind the back or leave them unfinished. Hands are very expressive and can distort into all kinds of shapes, and there are all those fingers to deal with. Where do you start? The secret that I have found to drawing hands is to not think about drawing hands. What do you draw then? For storyboarding we are not trying to make beautiful drawings but rather visualize the story into a series of pictures. These pictures are of a series of actions. So we simply draw the action. We draw simple hands that poke things, hook onto things, claw things, chop things, and bang things. Simply draw the line of action for the activity that you want and then add detail as necessary. You won't need much. It helps to think of a mitten shape.

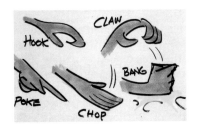

Think in terms of what the hand is doing rather than trying to draw all the parts. We are drawing the action verbs rather than the nouns. Nouns are passive while verbs express action. We are making moving pictures. I learned this idea from Walt Stanchfield.

Walt Stanchfield's Gesture Drawing Class

Draw the Story

When I was at Walt Disney Feature Animation I was fortunate to learn from the best gesture drawing teacher in the world, Walt Stanchfield. His students, including myself, would struggle to draw the pose of the model. We would struggle over the parts, the proportions, and the details, and sometimes we would get a decent drawing. Let me share with you what it was like in one of his classes.

Reality doesn't always match our expectations. I first went to Walt Stanchfield's gesture drawing class hoping to improve my drawing. I sat in front of the model and began drawing. Walt told me to "draw the story." What? What did that mean?

Walt explained that we have to draw the essence of the pose—draw what the character is doing and focus the energy of the drawing on that. He taught to feel the pose in our own bodies and "verbalize" what each part was doing. The ankle twists back here, the hips jut out that way, the neck dips down. It became a live process that slowly started to creep into our drawings. It is all about action verbs.

Walt created a weekly handout that included his drawing critiques of the student's work that revolved around some drawing theme he had chosen to talk about. The handout also included some of Walt's unique philosophical insights. Over the years I collected several volumes of them.

One time Walt critiqued a drawing that illustrated a pose of a woman huddled under an umbrella, peeking out to see if it was raining. The problem was that, being short poses (under a minute), the student didn't have time to finish the drawing. This in itself was not a problem, we often didn't have time to finish the drawings; the problem, Walt pointed out, was which parts the student left unfinished. The feet were nicely worked out.

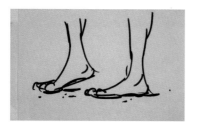

But the drawing didn't tell the story of a woman in the rain. There was no umbrella, no reaching out to check for rain. Walt then began to draw next to the student drawing and with very few lines, emerged a figure huddled under an umbrella reaching and peeking out to check for rain. He made it look so easy and effortless and completed it in about 15 seconds.

I looked at my drawing of the woman with the umbrella. Inspired by Walt's critique, I redrew it and came up with a drawing that I liked. It had a nice flow to it, felt spontaneous, and told the story.

Looking at this drawing years later, I realized that I lost the quality of her being huddled under the umbrella. The next sketch captures the action better.

Walt's advice to us was very simple as it was radical. He didn't want you to draw the model. This was gesture drawing. Walt wanted you to "draw the story." Focus on what the pose is doing, then you can always go back later to work out the details. The drawings his students made were full of life and stories.

He also suggested that we keep a sketchbook with us at all times, and that we draw with a pen rather than a pencil. It forced us to be confident and not afraid of failure. We couldn't rely on an eraser.

Each week, I looked forward to Walt's gesture class. I playfully challenged Walt on many occasions about drawing, and every time he ended up being right. Over time, and once in a while, my drawings would come to "life." Walt taught me a lot about life drawing, but Walt was more than just a great teacher of gesture drawing. More important, he inspired me with the kind of life that he led—outgoing, curious, adventurous, dedicated, and, above all, very generous with his lifetime of experience. It is in believing in his giving spirit, and love of the art, that I believe that Walt wouldn't mind me sharing with you a few of the quotes from his wonderful handouts. I hope they inspire you as they did me.

Walt's Quotes

A sure way to keep from making static, lifeless drawings is to think of drawing "verbs" instead of "nouns." Basically, a noun *names* a person,

place or thing; a verb *asserts* or *expresses* action, a state of being, or an occurrence.

—Walt Stanchfield

I like this drawing but it suffers from a bad tangent. Her nose is poking his shoulder. Bad tangents are poor alignments that flatten out space, because two levels of depth come together and touch. The classic example is the photographer who gets back her vacation photos only to discover that a tree is growing out of her child's head. Move the pieces around so they work well. In the next image, I moved her in so she overlaps the man. The pose also feels like she is more emotionally engaged in the action.

Conflict, in the form of tension, also adds interest to a drawing. One arm stretching *up* as the other reaches *down*; a person stooping *down*, picking something *up*; a person's feet wanting to walk to stage *right*, while the face looks to stage *left*, thinking, "Maybe we ought to be going the other way."

—Walt Stanchfield

Walt would have fun with this drawing. What is she standing on? Oops, I forgot to draw the base.

Gravity and Force

There are always two forces working on the body. Gravity never rests pulling down on the body. Fighting against this force is the life energy of the body allowing us to rise up. The muscles pull on the bones that support the rest of the body. Feel these forces in your own body when you draw. It will help your drawings feel alive.

The body always attempts to stabilize or balance itself. Here we have a paradox, for it seems that in order to balance itself and to maintain some stability and symmetry, the body has to establish some kind of conflict or tension. But this is as it should be, and a drawing without tension tends to be rigid and lifeless.

—Walt Stanchfield

In order to draw it faithfully and expressively, the artist has to be passionate about the gesture. He has to feel as if he were performing the action himself. To sit back and suppose that the model has done all the work and all we have to do is copy what's before us is folly. That is the purpose of drawing from life. The purpose of drawing from life is to transmute the essence of the gesture into our chosen medium drawing.

—Walt Stanchfield

One student had become frustrated with his attempt to capture this pose. The instructor saw that the student had lost control because he had been copying some of the lines that appeared on the model's body rather than the gesture of the body itself, to express the pose.

—Walt Stanchfield

Analyzing a gesture doesn't take a long time, nor does it use up a lot of energy (actually it's quite invigorating). All you have to do is decide what you want your character to do (that should take but a split second) and then without getting sidetracked by fascinating and eye-catching details, get it down on paper.

—Walt Stanchfield

More important than looking for things on the model to draw, is getting the feeling of what the model is doing. All the parts may be drawn, but if they aren't integrated to tell the story—they become just so many parts.

—Walt Stanchfield

So remember today's suggestion—have something to say, and keep it simple.

—Walt Stanchfield

Constructing drawings by using wrap-around volumes. Think of the lines on a globe.

Don't be deceived by surface decoration. Go for attitude, like this bunny here.

You can also use boxes to show the orientation of an object.

Size constancy gives a clue to depth. We usually assume that objects that are similar are also similar in size. If one of those objects appears smaller we assume that it is further away.

This drawing has some nice qualities but there is no gesture animating it from within. It looks like she is floating. She couldn't really stand that way and would probably fall over.

Getting Depth in Your Drawing

Walt also taught us some tricks to achieve depth in our drawings. If you look at a character that has stripped clothing you can watch how it appears to wrap around the form. You can draw these same types of stripes on your drawing that wrap around the form to represent depth on characters.

Playing with size constancy can be used to create some strange illusions. (In the next image, a bad tangent is used for a trick. Beware! Bad tangents can pop up everywhere!)

If it is hard to figure out how to draw a pose, draw it from the side. Then see how the parts line up. For example, normally the ears line up with the eye and bottom of the nose. When the head is tilted up or down, this relationship changes.

Foreshortening occurs when you look at an object head on. The trick to fore-shortening is to overlap your shapes. The second foreshortening trick is to exaggerate the change of scale. Things closer to the camera appear bigger.

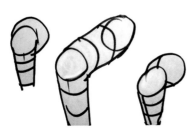

Use the Floor as a Stage

Walt taught us a great trick to see the spatial relationships of the pose. He had us draw a stage for the action. This could be a simple description of the floor the character was sitting or standing on. It really helps locate the figure in space.

Keep your drawings interesting by using angles for twists and turns. Walt would always point out how I stiffened up a pose. I would line things up and make them parallel to the picture frame. His quick critique drawings were full of angles that demonstrated how putting in those angles often defined the pose.

The Body's Acting Performance

Body language shows how a character feels. The body doesn't lie. Use it to tell your story.

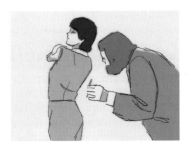

The part of the body leading an action defines the quality of that action. The same action can appear totally different depending on which part takes the lead. Let's look at walking.

When the head leads a walk it has a *Groucho Marx* ducklike quality. Why a duck?

When the head leans back with the feet leading, it feels more like the cartoon character, Mr. Natural.

The head down could indicate a depressed or submissive character.

Leading with the chest suggests a proud quality, like a king or soldier.

Let your lines flow.

Work toward achieving a rhythmic flow in your drawings. Let your lines flow together, suggesting how one muscle connects into the next. The body has natural rhythms to the muscle groups alternating between sides of the body and limbs. This is what gives it a feeling of gracefulness.

Caricature

Caricature is usually thought of as portraits with big noses. Storyboarding involves a caricatured style of drawing. Caricature drawing is capturing the essence with the least effort possible. You use the minimal lines necessary for recognition. In that way it is kind of like Zen—when done right, it looks effortless.

Caricature expresses its subject with the fewest lines possible. You look for the characteristic features of the person or object and exaggerate those. Unimportant details are ignored. One of the most important characteristic features is the gesture or life of the pose. If you can capture that you have achieved the heart of the pose.

Caricatures vary in the degree of distortion based on the style that you are using. In general, the more expressiveness that you put into your drawings, the more they will inspire the crew. This is particularly true for animation.

The distortion involved in caricature is not random exaggeration. You have to follow the structure of the form. The exaggeration of the face is based on a hypothetical "normal" face. If a feature is large then you push it bigger than normal. Conversely, if a facial feature is smaller than normal, it is pushed smaller.

Designing Interesting Characters

Work to create clear silhouettes with interesting shapes. Base characters off of simple shapes, like circles, triangles, or rectangles. Fruit shapes also work—apples, pears, and bananas. Try contrasting different shapes and sizes.

It is important to create a unified style to all of your characters so they feel like they belong in the same world.

Proportions Make the Difference

Artists often use the head as a unit of measurement. The average proportions of an adult human are about six heads tall. Deviations from this standard define other types. Cartoon characters are from two to four heads tall. They have a baby's proportions and that is why they are cute. Superheroes are seven or eight heads tall. Fashion models can be as tall as nine heads high.

Try out many types of designs when you are casting your characters.

Drawing Animals on Tiptoes

I used to have the hardest time with drawing animals. I just couldn't understand how their legs worked. We never drew animals in Walt's class. After studying them for a long time I realized that the bone relationships were just like people, except that they stand on their tiptoes. Suddenly, it became very easy. *When you understand something, you can draw it better.* Sculpting models with clay can really help your visual understanding.

The Story Drive of Emotions

There are four main emotions: fear, joy, sadness, and anger. For storytelling it is interesting to think of emotions in story terms. By this I mean that they go through changes based on events that happen. For example, once angry emotions are triggered, the action could start with a stare. This could lead to threats, either verbally or with the eyes. This could lead to a confrontation, maybe with yelling or pushing. Then it could lead to a rageful fight. The loser could develop desire for revenge. These all suggest being part of a sequence of actions that build because of a character's emotional reaction to the events of the story. Normally, people don't go from peacefully content to rageful in a few seconds. They build in intensity. Rage comes after someone crosses a point of no return.

Joy and happiness are not really powerful story drivers. Imagine a character who is happy for a whole film. It would be boring. Happiness is usually the destination emotion or used as a contrast for other emotions. Anything appears stronger if it is contrasted against something else. So the journey from a terrible loss back to happiness would make a good story arc of emotions.

Laughter is great for a change of pace. A funny scene could be inserted within a dramatic or terrifying scene to take the edge off it as comic relief and to provide contrast.

The five stages of grief are usually experienced in sequence: anger, denial, bargaining, depression, and acceptance. There is a clear progression of emotions and your audience can watch and identify with your characters as they struggle through the stages of loss.

Fear and terror are also powerful story drivers. Fear can force people to act under extreme circumstances. Paranoia could be classed as a fear that can be very interesting to watch, because you can present a situation where the character doesn't know if what he or she is afraid of is real or not. This makes for very interesting narrative questions. The audience will want to know if the threat is real or not.

Wonder and awe usually have a specific moment to appear in a film. This is when the character has an "a-ha" moment of insight and understands what is at stake beyond their immediate circumstances and how the situation affects their world.

Pride, envy, suspicion, and arrogance are great emotions for villains. These can also drive interesting narrative questions. Will pride go before the fall? What will their envy cause them to do? Are their suspicions founded?

Courtship and flirtation have a whole range of emotions associated with them that can drive a story in interesting ways. People in relationships go through a whole dance of acceptance and rejection signals often played out on the face and body. Shy, bashful, and coy emotions contrast with seduction and suggestiveness. Whispering secrets definitely gets the audience thinking about what was said.

Some of the most dramatically interesting emotions to watch are those when a character has something to hide. During the courtship example, one may hide how he feels when learning that the other party likes him. And, once outside the door, he will jump for joy, letting out his true feelings.

It is fun to watch people lying and trying not to get caught in it. People trying to hide their emotions usually will leak the real emotion in some subtle way. A poker face is the ultimate example of trying not to show what someone is feeling. If someone has been hurt and is trying to hide it, her smile might be big and forced, but her eyebrows might leak the sadness under the guise of everything is fine.

It is interesting to think of the verbal expressions that go with emotions. They help in giving story ideas: "If looks could kill"; "Pride goes before a fall"; and Pinocchio's lies were "as plain as the nose on his face" are several examples. In the film *Who Framed Roger Rabbit*, the characters are warned not to laugh, but can't help themselves and they "die laughing."

Drawing the Four Main Emotion Groups

When drawing emotions, the mouth and eyebrows are the main keys on the face to achieving these expressions.

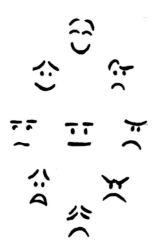

The eyelids can create subtle changes in expression.

Watch how just lowering the eyelids subtly changes the expression. Mad becomes evil by a simple lowering of the eyelids.

Live-action storyboards are a little different than animation storyboards. Expressions can be distracting from analyzing the storytelling aspect of the camera work. It also tells part of the story.

With animation we need to show the expressions of the acting. Showing a change of expressions shows the character thinking. Use a mirror and don't be afraid to act it out. See how it feels.

Changes of Expression Shows Thinking

When we see a character go through a range of emotions, we are watching his or her thinking process as it plays on his or her face.

When people think, they access their internal memory banks. Psychologists have noticed this and have even mapped out whether people are thinking about the past or future and images or words.[5] A person's eyes will look in different directions depending on what thoughts he or she is accessing.

Struggling.

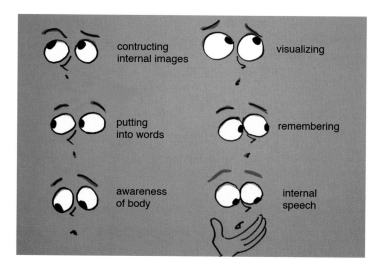

contructing
internal images

visualizing

putting
into words

remembering

awareness
of body

internal
speech

A Gallery of Emotions

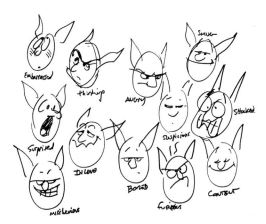

This is a sample expression chart of Goo. Animators use charts like this to keep consistency so everyone draws the character the same. More important, these charts inspire animators to come up with interesting acting.

Angry.

Plotting.

Annoyed.

Expressions come through from the shape of the eyes, eyebrows, and mouth. Body language reinforces facial expressions.

Frustrated.

Miscellaneous Drawing Tips

- Don't be afraid to redraw; search for the best solution to tell the story.
- Draw for clarity—one idea per sketch.
- When drawing eyes, darken pupils.
- Play straight lines against curves for interest.
- Have something to say in your image, don't doodle.
- If part of a drawing doesn't work cut it out and rework it.
- Avoid symmetry in drawing—it is boring. It can make your drawings look cut out. Use angles to avoid symmetry and rigid poses. Dynamic asymmetry is much more exciting.

Avoid symmetry in your drawing — it is boring. It can make your drawings look cut out.

Use angles to avoid symmetry and rigid poses. Dynamic symmetry is much more interesting.

- Draw bold and expressive.
- The important idea of the sketch should be highlighted and all else subordinated to it.
- Don't get too clever. Often choosing tricky camera angles just makes the drawing ambiguous.
- Show how the character feels. Feel the pose. Feel the emotion in your body as you draw.
- A person is always "doing" something. Express the purpose. Experience the pose, and feel it kinetically in your own body.
- Use straight line symbols for stretches, bent line symbols for squashes.
- Draw borders so you have to compose to them.
- Watch the body's landmarks where bones reach the surface, like hipbones and ribs.

One of my mentors was storyboard artist Vance Gerry. He had some interesting advice: "If you can't photocopy it, trace it. If you can't trace it, then you'll have to draw it."

Drawing for Clarity and the Use of Clear Silhouettes

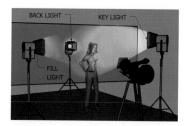

Here is the location of the three lights.

The back light creates a halo that separates the figure from the background.

Without the fill light the shadows are very stark. This is useful for film noir–type lighting.

You should be able to blacken in your drawings and still read what is happening. Keep decoration within the main outline. This keeps drawings from getting busy. Make sure the outlines of your drawings are interesting.

Basic Lighting

Light is extremely important because it allows us to see clearly. It fights the enemy of design—confusion. Light also creates mood or drama.

The most common lighting scheme is called three-point lighting. This is because it gives the most convincing illusion of volume. The *key light* provides the main source of illumination. It is kind of like the sun. The *back light* creates a rim of light around the edge that separates the figure from the background. Finally a *fill light* fills in the shadows created by the key light to soften them. Sometimes the fill light can be replaced by a reflector that bounces light back from the fill to the subject.

Three-point lighting gives a pleasing sense of volume.

The Drama of Light: Theatrical Lighting

Theatrical lighting uses light for expressive purposes rather than naturalistic representation. It is used to create mood or focus attention.

Shadows are another way to create mood and define a composition.

Chromatic lighting is light that takes on the quality of a specific color other than white. Here the overcast blue quality suggests the rainy mood.

Silhouette lighting and high contrast are two types of specialized lighting schemes that are very expressive and useful.

Mort Walker's *The Lexicon of Comicana*

Mort Walker is the cartoonist who draws the "Beetle Bailey" comic strip. He also created a virtual encyclopedia of cartoon devices that indicate motion and emotion in a graphic way.

The story of how the book came about is interesting:

In the early 30s, a humorist named Charles Rice attached labels to certain cartoon devices. He called sweat drops "plewds" and the dust clouds

behind a running person "briffits." This inspired Mort Walker to do some further research and, in 1964, he produced an article for the National Cartoonist Society magazine titled "Let's Get Down to Grawlixes." It was a tongue-and-cheek spoof of the plethora of "comicana" found in most comic strips. To his amazement the public took it seriously.[6]

This interest convinced Mort to take it a step further and created the book *The Lexicon of Comicana*. It is a wonderful satirical book but also a goldmine of instruction for cartoonists and animators.

You will see these kinds of iconic indications of things in comic strips all the time. They also can be very useful to bring storyboard drawings to life. Here are some examples.

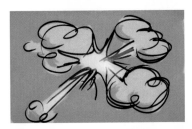

Explosions!

Speed lines indicate speed.

Fuming angry.

Technical Aspects of Storyboards

Procedures vary among studios but here are some guidelines for presenting camera work with storyboards. Often studios will have their own preprinted storyboard pages to work on. The page will contain panel boxes for pictures, instructions for camera and special effects, dialogue and action description, and the show name with numbers for show number, sequence number, scene number, and panel number.

SCENE .01 PANEL 001   CUT: SCENE .02 PANEL 001

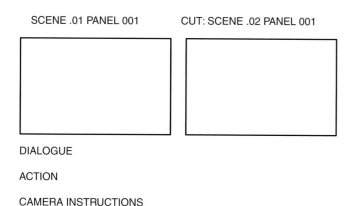

DIALOGUE

ACTION

CAMERA INSTRUCTIONS

Straight cuts are just labeled "cut" in the upper left of the incoming scene.

SCENE .01 PANEL 001   CUT: SCENE .02 PANEL 001

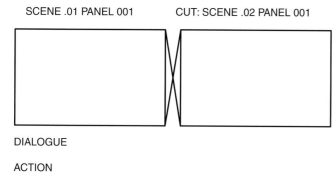

DIALOGUE

ACTION

CAMERA INSTRUCTIONS

Separate shots. Cross dissolves are indicated with an X between frames.

SCENE .01 PANEL 001   CUT: SCENE .02 PANEL 001

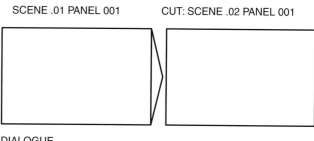

DIALOGUE

ACTION

CAMERA INSTRUCTIONS

Fades are indicated with > and <, or half a cross dissolve.

Pans are drawn in the correct aspect ratio for the film as start and end positions with an arrow indicating the direction of the pan. The aspect ratio is the ratio of the height to the length of the image. Television uses an aspect ratio of 3:4, widescreen uses a 1:1.85 ratio, and high definition uses a 16:9 ratio.

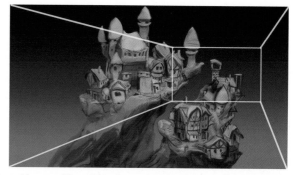

Zooms are indicated by a small box within the main panel with arrows indicating the direction. With the increasing use of three-dimensional computer graphics the camera has gained freedom to move all over. Resist the temptation to move the camera without a good reason to help tell the story.

Camera moves can be indicated by arrows. The difference between a zoom and a camera move is that during a zoom the camera stays in the same place but the focal length of the lens changes. Camera moves are much more dynamic because they actually move through the space while keeping the focal length constant.

Arrows are also used to indicate the path of objects.

Character entrances and exits into or out of the frame also use arrows.

It is time to return to Scheherazade. The night is growing late and she is growing tired.

Scheherazade feverishly draws.

She presents the drawing.

The sultan is enthralled.

Goo and Sticks are carried along by the current.

Sticks grabs a tree branch and pulls them to safety.

They sit waiting for their clothes to dry out.

GOO: "I'm never gonna find true love."

STICKS: "Look on the bright side, Goo. You had three girls chasing you."

[Smack!]

It starts to pour.

Goo and Sticks wander hopelessly lost in the woods.

Goo insists he knows the way home.

Goo and Sticks take shelter in a cave.

STICKS: "Do you think there're any bears in here?"

GOO: "Be quiet."

Sticks walks in and …

Trips …

Knocking over a suit of armor.

The helmet falls on Sticks.

The helmet is stuck.

GOO: "Shhh."

Goo does a double take!

The helmet comes off.

GOO: "Someone's coming."

They stand still pretending to be suits of armor.

They hear voices arguing.

CLOVER: "But I don't like any of them."

FATHER: "You have to choose one."

CLOVER: "I want to choose who I marry."

Goo watches.

Clover storms off.

They follow her father.

STICKS [Voiceover]: "What is this place?"

STICKS [Voiceover]: "Looks like a science project."

GOO [Voiceover]: "Quiet, I want to hear them."

STICKS [Voiceover]: "I think he said he's making a bro."

STICKS: "This place is kinda dusty."

Without realizing it Sticks leans on a switch.

Above them it sets off a chain reaction.

A metal ball rolls …

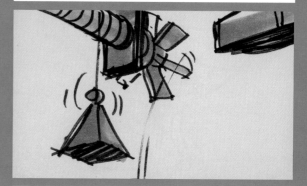

It turns a wheel releasing a weight …

GOO: "Huh?"

Suddenly the ground drops and Goo falls.

STICKS: "What are you doing down there?"

GOO: "Ahhh!"

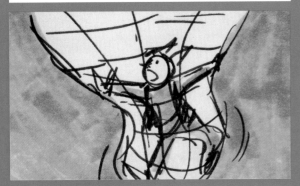

GOO: "Help!"

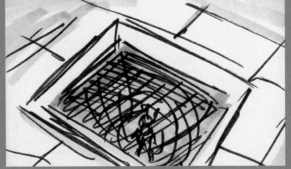

GOO: "Get me out of here!"

VOICE [Voiceover]: "There's a McClod in the castle."

VOICE: "Get him!"

The door shuts and all goes black.

Goo and Sticks are tied up and carried from the castle.

Scheherazade continues drawing.

SULTAN: "What happens to Goo and Sticks?"

She holds up the next drawing.

The Catfields toss Goo and Sticks onto the rope bridge.

Clover comes up behind the crowd.

She tries to peek over their heads but can't see.

Crowds gather on both sides.

Goo struggles to move in his ropes.

Up above unbeknownst to Goo flies CUPID.

He launches his arrow and . . .

Misses

CUPID: "Drat!"

Cupid lines up another arrow.

The arrow flies and …

Bingo! A perfect shot.

Goo turns to look.

Goo is shocked at what he sees.

Cupid smiles.

Clover climbs up in order to see better.

She tries to balance herself.

The clouds part, light streams down, and Cupid shoots.

Clover gets shot.

Goo looks angrily at Cupid.

Cupid points.

Goo looks.

Clover stands in front of a statue.

Goo sees an angel and falls in love.

Clover sees Goo and falls in love.

Clover's friend WEED nudges DAISY.

They look to see Clover bewitched.

They turn to see Goo.

Goo stuggles to get up.

Clover is betwitched by Cupid's arrow.

Goo is falling in love.

And falls.

Clover is shocked.

Sticks hangs onto Goo.

Sticks struggles to hang on.

Clover pushes through the crowd.

SULTAN: "What's gonna happen to Goo?"

Scheherazade has grown weary as the night grows late.

Scheherazade can barely keep her eyes open.

Her sister notices.

She yawns.

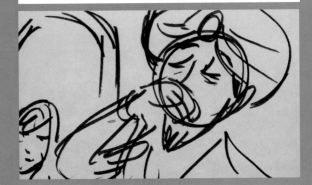

And it is contagious.

The sultan gazes over as well.

Scheherazade bows.

She blows out the lantern.

The sultan rises.

VIZIER: "Shall I follow the usual procedure, sire?"

SULTAN: "No, not tonight."

SULTAN: "I want to hear what happens."

They leave.

Scheherazade and Dunazade remain frozen.

DUNAZADE: "Your plan worked."

They hug in relief.

Will Goo fall in love or into oblivion? The pendulum swings to fear. Scheherazade survives the first night and the sultan wants to hear more. The pendulum swings to hope. But what will the next night bring?

Critique: 1001 Drawings

Go back over the story and analyze how the gesture poses and expressions of the characters tell the story of Scheherazade's 1001 drawings and her story of Dumb Love. Try your own staging and see if you can push the poses more extreme.

I hate my cleaned up drawings. When I draw my roughs, I am focusing on telling the story and the character attitudes. When I clean up drawings, I am focusing on putting them on model and thus I lose the life of the pose. To keep your drawings alive, work back and forth between the two.[1]

POINTS TO REMEMBER
- Carry a sketchbook and sketch, sketch, sketch!
- Sketch some more.
- Draw the story.
- Use gestures to help tell the story.
- Learn to draw the essentials fast.

- Try scenes a dozen different ways to compose them.
- Film always says one thing at a time, and everything must relate to that one thing.
- Draw the pose, not the parts. Don't blow it with too many details.
- Draw verbs (actions) not nouns (names of things).
- Don't stiffen up your poses. Think diagonals.
- Watch the Disney animated classics for examples of great drawings.
- Watch Hayao Miyaziki's films such as *Kiki's Delivery Service* or *Totoro* for great visual storytelling and drawing.
- Study comic books for great drawing and visual storytelling.

References

1. Wilson B, Hurwitz A, Wilson M. *Teaching Drawing from Art*. Davis Publications, Inc., 1987.
2. Ibid.
3. Jones C. *Chuck Amuck*. Farrar Straus Giroux, 1989.
4. Wilson B, Hurwitz A, Wilson M. *Teaching Drawing from Art*. Davis Publications, Inc., 1987.
5. Bandler R. *Time for a Change*. Meta Publications, 1993.
6. Walker M. *The Lexicon of Comicana*. Museum of Cartoon Art, 1980.

[1] Storyartist Toni Vian made this observation.

Part Two

Structural Approach: Tactics to Reach the Goal

Once upon a time ...

Director and CalArts teacher Alexander Mackendrick in his book, *On Filmmaking*,[1] shows the value of those traditional bedtime story phrases, such as "Once upon a time ...." He shows how these stock phrases illustrate dramatic structures. One could conceivably create a *Mad Libs*[2] to invent new stories. *Mad Libs* were children's books published by Price Stern Sloan of short stories with many of the key words replaced by blanks and instructions to replace the blanks with a name, verb, or adverb. The resulting stories were generally comical and surreal: Once upon a time in *name of place*, there lived *name of hero* who wanted *name of object* but couldn't get it because of *name of villain or obstacle*, but one day *description of event* caused *result of action* but meanwhile ....

What this demonstrates is that almost any content can fill the blanks of a story, but it's how these pieces fit together that makes it structurally dramatic. The basic structure is that a conflict is presented that leads to an inevitable confrontation and climax and then resolution. Each piece of the structure is required for the whole to work or it will feel like something is missing.

Let's quickly recap what we have covered so far:

- We watch movies for many reasons but mostly to feel good.
- We have to direct the audience's attention to one idea at a time using the speaking metaphor.
- Don't forget punctuation. The audience needs time to process information—give them pauses.
- Keep the audience's attention with intriguing narrative questions and then tease them by delaying the answers.
- Build story complexity by the hierarchical network of narrative questions that keep your audience guessing.

The structural approach to directing is based on what the audience is doing as they watch a movie. We want to give them an emotionally satisfying experience. To do that, we aim at the heart by working at the structure.

What follows is the beginning of a chart that will describe the tools that you will be able to use to work at the structural level. When used correctly, these tools will help you keep the structure invisible and your viewer "lost" in the story. Each of the following chapters in this book will add specific structural techniques and tools for making stories clear and dramatic. The chart presents the information sequentially, however, the mind processes all levels of this information unconsciously faster than we can think. Wait, this is how we think, we are just not aware of how much mental processing goes on outside of our awareness. Our consciousness is just the tip of a great iceberg.

In the beginning, when you storyboard and direct, there is so much to keep in mind, that it will feel overwhelming. It is like when you first tried riding a bicycle. You climbed on the bike unsure of what would happen. You shifted your weight and pressed on the pedals. The bike started to move. You probably wobbled all over the place and maybe even fell a few times. Over time and with practice you learned to ride smoothly. You learned to stop and go when you chose to. You learned to steer where you wished to go and I am sure it felt really good.

Now, with the practice to master these structural storytelling skills, I am sure you will be smoothly telling stories. Our goal here is to learn all of these skills and then forget them and work intuitively. You will use these techniques again when it is time to analyze your story to fix problems and make it more dramatic and clear.

Chart of Story Events and Structure

The **events**: What is going to happen next in the story?

The **threshold of awareness** divides what the audience pays attention to into what we notice and what we don't. We usually don't pay attention to what is below this line unless something catches our attention by being out of place.

Structure is how the story is told, through narrative questions, delays, and answers, using the "speaking metaphor" to show one idea at a time.

Let's make this a little more understandable, so we can learn to utilize this approach as a tool. In order to do that, I am going to show you a story.

MAN WITH STRING: "Some people say that the ...."

The audience doesn't hear background music in a movie.

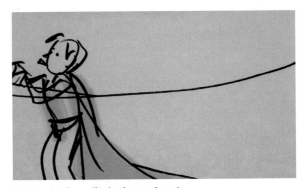

That is why they call it background music.

If the music is there, why can't they hear it?

Let's say this rope is our threshold of awareness.

Since we can pay attention to only one thing at a time ...

We don't notice everything below the rope threshold.

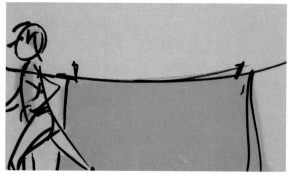

Let the story begin …

[Music swells.]

CREATURE 1: "Hey, do you hear music?"

CREATURE 1: "I think it's coming from down there."

CREATURE 2: "What are you doing?"

CREATURE 2: "Oh no. You crossed the threshold."

CREATURE 1: "I think I broke the story."

113

The clothesline is the threshold of attention. The puppets are characters involved in the story events. We watch and are entertained by their antics until one puppet notices something out of place and calls attention to it. The curtain is cast aside and the illusion is destroyed, just like the great Wizard of Oz. This is exactly what happens when we watch a film. We enjoy the antics of the characters until something happens to make us aware of the structural level and the illusion of being "lost" in the story is destroyed.

Most often we become aware of the structural level because the filmmaker has done something wrong. It can be a little problem, like a continuity error, or it can be a big problem, like the fact that the story might be boring. Either way we are bumped out of the story and that certainly doesn't make the audience feel good.

We watch stories to feel good but also to learn. This story is about a little puppet show gone awry, but it is also a story to make a point about focusing the audience's attention on the narrative questions of the story events.

Scheherazade continues weaving her spell on the sultan using every trick in the book. So far her plan is working since she is keeping his attention on the events of the story. He wants the narrative questions answered.

The story continues …

Daisy and Weed search for their friend Clover.

DAISY: "Clover?"

Weed taps Daisy to look.

Clover's lovestruck.

DAISY: "Clover?"

SULTAN: But what happened to Goo?

Scheherazade smiles and finishes the drawing.

She holds up the drawing for the sultan to see.

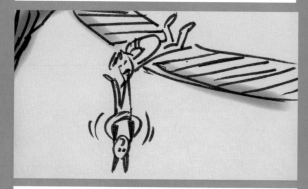

Goo still hangs by a thread, or actually Sticks' teeth.

Suddenly a hook reaches out and picks them up.

They are carried off.

Clover can't turn away.

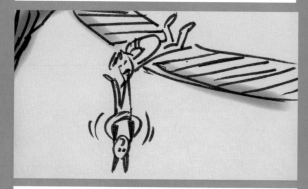

WEED: "She's falling for a McClod! This can't be."

The sultan waits for the next drawing.

She smiles at her idea.

She also scratches an itch and ...

Covers herself in soot from the charcoal.

She puts the finishing touch on the drawing and ...

Holds it up for view.

The sultan laughs.

Scheherazade is puzzled, the drawing isn't funny.

She looks back.

Dunazade points to her cheek.

Scheherazade turns to look …

In the mirror.

She sees what they are laughing at …

And notices the sultan is staring at her.

She smiles.

Well, Goo and Sticks have been saved from the brink and Scheherazade seems to be warming up to the sultan. The charcoal smudges bring a bit of levity to a tense situation. The pendulums have swung to hope. Let's see for how long.

Critique: Developing Character Relationships

The charcoal on Scheherazade's face is out of place. Instead of being on the drawing, it takes them out of the Dumb Love story temporarily, but what it serves is to reveal character relationships in the Scheherazade story. She is a little less uptight. It shows she is letting her guard down and that the sultan is warming up to her.

We are involved with the characters and what they are going through. We are "lost" in the story, not paying attention to the cutting, staging, composition, and all of the choices of the storyteller.

POINTS TO REMEMBER

- Aim at the heart by working at the structural level to create narrative delays that keep the audience guessing.
- Keep the structure invisible, don't call attention to it or you will create a hole in your story.

References

1. Mackendrick, A. *On Filmmaking.* Farber & Farber Inc., 2005.
2. Wikipedia. "Mad Libs," at http://en.wikipedia.org/, May 5, 2008.

What Do Directors Direct?

WORK HERE: STRUCTURAL LEVEL

DIRECTORS DIRECT ATTENTION

Threshold of Awareness

spotted. Finally, you can try not to think of it. It is a paradoxical trick that, by definition, can't be done. But we have directed your attention to something we told you not to pay attention to.

Why should we care about spotted elephants? What if you were on trial and the prosecutor lies and said that he heard that you were seen at the scene of a crime holding a knife. The judge tells the jury to disregard the comment. What does the jury do? They acknowledge that they are not to pay attention to the remark. But what has already happened in their minds? Yes, the jury has already constructed in their minds a picture of the defendant holding a knife at the scene. Or another example: What if a movie condemns violence yet portrays violent acts?

We begin our chart at the beginning. As we learned earlier, *the first thing the director has to do is capture and direct the audience's attention.* Don't worry; you don't have to be a wizard to do this. Wait, maybe you do. Let's look at some ways to direct attention. Try this experiment: **Do not to think of the spotted elephant.**

In order to complete the task, first you have to imagine an elephant. Then you have to add spots because elephants are not usually

I have continually talked about clarity, but there are times that call for a dose of ambiguity. We want controlled ambiguity—too much and you spoil the soup. We still need to be clear but leave room for the audience to puzzle over the exact meaning of what they see. An excellent example of when this is called for is when we want to withhold from the audience whether a character is guilty or not. In director Joe Wright's *Atonement*, Briony Tallis, a young girl who wishes to become a storyteller, sees an event but she misinterprets what it means. It is only when the audience is shown the event from another point of view do they understand the significance of the event and the consequences of Briony's distortion.

Director Alain Resnais plays with this idea in his film, *Last Year at Marienbad*, where a man is trying to convince a woman that they met last year at a hotel. She apparently doesn't remember. The film presents an enigma: Did this event ever happen? What is interesting about this film is that we get to see the stories that the man tells the woman. Are they actual memories or fantasies that never happened? As Chico Marx once said, "Who ya gonna believe? Me or your own eyes?"

How to Get Attention

What is it that attracts our attention? Shine a light, jump up and down, yell, and set off fireworks. It is easy to attract attention. You just have to do something to stand out.

As you read this notice the space you are in. What stands out for you? What "calls" to you? As a filmmaker, this is something to keep in the back of your mind. Motion, contrast, brightness, pointing at, and loudness all attract attention. Another way of directing attention can be done by trying another experiment. Next time you are in a group of people, casually look up. Even if there is nothing but sky above you, you will be surprised at how many people look up to see what you are looking at. You have directed their attention.

Strong contrast attracts attention. We can become aware of subtle changes, but if changes are too gradual then we might not notice them.

The Map Is Not the Territory

The fact that the map is not the territory sounds pretty obvious, but what is not so obvious is the fact that we really never deal directly with the territory. All of our experience of the world is through our maps of it. Our maps represent the world using images, sounds, words, and symbols—in other words, sensory information.

One of the functions of our brain is to act as a filter to protect us from information overload. If the brain didn't have this filtering process we would be continually overwhelmed with a bombardment of sensations. This filtering process organizes information into patterns. Humans continually seek patterns and notice even small changes to patterns. We deal with an overwhelming amount of information and organizing this information into patterns is a way for us to process it. The most obvious patterns are visual designs. But we are aware of patterns of weather, the way people speak, musical patterns, traffic patterns. Patterns are everywhere. Telling a story is organizing information into a pattern.

Neuro Linguistic Programming is the study of how language programs our minds. Language is kind of like the software for our brains. According to Neuro

Linguistic Programming theory we continually delete, generalize, and distort the information we receive about the world so that our brains don't go into overload.[1] In other words, we don't pay attention to a lot of information we are exposed to—we delete it. We also rely on stereotypes and clichés—we generalize. We distort the things that don't fit into our worldview.

> In many ways, we are cognitive misers, forever trying to conserve our cognitive energy. Given our finite ability to process information, we often adopt strategies of the peripheral route for simplifying complex problems; we mindlessly accept a conclusion or proposition not for any good reason but because it is accompanied by a simplistic persuasion device. According to the information-processing models, a persuasive message must successfully pass through a series of stages. First, the message must attract the recipient's attention; ignored messages will have little persuasive impact. Second, the arguments in the message must be understood and comprehended. Third, the recipient must learn the arguments contained in the message and come to accept them as true; the task of the advertiser and other persuaders is to teach arguments supportive of the cause, so that these arguments will come easily to mind at the appropriate time and place. Finally, the recipient of the messages acts on this learned knowledge when there is an incentive to do so; a persuasive message is learned, accepted, and acted upon if it is rewarding to do so.[2]

Selective Attention

Try this experiment and it will really make you aware of how selective our attention is. The next time that you are in a restaurant, close your eyes and just listen. Don't pay attention to any specific sound but just let your attention hear all of the different sounds. There will probably be many kinds of voices, some loud, some whispering. There will be the sounds of glasses clinking, silverware tapping on plates. Depending on the type of restaurant you might hear pots and pans crashing in the kitchen or the chef yelling out orders. There might be different kinds of music. There might be nature sounds like dogs barking. All of this you tune out when you listen to someone speaking to you at your table.

A tape recorder doesn't differentiate what it records. Early in my filmmaking career, I recorded some sounds for a film. I was surprised to find not only the sound that I wanted to record, but dozens more that the microphone picked up. It included car sounds and dogs barking that were more than a half of a mile away. I didn't hear this when I was recording. Our brains tune out all of this unwanted noise. But equipment like cameras and microphones do not have this selection process. The recorder does not know what you find important. That is why we need to be able to see and listen carefully so we know what we are presenting to our audience. We need to tune our sensitivity to light and sound.

Our attention is a very precious commodity. According to Tony Robbins, the motivational coach, what we pay attention to affects the quality of our life.[3] This is crucial information for filmmakers. Our ability to pay attention is affected by many factors such as fatigue, interest, state of mind, and expectations.

When we multitask, we feel like we are accomplishing a great deal of work. What we are really doing is juggling or shifting attention very quickly between multiple items. This is why people driving with cell phones are more likely to have accidents than other drivers. We think we are paying attention, but in reality our attention is split. Our minds can deceive us very easily.

Keeping Attention

Showing the audience new and exciting things will keep your audience's attention. This will work for a while, but if you have ever been in a great art museum, you have probably experienced that after a while you reach burnout.

Narrative questions about something we care about are what keep the audience's attention. But you must remember to give them a rest once in a while. The best cure for attention burnout is change. Create a change of pace or scenery. Take them someplace new. Scheherazade takes the sultan to a mythical place of feuding monsters.

Keeping Structure Invisible: Tricks of Attention

We have seen that we want to keep the audience lost in the story. So we work at a structural level. How do we keep the structure invisible? Well, luckily filmmakers have evolved a way to do this called *classical continuity editing style*. We will look at that in the chapter on meaning (Chapter 10). However, other types of entertainment artists have had to deal with the same issues only differently, and they can shed a lot of insight on the problem of directing the audience's attention. First, let's look at the art of ventriloquism.

In Chapter 1, we saw that a story is like ventriloquism. The film story appears to tell itself without anyone having to tell it. There are certain tricks involved to achieve this. Let's look at what ventriloquism can offer us.

DUMMY: "So how does a director keep the structure invisible?"

VENTRILOQUIST: "The director is like a ventriloquist. Ventriloquists use three techniques. First, they create a contrast in voices between themselves and the dummy. I speak normally and you talk funny."

VENTRILOQUIST: "Second, when the dummy speaks, he doesn't move his mouth. He "throws" his voice to somewhere else. Actually, you just talk with you lips almost closed with your tongue pressed against your lower teeth."

VENTRILOQUIST: "And third, they make the dummy's lips move when they want the dummy to talk. This distracts the audience. For example, when I want you to talk, I will move your lips and the audience will watch you."

DUMMY: "Are you calling me a dummy? I'll have you know I'm a vent figure. That is short for ventriloquist figure."

VENTRILOQUIST: "Oh, one more thing, they direct the audience's attention to the vent figure by looking at him and engaging with him as if he is real. Please don't hurt me!"
Source: Art by Jessica Dru.

The ventriloquist brings a character to life by giving it emotions and "acting" as if the dummy, I mean vent figure, is real. So in this case directing involves two aspects. First is directing attention to the vent figure when he speaks. Second, the ventriloquist misdirects your attention by keeping it away from himself or herself. Of course we know that the ventriloquist is doing all the talking, but when the vent figure speaks, he directs you where to look.

Remember the speaking metaphor? Show the audience one thing at a time. The conscious mind can only pay attention to one thing at a time. Note that I said the conscious mind. Our conscious mind is just the tip of the iceberg. Most of our perceptual organization happens with the automatic nervous system or before entering conscious attention. In other words, it happens at the part of the iceberg that you can't see.

A director directs the audience's attention through the arrangement of the presentation of the images and sounds of the film. First, you must capture the audience's attention, and then you must protect it from distractions. In this regard, a director is like a hypnotist. It is not under the viewer's conscious control.

When a film is presented clearly and dramatically, the conscious mind is following the story. However, our unconscious mind is picking up all kinds of information, outside the edges of our awareness. These subtle influences can affect how the audience thinks and feels. All of the structural elements can perform this function. As a quick example, the same scene in shadow versus direct sunlight can have a very different feel.

Milton Erickson Meets Bugs Bunny

Milton H. Erickson, M.D., was always fascinated by what makes people tick. There is a great story from Milton's childhood that illustrates his insatiable curiosity. One snowy morning he got up early, and while walking to school the young Milton did an experiment. He began to walk a very wavy path in the snow, zigzagging back and forth even though it was obvious that the path was fairly straight. When he returned in the afternoon, to his amusement, he found that people had followed his lead, their footsteps in the snow followed his, rather than the simple direct path. It was hard to resist Milton's lead. He grew up to become the world's leader of medical hypnosis.

Healing is the breaking of unhealthy limits learned in childhood. In *Uncommon Therapy*,[4] Milton Erickson shows that most people get stuck at life junctures. These are turning points from one life stage to another. The most common reason for getting stuck is fear from an earlier trauma. This fear has been learned and inappropriately generalized to other situations. Remember we delete, distort, and generalize our maps of the world. (This is where we often encounter film characters, when they are ripe for a change.)

In a story, the hypothesis "What if ...?" is presented as true. The writer is a masterful liar offering supporting details to flesh out a believable world in which the action takes place. The writer's truth is not the story but rather the emotions. Given this imaginary situation, this is how people would truly feel and behave. These hypothetical "what if" questions set off unconscious searches whereby the audience unconsciously seeks the answers from what is known of the story so far. If you don't continually ask highly charged questions, the audience will generate their own. You don't want them thinking, "When is something going to happen?" or "Why am I watching this?"

You want to put your audience in an anxious state of suspense. Anxiety usually comes from the unknown. The viewer finds the answers to the questions raised by watching the film and thus relieves the tensions from their lack of knowledge.

Erickson's Techniques

So how does Milton do it? What secrets does he know? In order to understand some of Erikson's techniques, I am going to allow Bugs Bunny to demonstrate them for us. We would usually find Bugs minding his own business when the hunter, Elmer Fudd, would arrive whispering, "Be very very quiet, I'm hunting wabbits." Bugs wanders nonchalantly over to Elmer who is obsessively involved in his task of pointing his shotgun down the rabbit hole. Bugs inquires, "Eh, what's up doc?" to which Elmer answers, "I'm hunting rabbits."

Bugs proceeds to ask a series of questions with obvious answers: Does he have a gray coat, like this? And a fluffy tail, like this? And long ears, like this? Elmer answers "yes" to each question getting more excited by the minute. Then Bugs casually replies, "I ain't seen him," and walks away. Then something very interesting happens. Elmer shakes himself as if waking up out of a *trance* and states, "That was the wabbit!" The chase is on.

Let's look at what Bugs was doing as he hypnotized Elmer. The first thing he does is to utilize what the person offers. Bugs accepts that Elmer is hunting rabbits. That doesn't deter him; in fact he uses it to accomplish his second objective. Bugs depotentiates Elmer's conscious state. In other words, the fact that the prey walks up to the hunter to ask what he is doing is not the normal state of affairs. It is very confusing. So Bugs confuses Elmer. In order to not be confused you have to go internal and make sense of the situation. Now he is primed and ready to go into a trance. Then Bugs asks a series questions creating a "yes" set. These are obvious questions that all result in a yes. Questions set off unconscious searches as the brain goes through its memories to try to find an answer. This leads the person internally deeper into a trance state. I was really surprised the first time a watched this cartoon after learning about Milton Erickson. My suspicions were confirmed when Elmer has to shake himself out of the trance.

This is not the only time Bugs hypnotizes someone. In *Wakini Wabbit*, Bugs is stranded on an island with two shipwreck victims. When a ship finally arrives he performs the ritual of sending them off, giving them lays, saying bon voyage, and shaking their hands. At the last minute he performs a switch and gets on the ship himself leaving them stranded.

A final example is from the classic cartoon, *Rabbit Seasoning*. Bugs and Daffy Duck argue whether it is duck season or rabbit season. The argument goes back and forth while Elmer waits impatiently. After Daffy states it is "rabbit season," Bugs simply agrees, "wabbit season." Without realizing what has happened, Daffy declares, "Duck season! Shoot him." And Elmer does. Daffy was locked into the pattern of saying the opposite of Bugs. So when Bugs switched sides Daffy didn't realize the implications, much to his chagrin.

Other Ericksonian techniques involve how to utilize embedded questions, presuppositions, and implications. We have seen that embedded questions do exactly what our narrative questions do. The audience seeks to find answers.

A presupposition is something that is assumed beforehand at the beginning of a course of action. Stories continually rely on all kinds of presuppositions. If you were to take a trip on a ship, you have already presupposed that the ship will float and move across the water to where you want to go. Erickson might have structured a presupposition like this: After you read the next sentence you might notice changes in your body. This statement presupposes that you will read the next sentence. It also leaves what you might experience in your body very open-ended. You might feel heavy, light, cool, warm. In this way any response you provide will be accepted as proof of a trance. Presuppositions lead us to think in certain ways. However, presuppositions are not always true. This is a powerful tool to mislead or surprise the audience.

Implication involves the listener arriving at a conclusion although the facts have not been directly stated. Many verbal arguments use implication to say things that might otherwise be unacceptable to state directly. It is a great way to make your character's dialogue more believable, rather than having them state the obvious. Implication and sarcasm are much more fun. Milton used all of these types of techniques for a reason. If he stated something directly, then his patient might offer resistance. Just like Bugs, Milton slipped right under the resistance. Scheherazade bypassed the sultan's defenses with her stories and now he is trusting a woman again.

I have a story that I am working on that some people might find mildly offensive. I got around this by having the main character tell the story to the other characters in the story. The other characters in the story think that the main character is crazy. I put the potential objections right into the story. This deflects anyone's objections to the story because it is just the ramblings of a "crazy person." It also adds a fun element to the story.

Milton understood the value of stories in people's lives and how to structure them to be very persuasive. He was a master of metaphor and stories that he told to his patients to help them through stages in their lives where they were stuck. Our movie stories have to have interest by creating metaphors about real human problems that the audience can identify with.

I don't know if you noticed, but we used an Ericksonian technique in the last chapter. It is known as *accessing early learnings*. I reminded you of the time you learned to walk and ride a bike. Directing and storyboarding feel overwhelming at first. By reminding you of something that you had to learn when you were young but were able to accomplish provides a positive framework to learn and grow rather than feeling overwhelmed and helpless.

The Power of Suggestion

So how is the director like a hypnotist? Sometimes it's stronger not to show it all but rather suggest it. The hypnotist knows how much the mind can create if it is offered interesting suggestions.

Much modern horror filmmaking seems to have forgotten this fact. There are two approaches to creating horror films. There are those that show all of the gory details and those that don't. The second group instead chooses to suggest what might happen and let the audience's imagination fill in all the details. Each type of film has its place, but I think that the kind that uses the audience's imagination can be more powerful, because you are utilizing their fears. They will take your clues and fill in the blanks themselves from their own personal experiences and associations. This will make it more meaningful for them—that is utilizing the hypnotic technique.

For example, let's say the audience is presented with a scene of a dark cave. They want to know what is in the cave. Well, at this point it could be anything. It is filled with the fear of the unknown. The minute that we show that the cave is filled with bats, the arachnophobic person who was imagining it filled with scary spiders loses some of their fear. Imagined fear can be worse than real fears; that is the power of movies.

There is also an economic benefit to suggestion. You don't need to create vast crowd scenes when you can suggest them. The audience's mind will give you casts of thousands. The Disney film *Bambi* had an incredibly vast forest, yet when you look at actual shots of the film, 98 percent of them are intimate close-ups. I only know of two or three long shots of the forest. It was all created in the mind of the viewer through the power of suggestion.

Sound can be very suggestive. The use of sound is what brings life to film. Disney's *Bambi* depicts man's presence in the forest with three musical chords. In Spike Lee's *Do the Right Thing*, he used flashing lights and the sound of helicopters to save his film budget the cost of real helicopters. Francis Ford Coppola's *Apocalypse Now* beach attack scene wouldn't have been the same without showing real helicopters. There is a time and a place for everything, including over-budget helicopters.

The suggestive power of images is beyond words. Consider this story about two hatcheck girls, Mary and Jane:

> One day Mary placed a dime on her plate as a decoy to entice tips from her customers, and Jane followed suit, but instead she put a quarter on hers. Two hours later, Jane collected two and a half times more in tips than her partner. She used salesmanship. She knew that sometimes a picture symbol—in this case a silver coin—speaks more eloquently than words. And more effectively.[5]

So before we burnout your attention, let's see what has been happening with Scheherazade.

Scheherazade finishes the drawing.

She looks up at the sultan ...

And holds up the drawing.

The sultan watches intently.

The McClod courthouse.

Goo and Sticks are dropped off.

Scheherazade continues her thankless task.

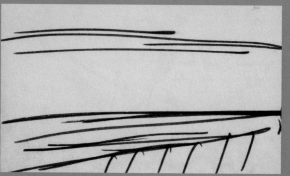

[Slam!] The gavel strikes!

Goo and Sticks stand before the judge. JUDGE VIC CON: "What were you thinking?"

JUDGE VIC CON: "Did you want to wake the dragon and destroy us all?"

GOO [Whispers]: "Did you see any dragon?"

JUDGE VIC CON: "Silence in my court!"

They look up sheepishly at the judge.

JUDGE VIC CON: "If you're ever caught on the ..."

JUDGE VIC CON: "Catfield side of town again ...

JUDGE VIC CON: "You'll face the hangman."

JUDGE VIC CON: "Do you two stooges understand?"

Goo and Sticks shake their heads yes.

The judge leaves the court.

Sticks sighs in relief.

Goo grabs Sticks ...

And pulls him out with him.

127

The McClod lookout shack.

Goo scours the Catfield side with a spyglass.

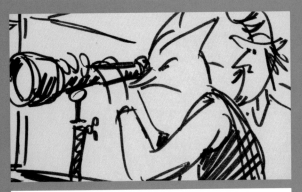

GOO: "Mmmmmm."

GOO [Offscreen]: "A-ha!"

GOO: "There's going to be a ball."

GOO: "I bet she'll be there."

GOO: "We're going dancing!"

STICKS: "Over there?"

STICKS: "Do you remember what the judge said?"

GOO: "He said 'if they catch us.'"

GOO [Offscreen]: "What could possibly go wrong?"

STICKS [Voiceover]: "We could be invited to a necktie party."

Will Goo risk death to see Clover again? Do you want him to? Has he gone mad? Is this new plan, to go to the party, hopeful or fearful or yet to be decided based on how things turn out?

How the Brain Organizes Information: Gestalt

What is a *gestalt*? Something you say when someone sneezes? Gestalt is a German word that means form or shape. It is an organized whole that is more than just the sum of the parts. Gestalt principles describe how our minds organize our experience. For example, the mind groups things that are similar or close together. The mind picks out things to look at and everything else fades into the background. When we read we see each word or clusters of words. What we don't notice is that the rest of the page recedes out of our awareness. It is like a flashlight shines on the words as we read them.

Francis Glebas has put together a really comprehensive and thought-provoking look at the art and craft of film making, specifically directing. His approach, which is to ask a lot of seemingly innocent questions, has much the same effect as the good flashlight storytelling he is trying to teach us....it draws us in and makes us think. I can't imagine anyone, in or out of our business, who won't find any number of helpful ideas as they work their way through the filmmaking jungles!

The way to use our speaking metaphor of telling one thing at a time is through gestalt principles. Gestalt principles work at every level of moviemaking, including perception of images, comprehension of plot, grasp of theme, and even sound.

A key concept of gestalt perception is that the mind tends to fill in the blanks. This power of suggestion is a filmmaker's greatest ally.

The Mind F lls in the Bl nks

I hope you noticed that there were missing letters in the previous heading. If you didn't, your mind took care of them for you. Our minds seek closure. If we hear a familiar musical theme or poetry with the last part cut off, we will fill in the missing piece ourselves. "Shave and a haircut...." The mind wants to hear the last phrase to complete the rhythm: "Two bits."

Visually if parts of a figure are cut out, there will be a tension in us that wants to close the shape. We tend to see complete figures. When we look at a close-up of a head on film we assume that it is connected to a body and not disembodied.

Grouping into Wholes

Do you see a collection of spots? Or something else? Grouping into wholes is a key gestalt principle that states that we tend to group individual items into clusters. The mind seeks closure and wholeness.

The	than	Parts	
the	Whole	of	the
Greater	Sum	is	

Gestalt usually states this in the following way: *The whole is greater than the sum of the parts.*

A little more information, in the form of a gray background, makes the figure emerge clearly. Closure is a related principle. We tend to perceive closed figures. The gray in the previous image provides the closure that the earlier image of spots merely implied. Closure works on various levels. It works on our perceptual level but it also works on our story level. We expect closure from our storytellers. In other words, we want all the loose ends tied up.

Figure/Ground

The second key concept of gestalt perception is that of figure/ground relationships. This relates to attention theory and our speaking metaphor. One figure becomes prominent at a time; we perceive figures and the ground recedes from our attention.

In this drawing it is hard to differentiate or separate the figure from the ground. The man blends into the line work.

Adding some tone helps separate the figure from the background. It is now easy to see the man. When we pay attention to the man the background recedes.

However, if we look at something else in the scene, the figure/ground relationship shifts to a different figure. What was once a figure now becomes part of the ground. Things in the background don't disappear; they are there if something shifts our attention to them.

Optical illusions can present reversible figures, whereby the figure becomes ground and vice versa. It is like two images in one, but we only see one at a time. Our perception switches between the two.

Is it a bunny or a duck?

Here we have a keyhole, a negative space. Wait; maybe it is a chess pawn, a solid volume!

Context helps specify the meaning of the shape. Here is the same shape but this time it is in the context of a keyhole.

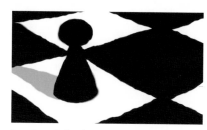

Now with the context of a chess board, the shape becomes a chess piece, a pawn.

Good Continuity

Good continuity states that we tend to assume things are whole not fragments. We assume continuous figures even if we can't see the whole image.

We see the outline of a person defined by a collection of spots. We don't see a collection of random spots.

Grouping by Proximity

Our perceptual processing tends to organize things that are close together or related in some way as a group.

Even when the shapes vary the principle still works. The proximity overrides the shape differences.

Grouping by Similarity

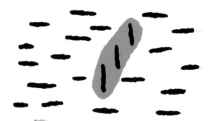

When objects are similar in some way, they are seen to belong together.

Grouping by Common Region

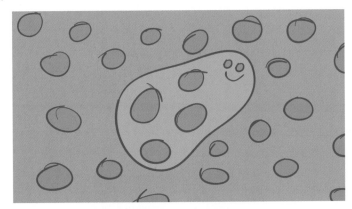

Items enclosed in a common area are seen to belong together.

Grouping by Connectedness

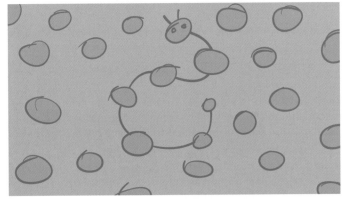

When items are connected in some way they are perceived as belonging together.

Symmetry

Symmetrical figures also tend to be clustered into wholes.

Utilization of Gestalt

Directing is directing attention and avoiding distractions. The director has to show the audience what to look at. Let's say we have a party scene. How do we make our main character stand out from the crowd? Well, we have seen that grouping applies to things that are alike in some way, which includes proximity or being close to each other. So we dress the main characters differently or have them stand apart from the crowd. If everyone is in muted colors and our hero wears black and white, the crowd will be perceived as a group and the hero will stand out. Another method is to have the hero facing the opposite way from everyone else.

What happens when there are two people? They organize into the gestalt of a "couple." We see them together and everything else fades into the background.

Perceptual Difficulties

Most of the time our perceptual process runs smoothly in the background of our minds. We see the world without having to think about it. There are times when this process is brought to our attention, for example, with optical illusions. It is possible for perceptual illusions to create seemingly supernatural effects.

I experienced this one night when I was a child. I had a flashlight and went to take my dog out for a walk. I pointed the light outside the glass door and was terrified. There, outside, was a horrible red-eyed monster! I ran. What actually happened was that my perceptual process saw the eyes of the dog reflected in the glass. In the same way that some photos illuminate people's eyes red, the classic red-eye syndrome, my dog's eyes looked red. The meaning I gave to it was that there was something outside with glowing red eyes.

Here we see a group of birds. We don't see individual birds—what we see is organized into the gestalt of a flock of birds. As we attend to things, gestalts keep shifting. Even our language is organized according to gestalt principles. We even have names for them: flock, herds, couples, and gangs.

Here Scheherazade and her sister stand out because everyone else is huddled under umbrellas forming a group. Scheherazade and Dunazade are not part of that group.

Our minds seek wholeness and closure. Figure/ground relationships see complete figures. Lighting is used in movies to effectively separate a figure from the background. Figures that don't provide this wholeness or closure create tension. The need for closure is what drives us to continue watching stories. When a story question is raised, it creates tension. We watch the story to dissipate this tension. This functions in music as well. If a piece of music is interrupted before the end our minds will fill in the blanks.

There is strong emotional power to closure—visually, musically, and with stories. Music score Beethoven's Fifth: Da Da Da … DAAAA!

Tension increases

Closure of Tension

This characteristic of the mind to fill in the blanks is a great asset to the filmmaker. It is the power of suggestion in action.

Good continuity is the gestalt principle that states we tend to assume things as continuing. Pictorially we tend to see lines continuing even if something obscures part of them. This is also why filmic cuts work. If we see one action and the action continues from a different angle, we assume it to be the same action.

The sultan is still in a state of tension from lack of closure. Scheherazade continues telling her tale wherein Clover consults the stars.

Scheherazade continues her tale of Dumb Love.

CLOVER [Voiceover]: "Where are you taking me?"

Daisy and Weed bring Clover to the fortune-teller, MADAME KNOWITALLISH.

They knock on the door.

MADAME: "Ah, I was expecting you."

CLOVER: "You were? I didn't even know we were coming."

Clover sits down.

The room darkens.

The crystal ball begins to glow.

Madame Knowitallish invokes the spirits of true love.

The ball grows brightly.

An image slowly emerges. It is a figure on the rope bridge.

We start to see who it is.

CLOVER: "It's Goo!" MADAME [Voiceover]: "Who?"

Daisy and Weed are startled.

They try to get Madame to steer Clover away from Goo.

The great know-it-all mystic doesn't get it.

As they continue gesturing, Clover senses something.

She turns …

Daisy and Weed smile sheepishly.

Madame still doesn't understand.

They point to Goo …

And express that he is the wrong choice.

Madame looks at them.

Finally the situation dawns on her.

MADAME: "This ball's on the fritz."

She pushes aside the crystal ball.

MADAME: "Let's try something else."

She begins dealing magic cards.

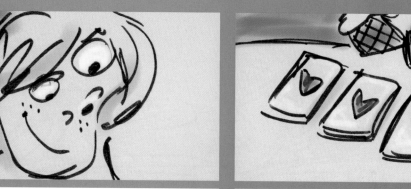

Clover smiles seeing the two hearts.

CLOVER [Voiceover] : "This is good isn't it?"

Madame Knowitallish is surprised.

MADAME: "This is quite rare. But 'true love' requires …

"Four hearts."

137

She is shocked.

She can't believe it.

Daisy and Weed are surprised too.

MADAME: "I think these cards have lost their magic."

MADAME: "Let's try the yes–no board."

MADAME: "It will spell out the name of your true love."

MADAME: "Place your hands gently on the dial."

MADAME: "This never lies."

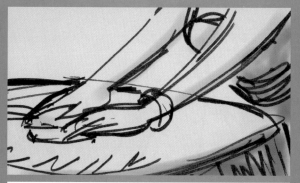

It begins to move by itself.

MADAME: "Yes, let the spirits guide you."

It lands on G.

CLOVER: "That's G for Goo!"

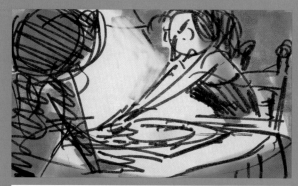

MADAME: "That can't be right."

She tries to pull it away …

But it stays put on G. It won't budge.

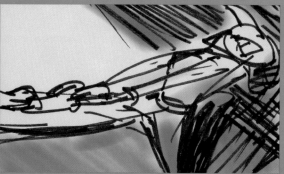

Madame Knowitallish tugs with all her might.

And it returns to G.

She screams!

And runs out of her fortune-telling parlor.

WEED: "This would be a great place for a capper joke."*
*A capper joke is the final joke of a scene that sums up the whole scene.

Daisy and Clover look at her.

The sultan laughs.

Scheherazade glances at her sister.

The next drawing is prepared.

The Catfield side of town is all lit up for the ball.

Goo and Sticks walk backward.

Walking backward they walk onto the rope bridge. GOO: "Great seeing you. Take care now."

The guard waves good-bye.

The guard stands at attention.

Suddenly it hits him.

He turns angrily to find …

Nothing. The bridge is empty.

The guard is more confused than ever.

Below the bridge, two figures make their way across.

GOO: "Sticks, did I ever mention I'm afraid of heights."

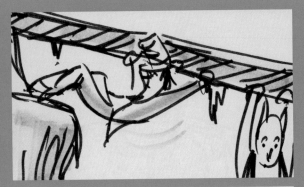

STICKS: "You'll be fine. Just don't look down."

A piece of the bridge falls off.

And falls into the ...

Abyss below.

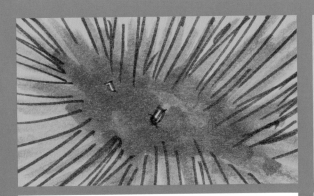

GOO: "Now you tell me?"

Sticks helps Goo up.

STICKS: "This moss sticks to everything."

GOO: "Wait, I've got an idea."

GOO: "Tonight, you're Stickarina. It's a perfect disguise."

GOO: "How do I look?"

STICKS: "Gooey!"

STICKS [Offscreen]: "Get it? Gooey."

[Smash!]

Goo and Sticks approach the entrance to the ball wearing their dresses and moss hair disguises.

GOO: "I'm finally gonna get to meet her."

OFFSCREEN VOICE: "There they are!"

Suddenly they are grabbed. GUARDS [Offscreen]: "Gotcha!"

Two Catfield guards take them.

The guards push them into a door.

[Slam!]

All goes dark.

GOO: "This doesn't look good."

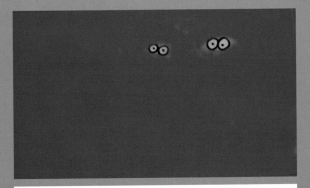

STICKS: "It doesn't look like anything, it's too dark."

144

[Flash!] A spotlight hits them.

They realize they are surrounded by people …

Who are waiting.

STICKS [Whispering]: "They think we're performers."

GOO: "What should we do?"

STICKS: "Follow my lead."

Sticks starts dancing.

The audience starts to dig them.

They begin the Macarena.

The band follows their lead.

Cupid appears next to Goo.

Goo looks and sees.

There in the back of the room …

Is Clover.

Goo lights up. GOO: "It's her."

Goo begins to walk offstage. Sticks notices.

He starts a conga line as a cover.

Sticks gets people to join the line.

The line grows.

The audience loves their show.

Goo weaves the line around to pass Clover.

Goo smiles at Clover.

Clover doesn't recognize Goo.

Goo is puzzled.

He takes off his disguise. Sticks freaks.

Clover recognizes Goo.

Goo is found out!

Everyone looks.

Goo is surrounded by Catfield swordsmen.

Goo goes to grab a sword …

He raises it in the air …

Too close to the candles …

It lights …

GOO: "Why is my sword on fire?"

Goo's sword is a Roman candle.

Fireworks shoot out of Goo's sword.

Clover is fearful for Goo.

Fireworks fly and the Catfields back up.

Scheherazade is slowing down.

The sultan notices. SULTAN: "The hour grows late."

SULTAN [Offscreen]: "Let us retire to our dreams and …

"Continue tomorrow."

Scheherazade blows out the candle.

The palace sleeps peacefully.

Well, Goo got to see Clover again but now he will have to pay for his transgression. The pendulum has swung back to fear. But this weaving between hope and fear has kept the sultan on the edge of his seat. Things are looking up for Scheherazade.

Director as Magician

The final art that we will explore about directing attention is magic. Nathaniel Schiffman, author of *Abracadabra*, asks a very interesting question:

[W]e have yet to answer the basic question, "What is magic ... really?" We know magic is fake. We know it relies on all sorts of deceptions, but why is it that some deceptions work while others do not? Why are some fakes plausible while others stand out like a sore thumb? For instance, a cartoon is fake—mere drawings on paper, that is pretty obvious. A sculpture is a fake made of rock. But when we observe the fakeness of magic, we don't interpret it as fake. We see it as very real. Even when we know in our hearts that a person cannot fly, that a silver sword cannot penetrate a body and come out bloodless, even when our eyes betray our common sense, we see magical illusions as real. Why is that? What is this stuff that magic is made of fake and yet real at the same time?[6]

He could have been talking about movies. We watch them and know that they are not real yet we go along for the ride and are moved to tears and laughter by them. How can they be fake yet real at the same time?

The unconscious mind cannot tell the difference between what is real and what is imagined vividly and emotionally. We rationally know that the movie is a fake, but our emotions and body respond as if they were real. We feel excited, the explosive release of laughter, shed real tears from being touched, while in our bodies our heart rate changes, our palms sweat, and we feel a rush of adrenaline.

Film needs to engage our conscious minds as well as our bodies. A movie can be about magic with centaurs and giants, but it must be plausible. We set up rules for the world and we must play within the rules or the audience will feel we have cheated and withdraw from our story.

Stage magic is like the professor's puzzle in the sense that magic is based upon invalid initial assumptions. The magician presents a logical "proof," but obscures the fact that the original assumption (that no trickery will be used) is actually the conclusion that we are meant to draw from the act. In any case, it is an invalid assumption because the magician certainly does use trickery in one form or another. A magician's proof consists of visual cues.[7]

These visual cues are how we direct the audience's attention.

Let's look at what magicians do to see if we can learn the secret. A ventriloquist is a type of magician. "[T]he ventriloquist misdirects us. He looks at the dummy and makes the dummy look at him when he talks. He acts as if the dummy is alive. That is the key to creating effective magic: acting."[8] So a good director is not really a director at all but rather a master of misdirection. "Furthermore as you watch magicians performing, you will often see the more experienced ones using one kind of misdirection as a cover-up for another kind. They make it look like they are hiding something spatially when in fact they are hiding it temporally. Sometimes they 'accidentally' mess up the trick along one misdirection to fool the audience into believing that is the method of secrecy they are using for that trick."[9]

In a sense, the whole film is a magic trick. In fact in German, an animated film is literally "trickfilm." The complete story is made from fragments, some of which never existed in the "real" world. The illusion is furthered by the mind linking up the sound with the pictures, even though, in reality, there may be no connection. It is an illusion whereby the whole truly is greater than the sum of the parts.

Magicians use the same type of structuring as storytellers. They tell a story about magical properties. This is known as *patter*. *Patter* is the magician's script.

Magic words, hocus pocus, abracadabra, and other nonsense words are still used, mostly for comedic effect nowadays, and sometimes to dramatize a particular moment in the course of an illusion. However, modern patter is more likely to be very straightforward and subsequently much more deceptively effective. Words are used to introduce an illusion, often by setting a scene of nostalgic childhood or faraway lands or by creating some other emotion in the listener. Words are used throughout a performance to enhance it with a fanciful story. And of course, words are used to misdirect and direct…. In ambiguous situations, the magician's words can be the extra shove that pushes people's minds to accept one reality over another. In selecting his words carefully, the magician "elicits certain perspectives and inhibits others."[10]

Magic wands and magical gestures serve the same function. The magician makes sure his or her gestures read clearly. Often he or she is directing your attention away from something. The trick is usually some common mechanical mechanism that is hidden from the audience's view. This is what Scheherazade is doing with the sultan. She is telling stories of high adventure while the trick is that she is teaching him moral lessons in an effort to heal and change him.

Patter and the trick have the same relationship as our story events and structure. Patter is the story of the illusion while the trick is the thing that remains hidden and makes it work.

| Story **events** | Magician's patter |
| Structure | Mechanics of the trick |

Occasionally, I perform magic tricks in my classes. I am the world's worst magician, but I do manage to teach my students something by using some simple tricks. One day I took a coin, placed it into my hand, and asked a student to repeat some magic words. The student repeated the words, "No it cerid sim." I opened my hand and to the class' amazement the coin vanished. What happened next was very interesting. Another student said, "It's in your pocket." I proceeded to empty my pockets and the coin was not to be found. The interesting thing is that this student had created a story to explain to himself where the coin had gone, because we all know there is no such thing as magic. *In other words, he created the story in order to make himself feel better.*

So how is a director like a magician? A magician performs a trick. As John Cassidy and Michael Stroud point out in their book, *The Klutz Book of Magic*, "Magic is not done, it's performed! Like any performance art, it withers away to nothing if it's not presented in the grand style. Moving your feet around is not dancing, reading the lyrics is not singing, and pulling a rabbit out of a hat is not magic."[11] The trick is a simple gimmick. It is the performance that creates the illusion.

While performing the trick, I told the class that I was the worst magician in the world and then asked the student to repeat some nonsense words. The coin disappeared and they took over creating a story of what happened to the coin.

Okay, a director is like a magician, so how do you apply this to film? Well, we perform the trick of simply juxtaposing images together. We can take unconnected images and put them together to make a story. We use images to implicitly ask questions and then we delay the answers engaging our audience in stories about characters on a quest for something they desire. The trick is how we structure all of the filmic elements in order to tell the story clearly and dramatically.

Subsequent chapters will be about specific ways to accomplish the task structurally in order to reach our goal of giving the audience an emotionally satisfying experience. Once we provide the audience with enough clues, they will do the work of constructing the story in their own minds. They will use gestalt to put all images together into meaningful wholes. They will use the gestalt principle of good continuity to see connections between shots that may have no connection at all in reality. They will use their presuppositions and assumptions to construct a story that is meaningful for themselves.

The Rules of Magic

There are several rules of magic you should know:

1. Never reveal the secret to how a trick is done.
2. Never repeat a trick. Remember when I said that you need to watch a movie twice to be able to see how it is put together? It is just like magic.
3. Use attractive magician's assistants, like movie stars. They are a great distraction. One more thing, try spelling "No it cerid sim" backwards. Sometimes one trick can cover another.

Hierarchy of Narrative Questions

Narrative questions drive the story. The questions are arranged in a hierarchy, meaning that some are more important than others. Some smaller questions will need to be answered before the bigger ones can be answered. In the chapter on the Scheherazade project (Chapter 15) you will find a hierarchy of the narrative questions of the Scheherazade story.

Narrative questions have to keep our interest. We have to care about the characters. We have to identify with their struggles and attempts at love, transformation, and redemption. Sometimes questions will be reasked or reframed because new information or new contexts require it.

I wonder if you know how questions are asked by a movie.[†] We direct the audience's attention to ask narrative questions by providing stories in which they wish to know what will happen next. Questions determine what we think about. "Question-asking can be a powerful persuasion device because questions structure our decision-making process. They do this by directing our thoughts about the issues at hand and by implicitly specifying the range of possible answers."[12]

Meaning is constructed from clues provided in the film that we put together in order to answer the narrative questions. We continually have to readjust the story of what we think is happening based on new clues we get.

Types of Narrative Questions

Let's look at some of the different types of narrative questions that we can use to structure our stories. The most common type is the goal outcome question. Will the characters achieve their goal? Most narrative questions are variations of this type. For example, another type of common narrative question involves the chase. Will they get caught or will they reach their goal of getting away? Will the plan succeed?

There are also dramatic questions such as will the truth come out? Emotional questions are common: How will they react when they learn that …? Finally, there are thematic questions. Will Pinocchio become a real boy? Rephrased: What will it take for Pinocchio to become a real boy?

Sequencing of Narrative Questions

Moving where the questions are asked and answered can make a scene more emotional, without changing the spirit of the script. The tactic is to delay the answer to a narrative question until after a boring part so the scene is kept alive by the tension of the narrative question. This often works well with passage scenes where the characters have to travel from one place to another.

In one scene I had to storyboard, the script called for a gag where a character had his hand stuck in a jar. The main character came in and pulled the jar off. Then several characters began a discussion that resulted in the main character having a little blowup about what was said. Answering the question about whether the character could get his hand out of the jar took all of the tension out of the scene. It was like a majestic ship when the wind dies, it may look great but it goes nowhere. Let's lay it out in a diagram.

Narrative question: Will he get free of jar?	Answer: Yes.	Boring talk.	Talk results in blowup.

Now, what if we move the second box after the third box? The scene starts with the narrative question: Will he get his hand out? But now let the main character have basically a tug of war to try to get it off. We are story-delaying. While this is going on, the characters talk. Right, when the talk heats up to the climatic moment, the main character blows up and the hand pops out of the jar leaving the main character to fall back onto the floor.

We have accomplished three things. First, the scene plays much more interestingly because the answer is delayed. Second, the scene is much more fun to watch because we have given the characters something to do besides talk. Finally, the blowup is much more dramatic because of its visual impact. It added a visual punctuation to the verbal outburst, kind of like an exclamation point.

Narrative question: Will he get free of jar?	Talk kept alive by tension.	Delay with tension.	Answer: Yes and blowup!

The pieces of moviemaking are narrative questions, delaying techniques and the answers. We have created a lot more interest just by moving pieces around.

Let's look at some of the narrative questions concerning Goo and Sticks.

Will *Goo* decide to see Clover against all odds? Of course we know that he will.

The first obstacle is can *Goo* and *Sticks* get by the guard. They accomplish this in a very unique way—they go in backwards, confusing the guard.

Now we want to know if they will succeed in getting across the bridge without falling.

They do manage to cross and find disguises. It looks like they will succeed, but they are caught.

Is this the end for *Goo* and *Sticks*? No, they have been mistaken as performers. But now we want to know if they can put on a show.

Goo sees Clover across the room. How will he be able to get to her? We are close to answering our main question: Will *Goo* get to Clover?

Goo forms a conga line to weave through the crowd to get to Clover. But she doesn't recognize him.

Goo and Sticks get caught. Will they escape? Goo draws a sword but it is a Roman candle.*
*A Roman candle is a type of firework.

So Goo still has not met his original goal of being with Clover. What will happen to him?

To learn more about magic, watch *The Prestige* and *The Illusionist.* They are both movies about the magician's art. One final thought: How do you not think of the spotted elephant? Simple: Focus on the gang of surfing purple giraffes. I just made the elephant disappear. You need to be wary when a magician tells you he is not that good.

Critique: Scheherazade Directs Attention

Combining the skills of ventriloquist, hypnotist, and magician, coupled with an understanding of gestalt principles, will give a director a powerful tool set. But never forget our goal: To give the audience an emotionally satisfying experience. "When you're able to touch somebody on an emotional level, that to me is magic. It not about tricks."[13]

Let's see how Scheherazade, a hypnotist and ventriloquist, works her magic. Is the fortune-teller's scene proof of the magical power of love continually leading Clover to Goo? Or is it Scheherazade as master ventriloquist tricking the sultan into thinking that the story is innocently telling itself? Or could it be that she is a hypnotist providing the sultan with a disguised parable of transformation?

Scheherazade uses narrative questions embedded in the story to maintain the sultan's interest. As she does this she keeps the pendulum swinging between hope and fear and always adding a dash of something unexpected to the mix.

POINTS TO REMEMBER

- A director must wear many hats in addition to magician, hypnotist, and ventriloquist. He or she must be a cheerleader, psychologist, mediator, shepherd, and explorer for the film and crew. And most important of all, we can't forget—entertaining storyteller.
- First and foremost a director directs the audience's attention and keeps directing it.
- Change the pace so your audience doesn't grow fatigued. Give them a chance to catch their breath and give them some new scenery.
- Misdirect the audience in order to entertain them. But make sure you are clearly directing their attention.
- Learn the gestalt principles and make them work for you.
- Analyze the hierarchy of narrative questions, delays, and answers in you film. Are the questions dramatically interesting? Do they maintain dramatic tension throughout the story? Would it be stronger if you moved some around?

References

1. Hall, L. M. *The Secrets of Magic*. Crown House Publishing, 1998.
2. Pratkanis, A., and E. Aronson. Age of Propaganda. Owl Books, 2002.
3. Robbins, A. *Awaken the Giant Within*. Simon Schuster, New York, 1991.
4. Haley, J. *The Psychiatric Techniques of Milton H. Erickson: Uncommon Therapy*. Norton, 1973.
5. Baker, S. *Visual Persuasion*. Boston: McGraw-Hill, 1961.
6. Schiffman, N. *Abracadabra*. Prometheus Books, 1997.
7. Ibid.
8. Ibid.
9. Ibid.
10. Ibid.
11. Cassidy, J., and M. Stroud. *The Klutz Book of Magic*. Klutz, 1990.
12. Pratkanis, A., and E. Aronson. *Age of Propaganda*. Owl Books, 2001.
13. Angel, C. *MindFreak, Episode 1*. A&E Television Network, 2005.

How to Direct the Eyes

look like the things that I was trying to draw? The problem was that I was totally unaware of where I was placing things on the page. When I began to learn photography I had the same bias. What was the content? I was unaware that a tree was placed to look like it was growing out of my brother's head. I was unaware of the patterns of light and dark—the essence of photography.

We have already looked at this issue in our building our chart.

Content of image.
Structure of image.

I was focused on the content because no one had taught me about how to structure the image—it was outside my threshold of attention. The structure doesn't have a form of its own. Structure is the form of the content. Any structural aspects in my art were intuitive or accidental.

In my early efforts to create art, I was ignoring a tool that could make my work more aesthetic, persuasive, and emotional. I didn't know that structure could "speak" more powerfully than content.

What I Learned from Watercolor Artists: The Missing Piece of Design

When I was in art school, one of the required courses was a design class. We learned a lot of cool stuff like how to make one color look like another color. Unfortunately, the class didn't teach me really

Visual Clarity

To understand a film a director must visually provide two things for their audience. First, the director must direct the viewers' eyes where to look. Second, once the viewers know where to look, they need to know what they are looking at.

This might sound obvious, but it is not usually how beginners proceed. I know from my own experience that when I started to draw, my concern was the content of the drawing. Did the drawing how to apply this knowledge for anything useful. It didn't teach me how to use design to make more dynamic narrative images.

Years later, I joined a group of storyboard artists who would go out on their lunch hour and paint watercolors. I wanted to learn more, so I got some books on watercolor hoping to learn some useful techniques. The books were not what I expected but extremely more valuable than some tips on technique. These books—by Edgar Whitney, Tony Couch, Frank Webb, Tony van Hasselt, and Judi Wagner—were all about design and how to use it to make more exciting narrative images. It was just what I needed, and on top of that, they made it easy and fun.

So let's look at the two tasks a director must accomplish visually.

Where Do I Look?

So how do you direct viewers' eyes? You show them where to look in three ways. First, by pointing the camera you choose what part of a scene they can see. Second, the camera frame includes what we see and cuts off what we cannot see. Finally, we direct the eye through designed composition within the frame.

Seeing Things

As we learned in our opening chapter, the audience is not just passively watching. Seeing is an active process. We search out and recognize things that have an interest to us. It is actually similar to hunting. In our world a more useful metaphor might be shopping. Think of when you are browsing in a bookstore. You scan book after book ignoring most of what you see. Finally something catches your eyes and your interest. It might be a word or an image or a design.

We actively seek not just what things are but what they mean to us. That is why we ignore most of the books. We just are not interested in them. When we seek out things in the world, we are interested in things like, is it a friend or foe? How can I use it? Is it edible? Is it in fashion?

Each object has its own identifying traits. Advertisers know this and enhance the uniqueness of their brand identities. As filmmakers we need to present our images so they can read easily; this means understanding objects' identifying features. There are several key traits that make identity possible as well as numerous subtle ones.

The first trait that is often overlooked is the characteristic viewpoint. This provides an object's characteristic silhouette. We normally see people from the front or side. We don't usually see people from the top or underneath because they are harder to identify. You would be surprised how many beginning storyboard artists often choose a high angle because it is "dynamic." It may be dynamic but often they chose the angle because it is dynamic, not because it supports the story. Most of the time this makes an image confusing.

We only need to present an object with enough characteristic traits that it suggests what it is to the audience. Their minds will fill in the blanks.

Objects in a film don't even have to exist in reality. Have you ever heard of the "flux capacitor"? Even though it doesn't exist, you would know one if you saw it, if you have seen *Back to the Future*. It is the part that makes a time machine work. All those computer banks in movies were just a bunch of flashing lights with a little design of the times added to make sure they appeared to be the latest models. The director suggests what it is and what it does and the audience goes along for the ride, "lost" in the story.

Where Do I Put the Camera? Staging the Action

The role of staging is to present the ideas clearly, in sequence, in a way that progresses the story.

The key question for the director should not be where do I put the camera, but rather, how can I stage this to be clear and produce the mood that will enhance the story? What are the secrets to directing the eyes?

The Great Eyes Learn to See

Let's begin with a parable on the genesis of "speaking" design.

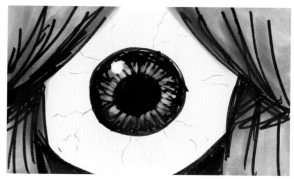

Once upon a time there was a great eye. It looked, but alas, it could not see.

This left the great eye *bored*. So the great eye summoned its most powerful wizard.

The wizard inquired, "What does your excellence desire?"

The eye explained that it wished to learn how to truly see.

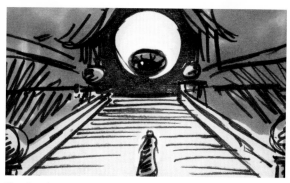

The wizard gestured toward the heavens.

All was dark.

Suddenly there was light.

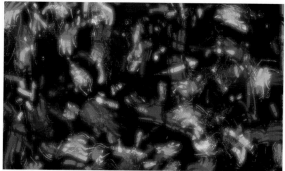

They all wanted attention but all the eye could hear was overwhelming noise. It was graphic noise.

The great eye could now see but it was *confused*. Everything spoke to the eye in confusing tongues. Everything cried out, "Look at me!"

159

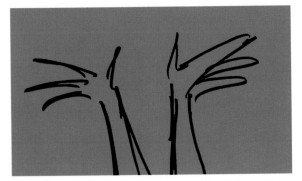

The wizard now needed to transform the graphic noise into well-orchestrated music.

The graphic noise had to be toned down. Like a musical conductor it had several sections play softly.

Then it asked for the melody to be heard clearly. It had to punch up the contrast.

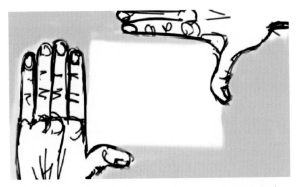

The first thing the wizard did was to create a frame to contain the chaos.

The frame had strange properties of attraction. It seemed to pull objects to it.

This force acted just like gravity pulling things down. Everything had a "visual weight."

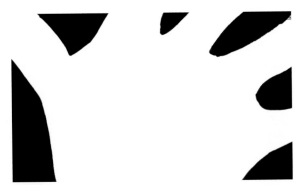

There was also a special place in the frame, a place of power. This is where important things went—the center. Height corresponded to power.

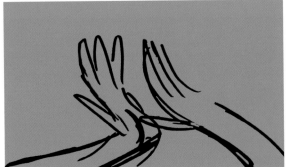

In order for things to take shape they needed space.

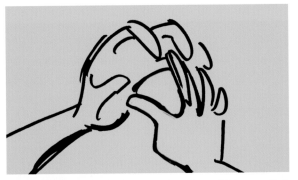

The wizard began to manipulate space to make a point in space. But it wasn't enough to make a point.

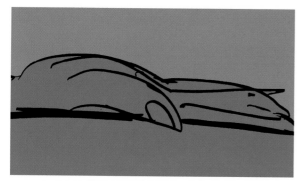

Space needed directions. Horizontals were very lazy but stable. Too much of them bored the great eye.

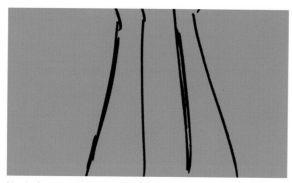

Verticals strove upward finding just the right balance against the force of gravity.

Diagonals were the most active of all, always suggesting the potential of motion.

And tension.

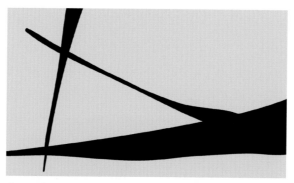

These different directions could be counterbalanced to control the chaos into some sort of order.

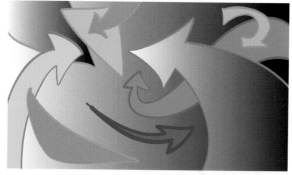

This directional aspect created arrows. The arrows said, "Follow me."

The wizard now could point the way for the great eye.

He gave the elements a name: points, lines, planes, edges, shapes, values, sizes, and colors.

But the elements were unruly and the great eye was still confused.

BALANCE,
POSITION,
DOMINANCE,
UNITY,
ALTERATION & REPETITION,
CONTRAST & SIMILARITY,
SYMMETRY, and
RHYTHM

The wizard put forth a set of principles—to create order in the chaos. These were rules for how the elements would interact.

The first principle was balance. This was an important life lesson; if you don't follow it you will fall on your face. Balance made the great eye visually comfortable.

Symmetry was the easiest way to create balance. It also could create stability.

The great eye always listened to who spoke the loudest. You had to punch up the contrast. When everything is similar, contrast is what makes differences visible.

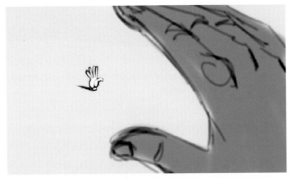

The wizard showed that size made a big difference. Each image needed one thing to be dominant, otherwise the great eye would be confused.

Size is relative. Something is small only in relation to something bigger than it. But with careful arranging, the small can have a "louder voice" to call attention.

The next principle was alternation. This requires repetition with changes.

When all of the elements were all subordinated according to the principles there was harmony.

The great eye was pleased but it wanted more.

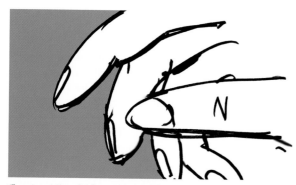

The wizard thought for a minute and then performed calculations.

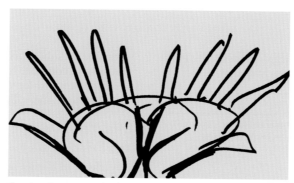

The wizard came up with a formula, the design equation. Form emerged from lines and graduations.

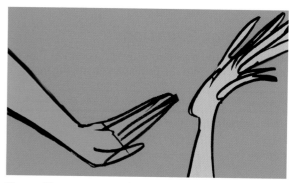

Lines could even suggest motion.

From edges and values the magical effects of light and atmosphere emerged.

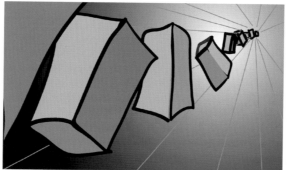

With overlapping shapes, diminishing sizes, and converging lines the image receded in depth.

With color and value the feeling of temperature emerged.

163

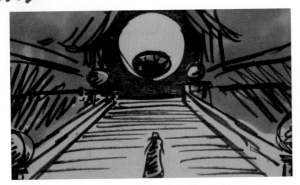

The great eye asked the wizard where it had learned to speak design.

The wizard told him that all of the principles could be found in the body. That is where he learned it.

The great eye still wanted more. But the wizard needed to leave to teach the great ear to hear.

The Design Equation

So what was the mysterious design equation that the wizard created? The elements of design plus the principles create the magical effects of design.

Elements +	Principles =	Effects
What is actually on the page:	How the elements are organized:	The representational illusions that the viewers complete in their own minds.
• Points • Lines • Planes • Edges • Shapes • Values • Sizes • Colors	• Balance • Position • Dominance • Unity • Alteration and repetition • Contrast and similarity • Symmetry • Rhythm	

Design is a very important tool to help make sure we present one idea at a time in a pleasing way.

Elements of Design: What Is on the Page

The elements of design are what are actually on the film frame, such as points, lines, planes, shapes, and colors.

Principles of Design: How to Organize What Is on the Page

The principles are how the elements are arranged for aesthetics and dynamic excitement. Principles such a unity, balance, and dominance require that multiple elements be subordinated to a greater principle. The most important design principle is contrast. It is extremely important to note that the principles of design are not just for visual design, but apply to every aspect of film, including actors' performances, lighting design, story design, and sound design.

Effects of Design: Illusions Created by the Elements and Principles

The effects of design are the illusions created on the flat screen such as light, depth, volume, form, motion, temperature, and atmosphere. These are created by the elements organized by the principles.

Good design is based on our own body's experience. The body contains rhythms, balance, grace, and directions; it reaches upward defying gravity. Let it be your guide. As we saw with gesture drawing, each activity has a dominant thrust, and all of the muscles are subordinated working together toward the main goal. The body also needs room around it in order to move. There needs to be negative space, or breathing room. Balance and counterbalance work throughout the body. Architecture is often a metaphor for the body. Landscapes are spoken of in terms of the body: foothills, shoulders of roads, mouths of rivers, and legs of a table.

The Enemies 171 of Good Design

My design class never taught me that there were enemies of design. The two main enemies of good design are boredom and confusion.

Boring! Evenness creates a lack of visual interest or excitement.

Better: The simplest change begins to create interest, in this case a simple gradation of tone.

Boring! Repetition or predictability can create boredom. We know what to expect.

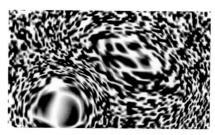

Better: Variety can create interest and a feeling of motion and surprise.

Boring! Symmetry can be boring.

Changing the angle can bring it to life.

Confusing! Bad tangents flatten space and catch the eyes.

Simple realignment creates interest and restores depth.

Confusing! Chaos, unless you are artist Jackson Pollack.

Work for clarity.

Confusing! Crowding.

Leave breathing room and negative space.

Confusing! High contrast and spottiness is hard to read.

Provide transitions and cluster darks together.

Confusing! Without a center of attention you don't know where to look.

Lead the eyes through the picture and make sure there is time to read it.

Use the design principles to avoid boredom and confusion.

Let's go back to Scheherazade and see how she designs her tale to continue to entertain the sultan. Meanwhile, Goo has his own problems.

DUNAZADE: "I have to admit your plan is working."

Scheherazade starts her drawing.

Clover stands on Daisy as Weed looks out.

Clover throws a small rock into the jail window.

The girls run off.

The rock hits Goo in the head.

GOO: "Ow!"

Goo looks at the rock …

And thinks that Sticks threw it.

167

Goo throws it at Sticks.

Sticks wakes up and rubs his head.

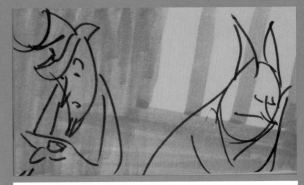

Sticks takes the rock and puts it in his pocket.

The sultan laughs.

Scheherazade prepares the next image.

Morning brings execution day for Goo and Sticks.

The executioner sharpens his axe.

The Catfields watch anxiously.

Clover steps out from the crowd.

She begins her plan.

GOO: "Sticks, I am sorry I got you into this mess."

Sticks is touched.

Sticks reaches in his pocket for a tissue.

But instead he finds the rock.

There is a note attached.

It is a drawing showing cutting the rope bridge ...

And Goo and Sticks jumping holding on to the bridge.

The plan dawns on Sticks.

169

He glances over and sees …

Clover at work on the bridge.

The ropes are almost cut.

STICKS: "Pssst."

GOO: "Can't it wait? We're about to be executed."

Sticks gestures for Goo to look.

GOO: "What's wrong with your eyes?"

Goo grabs Sticks and runs. STICKS: "Jump!"

GOO: "Jump?"

EXECUTIONER: "Jump?"

They jump onto the rope brigde.

It gives way.

They go flying . . .

To the other side.

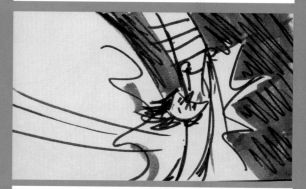

[Smash!]

STICKS: "We made it, Goo."

STICKS: "Goo?"

SULTAN: "Oh no."

171

SULTAN: "What happened to Goo?"

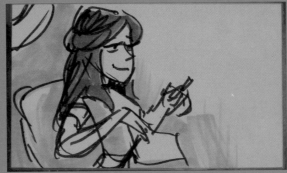

Scheherazade shows what has happened.

Goo is gone.

The sultan looks …

But he is looking over the drawing at …

Scheherazade.

Scheherazade becomes aware that she is being watched.

She turns away.

This exchange doesn't go unnoticed by Dunazade.

172

Scheherazade is slow to raise her eyes.

The sultan smiles.

She hides behind her drawings.

Clover screams.

Clover's father realizes that she has fallen for Goo.

The Catfields look over the edge.

High atop Clover's tower.

CLOVER'S FATHER: "What were you thinking falling for a McClod."

Clover hides her drawing of Goo.

Her father pushes her aside.

He takes the drawing.

He rips the drawing to shreds.

The pieces fall to the floor.

Clover gasps.

Tears fill her eyes.

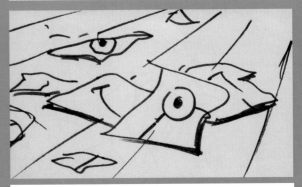

Goo's picture lies in pieces on the floor.

Clover mourns at her window, dropping the pieces like ashes.

They fall below …

Down …

Into the darkness.

Goo rubs his head, having slid down a lava tube.

SULTAN: "So Goo is alright?"

Goo looks up at the light as the pieces of paper fall.

He looks at the papers and doesn't notice that …

He is backing right into a giant web.

Struggling to get free, Goo gets tangled worse.

A shadowy form surrounds Goo.

Is this how it ends for Goo?

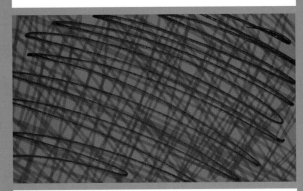

Finally finding his true love only to become an appetizer?

Scheherazade sets down the last drawing.

The sultan can't keep his eyes off of her.

She quickly blows out the candle …

Avoiding the awkward situation.

The sultan leaves for the night.

When he is out of earshot . . .

DUNAZADE: "Somebody's got a crush on Scheherazade."

Scheherazade glares at her sister.

Scheherazade walks out to the balcony.

DUNAZADE: "I think I hit a nerve."

Scheherazade doesn't stop.

She gazes up at the stars.

177

DUNAZADE [Offscreen]: "Scheherazade?"

Scheherazade turns to look and sees …

A sock puppet.

DUNAZADE: "Oh, Scheherazade, my darling …

DUNAZADE [Voiceover]: "My love for you is greater than …

DUNAZADE [Offscreen]: "All the stars in the heavens."

DUNAZADE [Offscreen]: "Kiss me."

Scheherazade begins to grow annoyed.

The puppets leave.

Dunazade pokes her head out.

And smiles at her sister.

Scheherazade is glaring.

She melts into a laugh.

Dunazade joins her sister on the balcony …

And they talk late into the night.

Well, things are not looking good for Goo. Everyone thinks he is dead and he believes he is about to be eaten by some kind of monster. This tension has worked on the sultan because he is surely falling under Scheherazade's spell.

Directing the Eye with Composition

"Composition is the positioning of all parts in a picture. It is the rhythm or repetition of parts in a picture. It is the arrangement of different shapes to unify everything around the center of interest or focal point of the work. It is always essential to good art."[1]

"Plato, the famous philosopher of ancient Greece, summed up the complex art of composition in a single phrase. He explained that composition consists of diversity with unity."[2] Diversity increases interest through variety. Unity gives a sense of belonging and order. These are two ways to fight the enemies—boredom and confusion—of good design.

Our visual goal is clear. Direct the eye to what you want the viewer to look at clearly and dramatically.

General Guidelines of Composition

We want to keep the viewer's eyes focused on the center of attention in an image yet allow the eyes to move through the image without leaving the frame. This statement implies three things.

First is the creation of a center of attention or focal point for an image. Dominance and contrast are used to achieve this. The viewer's eyes will focus on the area of greatest contrast in the shot. You have to direct the viewer's attention to the telling details of a scene. This is achieved in close-ups. It says, "Look here, this is important." Remember every shot is a close-up of what you want to say to your audience, even if it is a shot as wide as the universe.

Another way of creating a focus of attention is to use the camera to literally focus on what we want to show the audience and let the background dissolve into a soft focus field of blurred colors. This makes for a very strong figure/ground relationship. The figure pops right out at us. Using light can also accomplish the same goal. Either silhouette a figure against a light background or light a figure against a dark background and again the figure will pop out. Backlighting a character can create a halo effect that helps the character "read" against the background.

Second, we want to keep the viewer's eyes moving throughout the frame. This happens automatically; the viewer's eyes continually scan a scene looking for something that interests them. Our job is to give the eyes pathways. This is accomplished by using everything in a shot as an arrow or pathway for the eyes. Ideally, we want to create a loop that the eyes can travel and return to the focus of attention.

The third method is to make sure that there are not any unintentional arrows or pathways that lead the eyes out of the picture frame. We want to block the exits.

Pay attention to how your eye moves through this drawing. The bird in the foreground dominates the picture. We follow his look to the child bird looking at the book. We then follow the line of the book to the bright arm in the foreground and back to the main figure. The dark background keeps our attention on the silhouetted main figures. The light pictures on the wall help counterbalance the bright foreground figure. French artist, Honore Daumier is a master of this type of compositional design.

Directing the Viewer's Eyes—Look!

We have seen that every part of a picture graphically says, "Look at me!" One of the most powerful ways to direct the audience's eyes is to say, "Look where I am looking." The viewer's eyes will follow the eyes of characters in the scene. This follows the general rule of shots in cinema. First a character looks at something and this is followed by a show of what they are looking at.

Compositional Reading

When we look at a picture our eyes scan the way we read. We start to scan a picture from left to right and top to bottom. Why would this matter? Well, if you think of an image as a joke, if we follow the image from left to right then the punch line comes last. If it is reversed, the punch line comes first, and this is not what we usually want. However, this is relative to culture. If you have ever tried to read Manga in the original Japanese you know that they read from right to left.

The pig arrives at the house, or …

The second pig sees the first pig arrive.

In the flipped image, the pig at the house sees the other pig running up. It is a subtle distinction but very important, because the punch line of the story comes last.

Where Are We Going?

Another time the eyes reading point is important is when you are having characters go from one geographic place to another. It's useful to follow the standard map orientation. When we look at a map, we have the need to keep the west on the left and the east on the right. So if a plane is flying from New York to Los Angeles it should be pointing to the left.

Movie Composition Needs to Be Very Simple

Movement complicates the eyes reading. When you are driving 65 miles per hour past a billboard you are limited in how much information you can present. Always use significant movements and avoid undesired moves as they distract the eye. Position the camera to get good silhouettes and separation from the background. If the action moves we can move the camera along with it.

One way to achieve quickly readable compositions is to use simple shapes to base the composition on. Letter shapes work well such as C, S, L, T, X, and Z. Look in the mirror to see inverted versions of these. Other shapes that work well are spirals and sunbursts. Triangles are very powerful compositional shapes. Try interlocking your shapes like a jigsaw puzzle.

Circles can be tricky to incorporate into a composition because they have such strong closure it makes it difficult to integrate them with other shapes. It is often better to use partial circles.

Another way to think about composition is to subdivide the screen. Placing the focus of attention on thirds works very well. Avoid dividing the composition in half because this often is boring. If you want to center a figure in the middle of the screen you can add other elements to each side to make it less symmetrical.

In order to demonstrate these principles of composing pictures we are now going to analyze images from the Scheherazade and Dumb Love stories.

In this shot, even though Scheherazade is dominant in the frame, our attention goes to Dunazade's reaction. Scheherazade has already made up her mind and we no longer see her eyes, so we don't engage with her.

Even though the lovers are the smallest thing in this shot our eyes go right to them. We have a clear stage for their action free from distraction. The bridge functions as an arrow pointing to them.

The scientist's lab uses an upshot to show the enormous scale of the strange machinery. We feel small in this room. It uses a sunburst to unify the composition.

This is a great example of the viewer's eyes following the eyes of the characters. Goo is dominant and we follow his look to Clover's father and the scientist. Then our eyes flow to the rabbit who looks back at Goo and Sticks.

Here the shot is organized into overlapping planes of depth. There is a background, midground, and foreground with silhouetted figures overlapping the foreground. The overall composition takes the form of an X.

Goo and Sticks are at the base of a triangle here. Our attention also goes to them because they are in a pool of light. The judge's desk has a distorted reverse perspective that makes them feel smaller and more "in trouble."

Here Goo and Sticks are counterbalanced by the judge's desk. They lean together while the desk looms over them. This also divides the canvas in thirds.

Madame Knowitallish's parlor is presented in a triangular pool of light. Our eye knows exactly where to look when Clover is the one facing us. Light also establishes the mysterious mood of the scene.

There is a lot going on in this shot, but by grouping elements, our eyes go right to Goo and Sticks trying to sneak into the ball. Visually we are already saying, "They are surrounded."

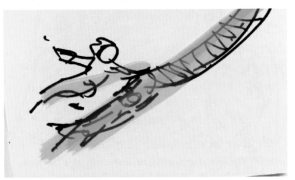

This is a U-shaped composition again with Goo and Sticks in a pool of light with a literal stage to act on.

The axe also points right at Goo and Sticks—a hint of things to come in this wedge-shaped composition.

Here we are right in the middle of the action. It is a very simple, clear, strong diagonal that falls with gravity to a vertical.

Here the light and dark lead the eye. Goo looks up toward the sliver of light. The space is closing in.

Another triangular composition with a pool of light for the action.

Here is a reverse L-shaped composition.

Here is an I shape tilted in what is known as a dutch angle. The slight skewing makes the shot more tense.

This reverse N shape has a lot of tension from the dutch angle and the asymmetrical balancing of Goo on the ladder.

Another reverse L shape with Goo breaking the L with the telescope, leading our eyes to him.

An X-shaped composition with action along the axis.

Graceful S-shaped compositions work very well.

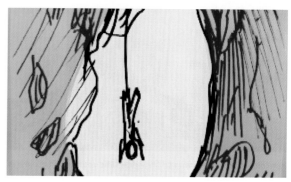

An O-shaped composition and closed in.

183

Sticks is the focus in this triangular pool of light.

Our eye shifts between the dominant Scheherazade and her looking in the mirror to the sultan behind her.

An upside-down U shape traps the light from above, closing them off.

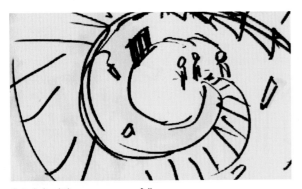

Spirals lead the eye very powerfully.

Here is a simple C shape on its side.

Criss-crossing lines provide a grid composition for Scheherazade and her sister to travel through.

Here our attention is drawn to the light in the doorway. Then our eye travels to the lighted sky and window. The door is centered in the composition.

Here the composition is created by the triangular light coming from the window. The sultan recedes in the shadows while his vizier is in the hot seat.

Finally, we have a radial or sunburst composition with light emerging from the center. This underlighting creates mystery.

A Magical Effect: How a Picture Makes You Feel

In the beginning of this chapter we saw that beginners pay more attention to the content of an image than the structure. Usually we are consciously more aware of the content because the structure is below the threshold of awareness. But even though structure is less visible it can often "speak" more powerfully than the content of the text.

Once again I would like to tell you a story in order to demonstrate the power of this next concept. Earlier I told the story of my storyboard work on *Pocahontas*. I am now going to show you how it applies to design, composition, and directing the eye.

The first pass of Pocahontas's farewell sequence was storyboarded directly from the script. The sequence was competently written, but it was all talk, which was fine if it was a novel. But it wasn't a novel; it was supposed to be moving pictures. Animation is told visually, not through dialogue. All writing is rewriting and this was simply the next rewrite, the first draft using pictures.

The sequence was about as exciting and heartfelt as the ending of a summer camp movie. Everyone, including Pocahontas, was standing around the dock as they watched John Smith and his ship leave for England—"See you next summer." Pocahontas was supposed to be feeling lost and alone. The images telling the story never showed Pocahontas alone, which is exactly how she felt. The images didn't match the story we were trying to tell. However, I felt that it could be more. So I asked for the opportunity to rework the sequence. Now, how would I do this?

Pocahontas had the unique distinction of being Disney's first feature to run counter to the Disney brand. This wasn't going to be a "happy ever after" movie. Originally, the film was to be modeled after *Romeo and Juliet* and *West Side Story*. They thought they had a tragedy.

What was the first thing I did? I started watching movies—all the sad movies that I could find. I watched *Romeo and Juliet, West Side Story, Ghost,* and many more. Then I watched a movie that helped me realize that they had the wrong paradigm for *Pocahontas*. It wasn't like *Romeo and Juliet* or *West Side Story*. It wasn't a tragedy.

Our paradigm was *Casablanca*! It was a bittersweet ending. We know that John Smith and Pocahontas love each other and they will both survive, they just can't be together for the greater good, just like in *Casablanca*. Now I had a clear direction. My drawings had to tell this story. This also was my chance to prove my boss wrong that my story work was not "emotionally cool." I called the sequence my heartfelt farewell.

The characters need to feel sad but not tragic. They are heroic. I thought about when I had left my home, friends, and family in New York to come work for Walt Disney Feature Animation in California. That was the feeling that had to go into the sequence—the sadness of leaving. However, something else was required to make it bittersweet. When I left New York, I was leaving for a great opportunity to fulfill my childhood dream.

The most important point of the sequence is how alone Pocahontas feels. How do you show how someone is feeling? Body language can say a lot. But what is body language? It is the shape the body makes when one is feeling different emotions, and unless you are a good poker player these emotions come through loud and clear. Doesn't visual language work the same way? The answer is yes. This is the secret: Every shape, line, and composition have a feeling associated with them. The technical term that I learned from Dr. Scott's Vocabulary of the Media Critic's class is known as analogical morphology. This is a fancy way of saying that they have a similar shape. So the shapes of our composition can tell us how to feel. Structuring in this way leads to a very important principle: Composition is subtext.

It was on *Pocahontas* that animator Glen Keane told me that composition is like visual subtext. When you tell a story there are always things that are unsaid directly but are profoundly significant. This is known as subtext. When the text and subtext are at cross-purposes they can create a great tension in a work. The subtext can often contain more truth than the text.

> **Composition is subtext.**

Visual composition, or how the image is structured, provides this role. Position in the frame is part of this subtext and it can be used to reveal power relationships between characters. Like the role of the music score, the images tell you what is going on but the compositional structure tells you how to "feel."

As an experiment, try to draw different emotions. Just use abstract images. What is truly surprising is how similar different people's images are of each particular emotion. Use this when you are composing your shots.

In the farewell sequence, I approached it in a shotgun fashion rather than a linear approach. I searched for key iconic images and then created the continuity around them. Thumbnail drawings were often drawn and redrawn many times to find just the right composition. Don't be afraid to throw stuff away. Keep experimenting. It pays off.

First I had to create a space for the action. Everyone standing around the dock would not be interesting enough. I wanted a more desolate location. The weather also had to set the tone. I chose to make it a foggy morning. Fog is mysterious and hides things from view.

It also wouldn't work to have everyone there already. Smith should have to wait for Pocahontas. This gives us a great narrative question that the original version lacked: "Will she come?"

The answer to the question is the arrival of Pocahontas. Like any star, she needed a big entrance. It should be a big deal that she is arriving. She emerges like a ghost through the fog leading her clan bringing food for the settlers.

We also needed to show that everyone saw Pocahontas differently now. Whereas before she was a "savage," now she was an Indian Princess. The men take off their hats in her presence to show respect.

Decisions are defining moments that reveal character. They should never be rushed and tossed aside. We need to see the internal struggle. She looks around and realizes she is needed where she is.

The good-bye scene itself must be pushed for all it's worth. It is not a peck on the cheek moment. It is their first, and possibly their last, kiss.

It has to be one of the most passionate kisses in film in close-up. It is as if their souls are one and should never be parted.

The moment needs to linger. How do you show they don't want to part? Their hands slowly, painfully part. Remember, it is all about story-delaying.

Pocahontas waves good-bye, the one Pocahontas taught to John Smith earlier in the film. It is all the more poignant because Smith had said let's stick with "Hello."

In order to convey how alone Pocahontas feels to the audience she must be shown to be alone in some way.

I thought when I leave someone, for example, at the airport, I wait and watch the plane leave, savoring that last moment. That is what I had Pocahontas do.

She races to her peak to watch as the ship disappears on the horizon.

This shot shows Pocahontas as very alone. Alone, she occupies her position as peacekeeper. The shot shows her dominating the frame suggesting her nobility and strength. This was one of those scenes where words fail. It was all about the "moving" pictures. They said it all, and the moody temp score.

I knew that I had achieved my goal when I learned that executives were crying when the story reel was shown. Give your audience an emotionally satisfying experience. An interesting aftermath of the screening is that Jeffrey Katzenberg said that we hadn't earned that ending yet. A film is a whole experience, each piece building upon the others, creating a dense network of meaningful connections. We still had some rewriting to do in Act Two.

Light and Shadows

Ultimately, film is about light and shadows. Be aware of the patterns of light and dark. *Notan* is a Japanese word that means dark light. "As a guiding principle of Eastern art and design, *notan* focuses on the interaction between positive and negative space, a relationship embodied in the ancient symbolism of the Yang and the Yin. In composition, it recognizes the separate but equally important identity of both a shape and its background."[3]

One of the key lessons that I learned about composing was to place light over dark and dark over light thus weaving together the elements. This is known as counterchange. The place where the values meet is called a value passage. These common values help unify compositions. American regionalist painter Thomas Hart Benton uses this technique to masterful effect.

POINTS TO REMEMBER

- Analyze your compositions, exploring each design element at a time, as well as overall. For example, check to see how just the color works, or the light-dark pattern, or the arrangement of lines.
- Design and composition principles apply to every level of film construction from single-shot composition to the overall structure of the whole film.
- As director, you are the conductor of the moving visuals. You need to control graphic noise in order to make music. Tone down graphic noise by lowering the contrast. Punch up the contrast on where you want the audience to look.
- Use composition to create visual drama.
- Composition is subtext. It tells the audience how to feel. Make sure you know what you are saying.
- Strive for visual clarity, simple but dynamic.
- Experiment with moving the camera around to stage the best composition.
- Make sure each shot has a focus or center of attention. Make sure this has the greatest contrast of value.
- Be aware of where your characters are in the frame and what their placement says about them.
- Use elements of your composition as arrows and pathways to direct the viewer's eyes.

- Group and mass similar things to simplify your composition. Mass your darks together to avoid making the picture look spotty.
- Weave your compositions with dark over light and light over dark.
- Watch *300* to study its dynamic composition.

References

1. Parramon, J. M. Composition. HP Books, 1987.
2. Ibid.
3. Bothwell, D., and M. Mayfield. *Notan*. Dover Publications, 1968.

Directing the Eyes Deeper in Space and Time

We are going to continue looking at how to direct the eyes, but for now focus on issues specific to the camera.

What Is Wrong with This Picture?

The problem is that the perspective is totally wrong. There are competing points of view like a cubist painting that flattens space. The background elements at times appear as close as the foreground elements. Size relations are ignored. It may be interesting as a puzzle but it is hard to orient yourself in a narrative sense. The enemy of good design strikes again! The picture is confusing—you can't understand the depth of the image.

We live in a world of three spatial dimensions. Our movie screens have two dimensions. Something has got to give. Remember, when we view our maps of the world we distort, generalize, and delete parts of the territory they represent. Well, we have to get rid of a whole dimension. But we don't actually lose it. We can suggest it and the viewer will see the missing depth. What kind of depth cues do we need to give the audience enough information to correctly locate our scenes spatially? Luckily we are not the first to encounter this problem. It was solved back during the Renaissance and it is called *perspective*.

"Perspective in art—often called 'artificial' or 'linear' perspective—is a system for representing three-dimensional space on a flat surface."[1] It is an optical system based on looking at a scene from a single viewpoint. Perspective creates the missing depth from our pictures but it also creates unity in the picture to a single viewpoint, thus directing our eyes.

The invention of the camera allows perspective to be taken care of by the optics of the camera itself. So even though we don't need to worry about it, the qualities that the camera imparts on our images are of utmost importance. We need to understand, not how the optics work, but the effects that are created by viewing a scene through a lens.

The camera also automatically captures depth cues. In addition to linear perspective, there is aerial perspective. Aerial perspective captures the fact that the more distance away an object is, the more atmosphere we have to look through to see it. Normally, farther objects take on a progressively bluish tint. They also lose contrast and detail. The extreme case of aerial perspective is a foggy day or under water. Sight distance is severely curtailed by the viewing medium, water or fog.

Overlapping objects indicate depth. An object in the foreground obscures those behind it, further away in depth. Size constancy is another depth cue. If we assume objects to be the same size, then if they appear smaller or larger, we translate that information into depth cues. Larger objects are closer. The scale of textures works like size constancy.

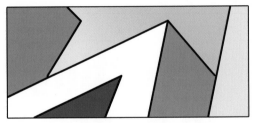

Line direction or surface lines can indicate depth. Diagonals often appear to recede into space, while horizontals and verticals are neutral.

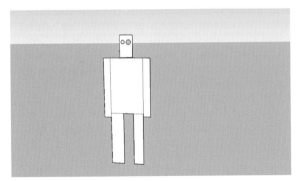

We start with the horizon. The horizon is the line where the ground plane meets the sky. This line is *always* located at eye level of the viewer.

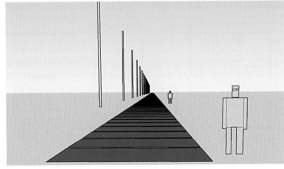

We are going to start with the camera on axis. This means we are pointing right along the length of our subject. All lines converge at a point on the horizon known as the vanishing point. This is called one-point perspective because there is one vanishing point. Our eye level is about waist high.

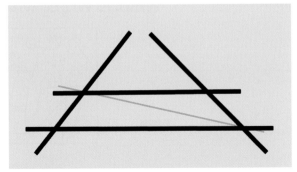

The size of each railroad tie also diminishes in scale. Let's look at how to space them so they appear evenly spaced. To do this we will use some simple geometry. First, set the placement of the first two ties. Now, we will draw a diagonal line from where the track meets one side of the tie to the other side of the next tie.

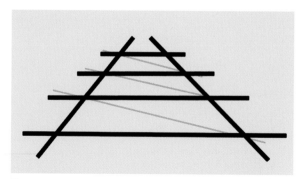

Now go back to the first side and draw another diagonal that is parallel to the first diagonal. Where this line crosses the track is where we place the third tie. We simply repeat this process for the rest of tracks.

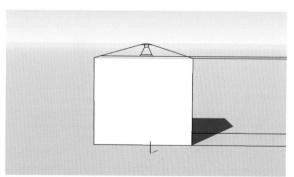

One-point perspective shows objects head on, on axis as this box shows. We can't see the sides of it.

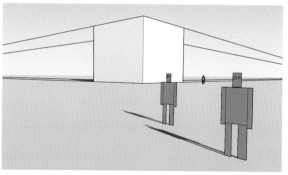

If we shift the camera to the side, lines now converge to two vanishing points. This box is now shown in two-point perspective. The horizon is at eye level.

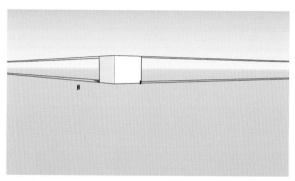

The placement of the two vanishing points is very important because it determines whether the view is wide angle or telephoto. The wider the points are apart the more telephoto they appear.

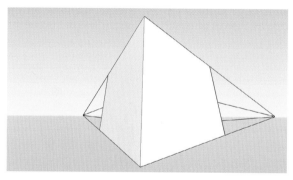

Here the vanishing points are close, giving a wide-angle view. Each type gives a very different feeling of space. The wide angle creates an expanse of space while the telephoto lens flattens out the space.

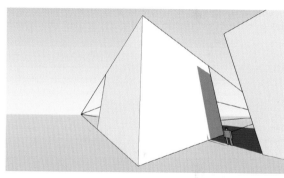

If we move closer to the ground plane we have a mouse-eye view. Low angles are very dynamic, creating a lot of diagonals.

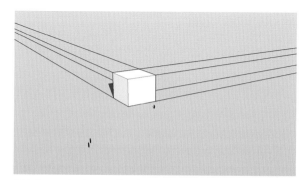

A bird's-eye view is great for showing location. Everything is clearly visible, but the image feels emotionally detached. We are above it all.

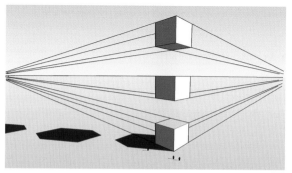

As we move objects in the space some will be higher and others lower than our eye line. We recede them all to the same horizon, wherever we have chosen to place it.

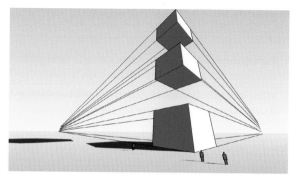

Three-point perspective creates the deepest space. The third point vanishes either very high or low. It is the effect of looking up at a tall building or down from one.

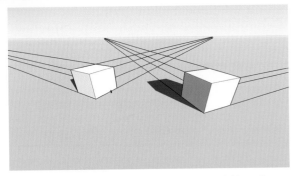

Objects oriented differently each have their own vanishing points on the horizon.

What happens when there are multiple ground levels? Each plane has its own vanishing points.

One difficulty that artists face is how to place figures in a scene so that they are in correct proportion and perspective. The horizon cuts all figures of equal height standing on the same ground plane, at the same place on the body, regardless of how near or far away they are.

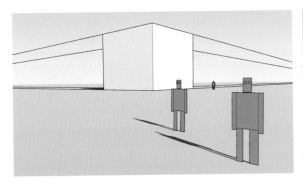

Here all of the figures line up along their eye lines.

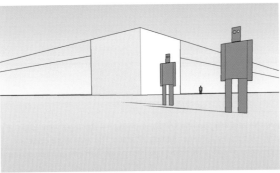

Here all the figures are correctly lined up at the knee eye level.

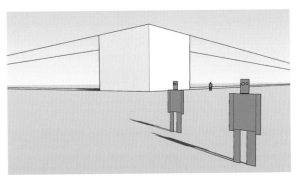

Figures that are lower than the horizon are each the same relative distance from the horizon.

Let's return to see how Scheherazade is faring with Goo. As you last remember things were not looking up for him; in fact, quite the opposite.

What has Scheherazade gotten herself into? What is the key for? What secrets will she unlock? Will curiosity kill the cat?

Scheherazade's unceasing hand continues its task.

Scheherazade draws with new energy and ...

Holds up the first drawing for the night.

Goo watches the shadow as it circles upon him.

HERMIT: "You're not a wild boar. What are you doing in my wild boar trap?"

GOO: "And you're not a dragon." HERMIT: "Dragon? There are no dragons down here."

GOO: "I'm Goo, and who are you?"

HERMIT: "Watch what I can do!"

GOO: "I need to get out. You got a bigger one of those?"

The hot-air balloon rises up.

She holds up the next drawing.

The sultan is relieved that Goo is alright.

SULTAN [Voiceover]: "Will Goo get out? It's a long way up."

HERMIT [Offscreen]: "Can't say I've ever tried this way."

GOO: "Hermit, I'm ready."

Goo says good-bye.

HERMIT: "Goo, remember to send me a rope, or a postcard. No, drop a line. Get it? Drop a line."

HERMIT: "Countdown. 100, 99, 98...." GOO [Interrupting]: "Start at 10."

HERMIT: "... 3, 2, 1—Let the *Goo* fly!"

[Smash!]

The hermit cringes.

Goo lies on the cavern floor.

The hermit runs over and ...

Shakes his hand. HERMIT: "Nice to meet you. I don't get many visitors."

SULTAN: "I don't get many visitors. That's a good one."

The storytelling ends for the night.

Scheherazade desires to know more about the sultan.

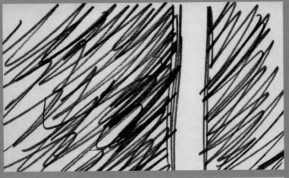

Why does he act as he does? What happened to change him?

And where are all of his other brides?

Scheherazade can't contain her questions and …

She takes action.

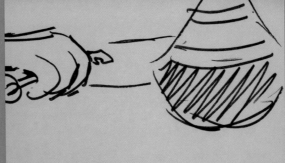

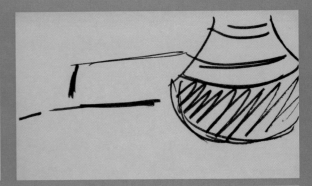

What to Use: Telephoto or Wide-Angle Lenses?

Let's compare how a camera moves with a telephoto lens and a wide-angle lens and see why you would use one over the other.

Telephoto Characteristics

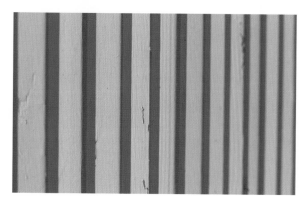

- Little distortion.
- Used for beauty shots.
- Flattens space.

Wide-Angle Characteristics

- Narrow depth of field.
- Verticals and horizontals remain neutral.
- Brings distant objects near.

- At fish-eye wideness, extreme distortion.
- Unflattering to faces.
- Expands space.
- Deep depth of field.
- Verticals and horizontals shift to create dynamic diagonals.

Telephoto Lenses Truck In*

Telephoto lenses have a narrow depth of field and very little distortion.

When the telephoto lens trucks in the image stays relatively similar, only getting closer.

Notice how there is a narrow range of objects in focus.

---

*   In a "truck in" the camera actually moves closer to the subject, whereas in a "zoom in" the camera stays in place but the lens focuses on a smaller area.

Wide-Angle Lenses Truck In

Wide-angle lenses have a very wide, deep depth of field.

As we move in with a wide-angle lens we start to notice a lot of change in the frame.

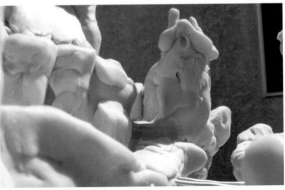

We also experience distortion as the lens dramatically pushes apart the space. This is great for action movies.

How to Use Framing to Tell a Story

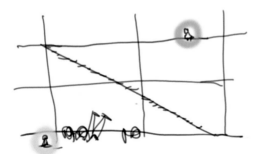

In *Fantasia 2000's Pomp and Circumstance*, which I directed, we had trouble with the idea that Donald and Daisy Duck kept just missing running in to each other. We tried showing them far apart, on opposite sides of the ark, with Donald on the top deck and Daisy below. It was the recurring speaking problem of trying to say more than one idea at a time—you didn't know where to look. What we realized was that these were "near" misses, not "far" misses. The characters had to be near the same spot on the screen but something keeps getting in their way of seeing each other. This made it fun for the audience to watch.

The following example demonstrates the problem of too much happening in a shot. Donald Duck was looking for Daisy Duck while Daisy was entering the ark without seeing Donald or him seeing her. The animation director, Hendel Butoy, came up with a very elegant solution by using camera framing to show only what we wished the audience to see. The interior red frame represents what the audience got to see, the rest remained offscreen.

First Donald comes out of the ark door frantically looking for Daisy.

Donald climbs up on the elephant and exits the frame, just as Daisy enters the frame from the other side. We are showing one thing at a time. *The motion of entrances into the frame catches the viewer's eyes.*

Daisy walks ahead of the elephant.

Just as Daisy exits the frame, Donald jumps down off the elephant, reentering the frame. Again, focus only on one thing at a time.

Now we cut to a close-up of Donald looking for Daisy. His head obscures the fact that ...

Daisy is entering the ark. They have just missed each other. If only he would have turned around.

Back to our story. So Goo is stuck, but at least he is alive! But why has Scheherazade stolen the sultan's key? Observe how perspective is used in the palace scenes.

Later that night.

Scheherazade shows her sister the key.

DUNAZADE: "What are you thinking?"

Scheherazade draws.

DUNAZADE: "I know you want to understand the ..."

DUNAZADE: "... But I don't want you to die doing so."

Scheherazade sneaks out of her room.

DUNAZADE: "Scheherazade, wait."

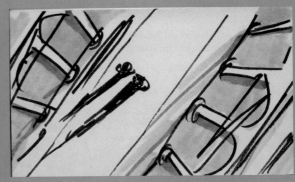

DUNAZADE: "Your plan is working."

DUNAZADE: "The sultan is falling for your stories ...

DUNAZADE: "And he's falling for you."

DUNAZADE: "This is dangerous."

DUNAZADE: "You've got to stop."

DUNAZADE: "I'm serious. We could both be killed."

They hear a sound and turn.

There is nothing there.

They continue on.

DUNAZADE: "Are you sure you want to do this?"

DUNAZADE: "Please, let's go back now."

Scheherazade puts the key into the lock

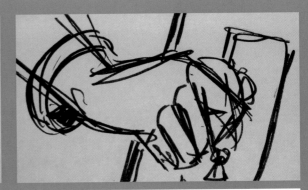

[Click.]

204

Dunazade nervously looks around.

The door opens streaming light into the pitch black.

Scheherazade lights a candle.

They descend the steps.

Scheherazade stops dead at what she sees.

The catacomb is filled with tombstones.

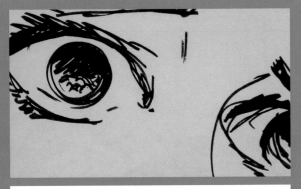

Terror fills her eyes.

Dunazade walks over to one.

She dusts it off and reads.

DUNAZADE: "It is our friend Dawn, and it is dated the day after her wedding to the sultan last year."

Dunazade breaks down crying.

Scheherazade, herself, fights back the tears.

She tries to comfort her sister.

Dunazade looks up . . .

As a new emotion fills her sister …

Rage.

She begins to draw.

Scheherazade holds up the drawing.

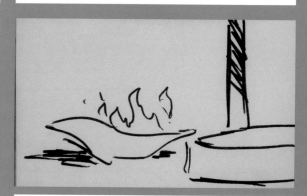

Dunazade can't believe what she is suggesting.

Scheherazade holds the drawing up to the candle and lights it.

It falls …

Burning on the floor.

Scheherazade is overconfident and her curiosity about the sultan has driven the story into a new direction. This is a turning point. She starts out seeking understanding, but finds more than she bargained for. The pendulum has swung back to fear. Scheherazade now knows the truth about the sultan's previous brides. What did she draw?

Camera Mobility

With new computer graphics the camera is no longer bound to the earth. It can swing along with Spiderman. But, as Spiderman might point out, with the freedom of camera movement comes great responsibility. You can create great excitement with camera movement, just remember the enemies of good design. Too much camera movement can be confusing, and if your audience is confused then boredom is not far away. Don't be turned by the dark side of technology. Just because you can do a 360-degree spin with the camera doesn't mean you should. Don't let the camera work break the threshold of awareness. Actually, this was used to comic effect in Mel Brooks's *High Anxiety*. As a tribute to Hitchcock's camera work the camera took on an ominous presence as it slowly trucked into a large picture window. The camera hit the glass causing the actors to notice it. The camera then sheepishly backed away. I am using ominous and sheepish to describe the camera because that is how it felt in the shot. The camera has expressive power.

In this next example from *Fantasia 2000's Pines of Rome* the camera tracks a flock of flying whales as they first head over the horizon toward us. Then the camera rotates to track them as they fly overhead and rotates again as they fly away from us into the sunset. It made for a very dramatic shot that put the viewer in the middle of the action.

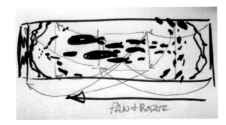

Alternative Approaches

Perspective drawing is a projection system that maps out the view in points in space. There are actually several types of projection systems including classical perspective, oblique projection, and orthogonal perspective. The problem with the classical perspective that we have been demonstrating is that it is best suited for rectangles.

Author John Willats, in *Art and Representation*, does an excellent job analyzing and demonstrating the various methods of representing the three-dimensional world in two-dimensional pictures. Caricatures, children's drawings, maps, and schematic diagrams are based on topological geometry rather than a system of projection. "Topological geometry is based upon the most elementary and general types of spatial qualities, which include relations like touching, separation, spatial order, and enclosure. More special kinds of properties like straightness (preserved in projective projections) and true (scale) sizes and shapes of faces (preserved in orthogonal projections) are not preserved in topological transformations."[2]

I would like to show you another way to plan a picture that art director Bill Perkins taught me. The idea is to separate out simple layers of depth kind of like stage flats. There is a background, possibly multiple layers of midground, and a foreground.

It turns out that this is exactly what Walt Disney Studios did with their multiplane camera. This was a special type of animation camera used to create the illusion of depth with flat animation. When the camera panned objects in the foreground it moved by faster than those in the background thus creating the illusion of depth. It also allowed for depth of field illusions whereby only one zone of depth is in focus and the rest are blurred.

If you plan and keep your value ranges of colors within those allowed for that layer you can create atmospheric perspective and achieve a great illusion of depth. The foreground will contain your greatest contrasts, say from 95 percent gray up to white. The midground will contain values from 70 percent to 15 percent grays, and the background will have the narrowest value range, perhaps 40 percent to 20 percent gray.

Eastern artists have used this approach for centuries. Now you may think that some of these other approaches are only suitable for animation, however, if you watch Baz Luhrmann's *Moulin Rouge*, Michel Gondry's *Science of Sleep*, or Dave McKean's *Mirrormask* you will be exposed to new worlds of spatial possibilities.

A Trick for Planning Scenes

In his book, *Composing Pictures*, Donald W. Graham suggests to work out the placement of figures and items in a composition from a simple plan first, and then proceed to drawing the scene or staging it for the camera.

In the plan it is easy to move the pieces around so that you don't obscure something important when you stage things in depth. The scene clearly stages the two main standing characters without obscuring the seated bystanders. This tool becomes even more powerful when you realize that you can plan your blocking and camera moves with simple arrows and still know that your compositions will be clearly staged.

Proximity

Proximity, or how close we are to something, affects how we feel about it. I am sure you have been around someone who "got into your space." You probably felt uncomfortable because they were too close. Well, when watching movies the audience is keenly sensitive to spatial distance and it affects how they feel about certain characters.

When I have wanted to remind the audience that Scheherazade was telling the story, but not focus on her but rather the story she was telling, I kept the scene in a wider shot showing the characters in the room. This way we really didn't engage with the characters at these times. Silhouetting the characters by backlights also contributes to this distancing effect.

Alternately, when I wished to follow her actions and have the audience engaged, I moved in closer. Now we feel like we are with a friend.

In fact, if you move in too close, the audience can feel like they are inside the character's thoughts.

Proximity is extremely important in scene transitions when we wish to transfer the audience's attention and involvement to another scene. The classic case is the riding off into the sunset scene. At the end of a Western, the characters ride away from us, disengaging our interest until we can no longer see them and the film is over.

Blazing Saddles has a great gag based upon this ending. The heroes have defeated the bad guy and ride off toward the sunset. They stop after a distance, dismount, and enter a limo. It is funny because it is unexpected, but the limo driving away still performs the function of disengaging us from the characters.

The engaging aspect of proximity is another reason that every shot needs to be a close-up of what we want to say to our audience. It pulls them into the story.

Point of View: Subjective Camera

In a point-of-view shot, the audience assumes that what is shown in the frame is a character's point of view. This is often shown as a shot of a character looking, followed by a shot of what he or she sees. This is known as a shot-reaction shot sequence.

Compose your compositions to allow for offscreen space. Characters need breathing room in the direction they are looking. Don't cramp them at the edge of a frame.

The Town of Dumb Love and SketchUp™

Filmmakers use all sorts of tools and models to help them plan and envision their shots. In order to create the organic-looking town of Dumb Love, I built a model out of Super Sculpey®, a wonderful modeling compound available at most craft stores.

This model of the town of Dumb Love was modeled with Super Sculpey®. It works like clay but creates fine detail and can be baked in a regular oven.

For the sultan's palace I used a program called Google SketchUp™. It is available for free for Mac and Windows operating systems. It makes creating architectural three-dimensional models child's play. It is an excellent tool for exploring perspective and camera views. The professional version allows you to create animations flying through a scene as well as more modeling tools.

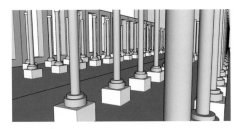

Beware of Depth Killers

The following list are things to watch out for that can destroy the illusion of depth. Interestingly, these can be useful. They often are used in posters. In film they can be very useful in the design principle of contrast. We can contrast flat scenes versus deep-space scenes to enhance our visual storytelling. Producer and film professor Bruce Block describes how to visually enhance a story using contrast with all of the design and spatial elements in his book, *The Visual Story*.

- Lines that are parallel to the picture frame will tend to flatten out space.
- If you ignore size constancy using incorrect sizes of objects, it will destroy the illusion of depth or create a surreal effect.
- Shadows that are all black can create holes in a picture. Highlights that go all white can look pasted on top of a picture.
- Objects that don't all have the same horizons also kill depth. They feel like they don't belong in the same picture.

POINTS TO REMEMBER
- Make sure you give your characters breathing room.
- Stage from a simple plan and use arrows like a football play.
- Use camera movement and framing to help tell the story one idea at a time.
- For beauty shots use telephoto lenses.

- For dynamic excitement use wide-angle lenses to keep maximum movement through the frame. Shoot on the camera's axis.
- Use proximity to determine the level of engagement with your characters appropriate for the stage of your film.
- Watch *Lawrence of Arabia* for a great exploration of screen space.

References

1. Cole, A. (1992). *Perspective*. Dorling Kindersley, 1992.
2. Willats J. *Art and Representation*. Princeton, NJ: Princeton University Press, 1997.

9

How to Make Images Speak: The Hidden Power of Images

After we see images, we need to "read" them to see what they really are.

A Fancy Word for Clues

I first heard the word "semiotics" in the 1980s. I had to take a course called Vocabulary of the Media Critic. I thought with a title like this, it had to be boring. Well, I learned not to judge a book by its cover, or in this case, a class by its title. This class was the most educationally mind-blowing class that I have ever taken. Dr. Alwyn Scott taught the course at the New York Institute of Technology. I have mentioned that he taught his class to aim for the heart by working at the structural level. He also told us that if we wanted to make significant films, that we should study semiotics. Study what?

I had never heard of semiotics. It was unfortunate that he didn't teach us how to aim at the heart by working structurally and equally unfortunate that he didn't tell us how to use semiotics. Well, with Dr. Scott pointing the way, I started studying it, and about 20 years later, when I was directing the *Pomp and Circumstance* sequence of *Fantasia 2000*, that I found that semiotics was exactly what I needed. But what is semiotics? For our purposes, we can think of semiotics as a fancy word for clues.

They say Eskimo have over 50 words for snow. This is because for them it is crucial to differentiate between the different types of snow. It could mean the difference between life and death for them. For filmmakers clues are important. A general word, "clue," like the word "entertainment," doesn't give us a lot of information about how to structure our movies. Semiotics will show us that there are many different types of clues that we can use as tools to convey information to the audience in many different ways. The audience will use all of these different types of clues to construct the story for themselves.

Why Should You Care about Clues?

In the retelling of the Noah's Ark story of *Pomp and Circumstance*, Donald Duck plays the role of Noah's assistant responsible for getting all the animals on the ark. This idea brimmed with comic possibilities. We layered a secondary plot onto this to give the story great emotional resonance. Donald and Daisy both think that the other didn't make it onto the ark, and they both mistakenly believe that the other has been lost to the storm. While this gave us great heart for our story, it presented a new problem. We needed to be careful with this idea because it could have easily gotten morbid. But a bigger problem was how do we refer to something that is missing?

We had to show that Donald was missing Daisy so we drew an image like this one. Unfortunately, this image doesn't say that Donald is missing Daisy. Look at it carefully. All it shows is Donald looking over the side of the ark looking sad. How is the audience supposed to know that he is not just seasick? Semiotics came to our rescue. No, semiotics is not a seasickness cure.

Now, *Fantasia* is known for creating visual stories to accompany great classical music. *Fantasia* stories contain no words; the stories are really like silent films. Therefore, we couldn't rely on the characters to say how they felt. We were totally dependent on the visuals to tell the story.

Our problem was how do we tell the audience, without words, that Donald is missing Daisy? Or in other words, how do we signify something is missing? When I remembered semiotics, the question was reframed to, "What signs could we use to signify to the audience that Donald was missing Daisy?" With the question reframed we knew what we were looking for—some iconic sign that represented each of them for each other, a symbol of their love. An icon is a type of sign that works by resemblance; in other words, it looks like what it is supposed to represent. Drawings and photographs are iconic signs. So we gave Donald a drawing and Daisy a locket. Now standing at the edge of the ark, Donald could pull out his icon of Daisy and the audience knew exactly what he was feeling. The icon signified something missing.

Donald's icon of Daisy.

Daisy's icon of Donald. (*Credit:* Art by Aernout Van Pallandt.)

What other devices could we use to say that Donald is missing Daisy? The design principle of contrast is used to compare two things. If we showed Donald all alone on the ark and compared him with all of the animals of the ark paired off two by two, then by contrast he would seem even more alone.

Donald by himself + animals paired off = Donald even more lonely.

Contrast of scale helped us convey the theme of *Pomp and Circumstance*. This was a love and forgiveness story set in a storm of epic proportions. We wanted to relate this to our audience, so I needed to convey the importance of scale to my art director, Dan Cooper. I drew a little sketch that looked like the next image.

I drew it from the center out and described it as I drew it for him. First, I drew Donald and Daisy. I told Dan that they were dwarfed by all of the animals that they had to get on the ark. The scale of the enormous ark dwarfed all the animals including Donald and Daisy. But the ark itself was tiny when compared to the biblical storm. However, that wasn't the end of the story. Finally, even the storm was dwarfed by love, indicated by the heart.

Donald's checklist was another great use of semiotic icons. We needed a device to show Donald's realization that Daisy was missing. Donald has a big list with pictures of all the animals and he checks them off as the animals board the ark. When he gets to him and Daisy he realizes she is missing and goes off to search for her. Once again semiotics helped us signify that something was missing.

(*Credit:* Art by Aernout Van Pallandt.)

How Movies Speak to Us

Let's start with an image. It doesn't appear to say much. But don't judge an image by its mere appearance.

What is this?

After drawing this image on the board, I always ask my storyboard class, "What is this?" The answer: a bundle of sticks. So then I ask, "What else is it?" The answers come back: a pile of trash, a whiskbroom without the handle, a bundle of firewood, a harvest.

Sometimes the first answer can get them stuck in a rut of only thinking about it in one way. I need to prompt them out of that rut. I ask how else they could describe it. One time, I was surprised when a student answered a "Christmas present for a beaver." This got them out of the rut. I suggest it could be a drawing on a blackboard that represents a bundle of sticks. It reminds me of the surrealist painter, Magritte, who wrote, "This is not a pipe" over a picture of a pipe.

THIS IS NOT A PAINTING BY MAGRITTE

Pomp and Circumstance also had a semiotic gag, kind of like Magritte's painting. Donald is directing the pairs of animals onto the ark and a pair of ducks walks by. What does that make him?

(*Credit:* Art by Aernout Van Pallandt.)

But our story digresses.... I jump to another level and ask the class how the drawing of a bundle of sticks makes them feel. The answers now cover a wider range. It is warmth, strength in numbers, unity, togetherness, and uniformity. I then start to analyze each of the answers.

We start with the fact that it represents a bundle of sticks. That is what is called a *denotation*. This is the dictionary or literal meaning. The fact that it is a drawing doesn't change its denotation. It is still a "bundle of sticks." A whiskbroom or kindling wood are also denotations of the image. But there is another level. It has associations connected to it. These are the things like warmth, unity, or togetherness. These are what are known as *connotations*.

So the image has a denotation or literal meaning and a bunch of connotations. So what? Does this help us make a better movie? No, not yet. But, there is more. Some connotations are common. We have all experienced the warmth of a fire, so we know the connotation of "warmth." What if someone said "pain"? Most of the class didn't understand the connection, until the student explained that he had watched workers carrying big bundles of wood and they looked like they were in pain. Everyone now understood. They now shared a new connotation to the bundle of sticks.

What if we could make images speak for us? Then it might be useful for us as filmmakers. In the film *The Straight Story*, director David Lynch tells the story of Alvin Straight's journey across Iowa on a lawn mower. When he learns that his estranged brother is ill he decides it's time to make amends and visit him. The problem is that his eyesight is failing so he can no longer drive a car. Driven by his need to make amends, he embarks on a 300-mile journey across state lines driving a lawn mower tractor towing a small trailer.

Along the way Alvin passes a girl who is hitchhiking. That night at his campsite she catches up with him. He invites her to sit and share his meager meal. "When are you due?" he asks her. His worldly experience allows him to grasp that she is running away from home because she is going to have a baby. In other words, he saw and pieced together the clues.

He offers her some dinner and a metaphor. He tells her about his own feud with his brother. But now his brother is sick so he is going to visit, and that is why he is on his journey. Alvin tells her that families are like bundles of sticks. It is easy to snap one stick, but put them in a bundle and they have real strength. The night grows late and he offers for her to stay in the trailer. She says she will sleep in the chair by the fire.

The following morning he comes out of the trailer and the girl is gone. I was expecting to see a shot of a note, but instead David Lynch chose to show a shot of the chair and on it was a bundle of sticks tied together with a ribbon.

It was an extremely powerful shot that condensed multiple layers of meaning into one shot. The shot said, "Thank you. I am going home to my family." In addition, it implied that she could get emotional and physical strength and warmth from her family just as the sticks signified strength and their utility as firewood. The fact that the sticks were wrapped in a ribbon suggested also that this was a "gift" in return for his sharing his personal story and advice in the form of a metaphor.

What he did was stack the connotations upon each other and each one recalls the other and the whole stack. This stacking can become quite complex. Associations can stack up like, well, like a bundle of sticks. Let's look at how it works.

First, we have the denotation that it is a bundle of sticks tied with a string. Second, this image connotes strength, warmth, and unity. Third, this suggests the good qualities of a family. Fourth, it connotes the story as a gift given. Fifth, the image becomes a way of saying "thank you." There is another layer of connotation now that I have told you about *The Straight Story* that becomes a signifier of the movie.

What is going to happen the next time you see a bundle of sticks? What will you remember? Like the proverbial string tied around your finger, you will remember this lesson in semiotics and how images can be made to speak. You just have to share with your audience what the personal connotations to the images are and then you are free to call upon them at any point later in your film.

So can semiotics help us make better films? I will answer with the next image.

Remember though, when leaving clues for the audience, it is important to point at them so they don't miss them.

Denotation

Denotation is what a thing is in common language. It is the literal dictionary meaning of something. Let's say we have a picture of a tree. The denotation is "tree."

Connotation

Connotations are what are evoked in the mind of the viewer by what they see. They are the associated meanings to something. A tree can be something to climb or a place for shade. These associations branch out like branches of a tree. These can be stacked on top of each other so one thing will trigger another and then another and so on—every branch can have its own tree. These are the shared connotations that images evoke.

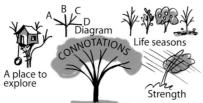

Tree denotes: tree, a trunk with branches

The underground secret is that trees also have roots. These are the hidden or private associations that can be evoked. Once the filmmaker uses them they can be recalled just as the branches can. It is up to the filmmaker to decide how explicitly he or she wants to bring out the association. Not only every sign, but structures can also have emotional associations.

The Mind Makes Associations

Our minds basically work by using associations. Logic requires a lot of thought. Associations are immediate. Remember logic doesn't persuade people, stories do, and stories evoke associations.

So how can we create these associations for our audience? It is thought that primitive people and children think mainly through association as a form of magic. The clearest expression of this type of thinking is the Voodoo doll. The idea behind Voodoo relies on the association between the person and the doll. When a part of the person (hair, fingernail, etc.) is put on the doll, whatever happens to the doll is supposed to happen to the person by association of the piece of them attached to the doll. The fact that, in some cases, it appears to work is based on the power of suggestion.

We all have experienced this type of behavior. It is known as *superstition*. Let's say someone calls and then we get hurt. If they call again we may worry about being hurt. We have unconsciously associated the call with getting hurt.

So what is responsible for the association? Our minds are always searching for patterns of cause and effect. Things that are similar in some way or happen at the same place or time often get connected together as cause and effect. Remember gestalt? Things that are in proximity get clustered into a group. It is like magic.

How many signs do you see?

In the last image, how many signs do you see? If you just said some road signs, then turn in your detective badge because you missed a lot of clues. Just for starters there is the type of terrain, style of architecture, utilities, clothing style, modes of transportation, weathering signs, types of materials, types of vegetation, colors, and more. Every image is filled with signs, and that is why they can say a picture is worth a thousand words.

Sometimes signs can compete with each other as in the stop sign in the next image that doesn't allow you to stop at anytime.

Semiotics studies how signs signify something and how meaning is constructed from sequences of images. Signs refer to things in our world. Semiotics began with the splitting of the sign into the signifier/signified pair. For linguistics, this event was equivalent to the splitting of the atom for physics. The sign is comprised of two parts, the signifier and the signified. The signifier is the physical support of the sign. It is what we hear or see—the verbal phonemes (parts of words) or images. The signified is the concept that the sign represents for us in our minds.

Sign = Signifier, the physical support of the sign

Signified = the concept created in the mind

There are three types of signs: icons, indexes, and symbols.

Iconic Signs

Icons speak by resembling what they are. Film is iconic. We recognize what we see when we watch a film. It is based on images. Drawings, pictographs, photographs, and computer screen images are also iconic.

Index Signs

Indexes are connected by a causal relationship. The expression "Where there's smoke, there's fire" refers to an indexical relationship between smoke and fire. Smoke indicates that fire can't be far. The speedometer in a car is an index of how fast the car is going, just as a heart monitor tells how fast a heart is beating. Windblown trees are an index of how hard the wind is blowing. Shadows on the wall are indexes of the objects that cast their shadows and of the fact that there is a light to create a shadow.

A footprint is an icon and index. It looks like the foot and signifies that someone walked there.

Symbolic Signs

The last type of sign is the symbol. These are signs that have an arbitrary relationship to what they signify. They don't resemble their referent or have a causal relationship. Their relationship is based on an agreed-upon convention; in other words, you have to be taught what they mean. Language is symbolic because we must learn what letters and words mean. If you don't know the code you won't know what the symbol means.

There are other types of symbols as well. Religions and other organizations have symbols that bring up a whole host of meanings for those who understand them. For those who don't know them, these signs are an enigma. Sometimes symbols are unconscious. In other words, even those who created them do not understand them. Ultimately, the audience decides the meaning of what they see.

When we last left Scheherazade, she left behind a sign. Read on to see what it signifies.

The drawing continues to burn as they leave.

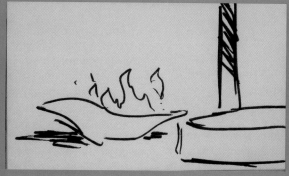

A hand reaches in and picks it up.

It shows the sultan toasting wine laced with poison!

The evidence burns before …

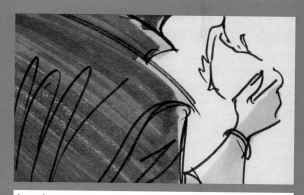

It can be put out.

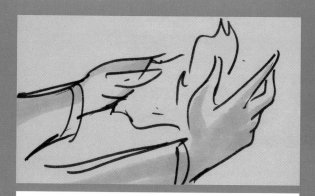

Only ashes remain.

Crime Story Clues and Signs

I don't think that crime and detective stories could be told without semiotics. Detectives look for clues. Clues are nothing more than signs of a crime. In fact, they rely on them so much that these stories could also be called semiotic stories. They are also filled with significant objects, in this case, incriminating objects. These suggest nothing less than a character's guilt or innocence.

As most detective shows make clear, clues are ambivalent. There are always multiple possible stories to apparently account for them. The detective's job is to narrow down those stories to the true one that accounts for the facts of the crime with the motive and opportunity of the criminal. The director's job is to misdirect the audience into thinking of those other possible stories. What if this person did it or suppose it was that person? That is part of the fun of watching crime stories—playing armchair sleuth.

Hitchcock's *Rear Window*

Speaking of armchair sleuths, Hitchcock's *Rear Window* demonstrates this process of trying to make up stories to fit the evidence and a metaphor for the film viewing process itself. Film viewers search for clues and makes up stories to explain to themselves the things that they think they see, just as the characters do in the film. As filmgoers we are all guilty of this voyeurism—a desire to know. Stefan Sharff analyzes this process in *Rear Window* in scene by scene detail.[1]

Hitchcock and His McGuffins

Objects in Hitchcock's world can be very functional. He uses three types of objects. First are his McGuffins. "It might be a Scottish name, taken from a story about two men in a train. One man says, 'What's that package up there in the baggage rack?' And the other answers, 'Oh that's a McGuffin.' The first one asks 'What's a McGuffin?' 'Well,' the other man says, 'It's an apparatus for trapping lions in the Scottish Highlands.' The first man says, 'But there are no lions in the Scottish Highlands,' and the other one answers, 'Well, then that's no McGuffin!' So you see, a McGuffin is nothing at all."[2] McGuffins are objects that set the story in motion, an object that everyone wants. It doesn't matter what it is, only that everyone wants it.

Besides his McGuffins, Hitchcock used two other types of objects, symbolic objects and threatening objects. Symbolic objects become dangerous when you know what they signify.

In *A Shadow of a Doubt*, the ring that Charlie gives his niece is one object that takes on different significations depending on how much information is known about it. First, his niece accepts it as a gift of love. At this point all she knows is that her loving uncle gave her a piece of jewelry. In the next phase, it becomes an object of suspicion as she discovers someone else's initials on it. When she learns the initials match a murdered woman it becomes an object of horror. When she

returns the ring to her uncle, it signifies that she knows that he is the murderer. Mladen Dolar describes this transformation of Hitchcock's objects in great detail in *Everything You Always Wanted to Know about Lacan But Were Afraid to Ask Hitchcock*.[3] If objects could talk, oh, the stories they could tell.

Hitchcock's other type of object are those oppressive objects that threaten with their sheer silent presence. The house in *Psycho* does not have the appearance of a happy home inside or out. Height functions as a continual threat with the tower in *Vertigo*, Mount Rushmore in *North by Northwest*, and even the Statue of Liberty in *Saboteur*. Finally, in Hitchcock's world we are not even safe from *The Birds*.

Significant Objects

How do you represent something that is not there? The value of semiotics comes into play when we need to refer to something that is not present onscreen. We do this with language all of the time. Words continually refer to things that are not physically present: the gold of Fort Knox, the ends of Earth, the planet Mars, or dinosaurs. Semiotics gives the filmmaker tools to refer to what is not currently on the screen visually, without resorting to words by the play of signs. Sometimes these signs can be very significant and carry great meaning in a film. Here is a sampling of how significant objects have been used in various films.

Even names can be full of significance. In *Star Wars*, the name Darth Vader signifies the dark father. The name sounds like dark invader. Luke Skywalker has the prophet's name, Luke, and the description of walker of the skies. We meet Luke living in the desert signifying that he has nowhere to go. The cars are hovercraft signifying advanced technology. The light sabers signify high technology while their swordlike qualities invoke memories about swashbucklers and codes of chivalry. Then there is the planet that isn't a planet. It is the fully operational death star. (*Credit*: Art by Aernout Van Pallandt.)

In *It's a Wonderful Life*, George Bailey during a string of bad luck wishes he never existed. In order to earn his wings, Clarence, the angel, must help George. He does so by showing George what the town would have been like without him. George can't believe that this is happening. He reaches in his pocket for flower petals that his daughter, Zuzu, gave him. They are not there. She never existed! Later, when George learns the lesson that his life is valuable to others, the return of Zuzu's flower petals signifies that the nightmare, that George didn't exist, is over. The bell ringing on the Christmas tree signifies that Clarence got his wings. The bell has additional significance for us, the audience, and George for we know that it is Clarence getting his wings. The book signed by Clarence signifies that George's experience was indeed real.

Timothy the mouse believes the way that Dumbo got into the tree was that he flew up using his ears as wings, but Dumbo isn't convinced. The crows, standing in for Dumbo's missing father figure, give him the added push he needs to believe in himself in the form of a wonderful symbolic placebo, the "Magic Feather." The scene is driven by a wonderful narrative question: Will Dumbo really be able to fly? He flaps his ears and the scene is enveloped in a cloud of dust. We don't know if the Magic Feather worked. It is only when we see his shadow, an index of where he is, that the question is answered. During the death-defying circus show Dumbo loses the Magic Feather. The placebo, like Alfred Hitchcock's infamous McGuffin, means nothing, except that it enables people to believe something that they normally can't. Finally, in the crisis of falling, Dumbo accepts the truth that he can fly, and he soars above the crowd! With Timothy's help he changed the impossible to the possible.

In *A Christmas Carol*, Tiny Tim's cane signifies Scrooge's redemption or damnation.

Popeye, of course, has his spinach, a symbol of strength. (*Credit*: Art by Aernout Van Pallandt.)

In *Piglet's Big Movie*, Piglet's book of memories "remembers" him. His friends use it to find Piglet. (*Credit*: Art by Aernout Van Pallandt.)

In *Bladerunner*, a dove flies off when a replicant dies. Does this signify that they have a soul? (*Credit*: Art by Aernout Van Pallandt.)

Objects can suggest a vast variety of ideas such as love or hate. Clocks, calendars, seasons, weathering and erosion, and the rising tide all signify time. Uniforms, medals, clothes, costumes, and masks all suggest character and social class. The weather, lighting, architecture, environments, and open and closed spaces, as well as the sound ambience of places provide the filmmaker signs to suggest meanings.

Love can be expressed in myriad ways—love letters, flowers, and gifts. But objects can also signify changes in love, such as buying a crib for a coming baby, or taking off a wedding ring signifying a divorce.

Death has its own collection of objects that silently state its presence. At one end of the spectrum we have the pirate's skull and crossbones and at the other we have the flat line of the high-tech heart monitor.

Doors represent the passage from one place to another. These places might be states of mind. Doors, windows, and mirrors are all objects that have great potential to speak without words telling us what is going on between characters or inside a character's mind.

How Images Ask Questions

We continually ask questions. That is how we think. We ask a question and decide the answer for ourselves. When we see images we want to know what they signify. It is like a child playing in an airplane cockpit—they want to know what all those buttons do.

- What is it?
- What is going on?
- Why do I care?
- Why should I care?
- What do the characters depicted want?
- What will happen next?
- What may change that can set something in motion?

We think in terms of stories. Then the director presents images that ask questions that are driven by character desires, wishes, and fears, and then delay the answers.

And speaking of delays, let's go back and see how Scheherazade handles the news that the sultan is an insane murderer. How will her state of mind affect her storytelling? How can we show that it does?

The group gathers for the story session.

The vizier enters.

He approaches the sultan.

And …

Whispers in his ear. The sultan's expression changes.

Scheherazade lights the lamp.

Scheherazade isn't paying attention.

She burns her finger.

Dunazade and the sultan watch concerned.

Her new knowledge of the sultan makes it difficult to draw but she continues on.

Clover's tower.

Daisy and Weed approach.

Clover waves.

Daisy and Weed wave back.

Clover struggles to open her locked door.

She slams into the door.

[Crash!]

Unfortunately, she knocks out her third eye.

It rolls out the door ...

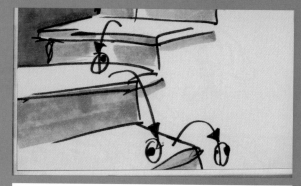

Bounces down the stairs ...

Past Daisy and Weed ...

And out onto the street.

VOICE: "Hey, look what I found!"

A wild-haired kid holds up the eye.

KID WITH HAT: "Throw it over here."

The wild-haired kid throws it, but the kid with the hat can't reach it.

He turns to watch it fall over the edge.

It sails down into the chasm below.

KIDS: "Sigh."

Deep in the chasm …

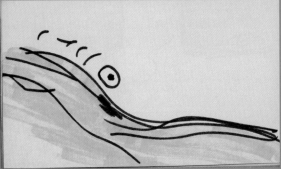

The eye reaches the bottom and continues to roll …

And stops by the hermit cooking dinner.

Goo tries his latest scheme to return to his true love.

Goo takes aim and …

Fires!

226

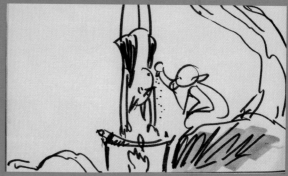

The arrow flies skyward.

The rope goes taut.

And carries Goo up with it …

Right over the roasting fire …

Just as the hermit sprinkles salt on his wild boar.

The sultan laughs.

Scheherazade struggles to hide her contempt but she must continue on …

Or suffer the fate of her friends. SULTAN: "Vizier, let the wine flow."

VIZIER: "Yes, sire."

The sultan holds out his glass, unaware of changes it may bring.

The sultan toasts.

Dunazade wonders if her sister could have followed through with her threat.

Scheherazade pauses from drawing.

She holds up her glass ...

And drinks.

228

Dunazade watches her sister and …

The sultan sip the wine.

Dunazade is relieved.

Scheherazade holds up the next drawing.

The sultan continues to be lost in the story, unaware of the events happening right under his nose.

CLOVER: "I'm seeing something."

DAISY [Offscreen]: "What is it?"

CLOVER: "It's Goo. He's lost in the underworld."

Clover races to her bookcase and pulls down a book.

She flips through the pages and stops. CLOVER: "That's it! That's what I saw!"

WEED: "It's an underworld soul eater." DAISY: "It says they torture their victims by eating them for eternity so they die over and over."

CLOVER: "I've got to save Goo!"

How does Scheherazade's new knowledge affect the story she tells the sultan? Clover and Goo are both trying to escape their respective trapped situations. This is exactly how Scheherazade feels, wanting to escape. Now, I could say that this pairing up was totally planned letting one part of the story comment on another, yielding greater resonance, but I would be lying. I didn't see this connection until I wrote the text for this section. It was unconscious. That is how to use intuition. Look for these types of connections and build upon them. In contrast to Murphy's Law, happy accidents are those times when things go right.

Scheherazade's regained some control in deciding not to poison the sultan. Does she have a new plan? Clover has a new problem: Can she save Goo from the soul-eater demons?

Speaking Indirectly

Semiotic signs have shown us some ways that images speak. All language is used to say something else. We always say more than we literally mean. We can't help it, because once we release a signifier onto the world it mingles with others, growing in complex webs of associations like six degrees of separation. Besides, most of the time we are not just conveying information, like giving someone the time, but rather we are implying, insinuating, and suggesting. As filmmakers we can also reveal information in a way that is not direct and the audience has to put together the information and decide for themselves what it means.

Once a director has mastered how to tell a story with pictures clearly and directly, then real persuasive power comes from learning how to speak indirectly using rhetorical devices and figures of speech, or tropes. In Chapter 1, I told you

to say one thing at a time. My reviewer, the director, animator, and author Nancy Bieman, pointed out that I was wrong in suggesting that we can only say one thing at a time. Yes, she is correct, but we needed to walk before we could swim, so in the beginning I suggested to tell one thing at a time. I have seen so many beginners presenting two centers of interest in a shot without even realizing it. However, I didn't say that what you present couldn't be multilayered. Nancy pointed out that double entendres do just this. Language is always multilayered, but even though a double entendre may branch off into multiple meanings, it is clear. Let's now look at some ways to speak indirectly.

Four Master Tropes

Tropes are figurative uses of words. When I say a trope is like a tool for understanding, I am comparing a trope to a tool. They help us understand the world by rendering the unfamiliar more familiar. How can figurative uses of words help us with visual stories? We are using a speaking metaphor, and it so happens that all of the tropes can be used in a visual form. The vast array of tropes with their fancy-sounding names can be broken down into four main types: metaphor, metonymy, synecdoche, and irony. Let's look at each of them and see how they can help us visually speak indirectly.

Metaphor

Far from being a fancy device used in poetry, George Lakoff and Mark Johnson suggest that "Our conceptual system thus plays a central role in defining our everyday realities. If we are right in suggesting that our conceptual system is largely metaphorical, then the way we think, what we experience, and what we do every day is very much a matter of metaphor."[4]

Consider another wonderfully surprising image from *The Straight Story*. Alvin's lawn mower tractor has died. We see him depressed and taking out his gun. He is not going to end his misery, is he? We are in the kitchen when we hear the shot. We look outside the window to see what happened and we are presented with the lawn mower tractor on fire. Alvin put the lawn mower out of its misery.

In this scene, David Lynch misdirects us leading us to think that Alvin may do something to hurt himself out of his frustration. He gives us the sound of the gunshot, but lets our imagination fill in the blank as to what happened. Then after a perfect story-delay he shows us the tractor in flames. We laugh with relief.

Lynch is using a visual metaphor here. Alvin is a farmer and in the context of farm life, when an animal is hurt, one shoots it to put it out of its misery. Lynch is comparing the tractor to a dying animal. Metaphor works by taking something that is known and mapping it onto something that is unknown. This mapping process provides a flash of insight allowing us to understand the unknown a little better.

Known: We know what a fish is like surrounded by water.

Unknown: Just like a fish that can't see that it is in water, it is hard for us to understand we are swimming in signs.

Using a metaphor generates understanding. As professor Daniel Chandler points out, this interpretative effort of understanding metaphor is experienced as pleasurable. It is like a narrative question being answered.

In terms of the signs involved, "Metaphor can be regarded as a new sign formed from the signifier of one sign and the signified of another. The signifier thus stands for a different signified; the new signified replaces the usual one."[5]

Metaphors are based on a resemblance between two things, and in this sense they are iconic in nature. "Metaphors need not be verbal. In film, a pair of consecutive shots is metaphorical when there is an implied comparison of the two shots. For instance, a shot of an aeroplane followed by a shot of a bird flying would be metaphorical implying that the aeroplane is (or is like) a bird."[6]

(*Credit*: Art by Karen Yan.)

Since film is composed of pictures and pictures are particular and concrete, metaphors allow us to express ideas that are abstract such as the theme of a film. Some of the metaphoric uses listed by N. Roy Clifton include using a metaphor to convey a character or using a metaphor to convey an inner state. Alan Parker's *The Wall* is one extended metaphor about the difficulty of the main character not being able to break down mental walls that prevent him from connecting with others.

Intercutting two parallel stories is a way to invite the audience to metaphorically make comparisons between them. Camera angle, lighting and shadows, movement, sound, manipulation, and using montage or juxtaposition are all ways to use the structure to make metaphorical comparisons.

Metaphor is also a way to utilize the film frame to convey relations of power to the audience. Consider this shot from *Ivan the Terrible*. Without a word, Sergei M. Eisenstein makes it very clear who is in charge.

Metonymy

Metaphor and metonymy are the major rhetorical devices used to speak indirectly. In *The Straight Story*, director David Lynch uses a pile of sticks to say "Thank you very much. I'm going home to my family." Hitchcock in *A Shadow of Doubt* uses a ring to imply love, betrayal, discovery, guilt, and acknowledgement. That is powerful filmmaking. They do it by going beyond the denotation of the objects, to connotations that have been defined earlier in the sequence or by new information that changes the perception of the objects. Most intuitive filmmakers don't know that connotations can be stacked upon each other to give these very resonant meanings in a film.

Everyone who has had a high school English class has heard of metaphors. Metonymy doesn't have the same claim to fame but it is very valuable for filmmakers. Let's go back to professor Daniel Chandler for some illumination on the subject. "While metaphor is based upon apparent unrelatedness, metonymy is a function which involves using one signified to stand for another signified which is directly related to it or closely associated with it in some way. Metonyms are based on various indexical relationships between the signifieds, notably the substitution of effect for cause. The best definition I have found is that 'metonymy is the evocation of the whole by a connection.'"[7] Metaphor and metonymy are both ways in which we understand the world but function differently.

> Metaphor is principally a way of conceiving one thing in terms of another, and its primary function is understanding. Metonymy, on the other hand, has primarily a referential function, that is, it allows us to use one entity to stand for another. But metonymy is not merely a referential device. It also serves the function of providing understanding. For example, in the case of metonymy, the part THE PART FOR THE WHOLE, there are many parts that can stand for the whole. Which part we pick out determines which aspect of the whole we are focusing on.[8]

"As with metaphors, metonyms may be visual as well as verbal. In film, which Jakobson, regarded as a basically metonymic medium, a depicted object which represents a related but non-depicted object is a metonym."[9] Thus in *Pomp and Circumstance* we were using the icons of Donald and Daisy to metonymically stand in for the real Donald and Daisy.

Metonymy also works visually by visual continuity. Consider a pan along a body. Each part leads to the next part. When one part is shown it evokes all the other parts, metonymically linked, even if the shots have been "Frankensteined" together from shots of different bodies.

"Forty Sail," where the part stands for the whole. (*Credit*: Art by Rajbir Singh.)

N. Roy Clifton, author of *The Figure in Film*, offers some visual applications of metonymy. A thing can stand in place of its owner. The lawn mower tractor can stand for Alvin Straight. In fact, his name stands for him. A badge could represent a person. A map could represent a territory. Stanley Kubrick's *The Shining* uses this in a great transition shot. We see Jack Torrance looking at a model of the maze at the Overlook hotel, and then the camera trucks into the model, which dissolves into the actual maze where his son is playing.

Each part of something can represent a whole web of connected ideas. A simple storyboard drawing could trigger all of the ideas in this book. Or a drawing of forty sails would lead you to expect the next image.

(*Credit*: Art by Rajbir Singh.)

I bet you weren't expecting this to be at the bottom of "Forty Sail." How is that for metonymical misdirection? I draw this image in my storyboard class and the unexpected quality of this image never fails to provoke laughter. Monty Phython uses metonymical misdirection to comic effect in *Monty Phython and the Holy Grail*. The scene is of the great knights of Camelot riding in quest of the Holy

Grail. The camera pulls back to reveal the knights riding pretend horses followed by serfs who clomp coconuts to provide the galloping sound.

Synecdoche

Synecdoche is often considered a subclass of metonymy. Synecdoche is a relation of the part to the whole or a relationship between the parts.

> In photographic and filmic media a close-up is a simple synecdoche. Indeed, the formal frame of any visual image (painting, drawing, photograph, film or television frame) functions as a synecdoche in that it suggests that what is being offered is a "slice of life," and the world outside the frame is carrying on in the same manner as the world depicted within it.... Any attempt to represent reality can be seen as involving synecdoche, since it can only involve selection.[10]

Irony

> Irony is the most radical of the four main tropes. As with metaphor, the signifier of the ironic sign seems to signify one thing but we know from another signifier that it actually signifies something very different. Where it means the opposite of what it says (as it usually does) it is based on binary opposition. Irony may thus reflect the opposite of the thoughts or feelings of the speaker.... It can also be seen as being based on substitution by dissimilarity or disjunction. While typically an ironic statement signifies the opposite of its literal signification, such variations as understatement and overstatement can also be regarded as ironic. At some point exaggeration may slide into irony.[11]

A key point in this statement is that it appears that irony requires two signifiers. The one signifier represents something and the other signifies that it is meant to be taken ironically. A knowing smile could suffice as the second signifier. The context often is what provides the qualifying signifier.

Ironic juxtaposition is where one image or shot can comment ironically on another. This is a great way to create transitions between scenes where the last line of dialogue from the first scene comments on the opening image of the next scene.

Singing in the Rain—ironic or sincere?

Speaking Indirectly in Time

Once something is said or shown, the story is not over, it is also affected by what will be said or shown. It has a retroactive effect on the signified. The meaning of the signified can shift until the meaning is anchored at the end of the sentence or film. Mysteries make you connect a clue with one person so you begin to suspect that person of the crime. Then they reveal a new context so the meaning shifts suggesting another reading and another suspect. When the mystery is finally solved at the end of the film all the signified are anchored into place, like when Charlie's niece pieces together the story of the ring. Only when the ring has traveled from the dead woman to Charlie, then to Charlie's niece, and then back Charlie, do we know the full story.

So can Clover save Goo from the depths? And what does it have to do with dental floss?

Daisy and Weed approach the guard at the base of Clover's tower.

GUARD: "What's that for?" DAISY: "Ah?" WEED: "It's Princess Clover's dental floss."

WEED: "Can't be too careful with your teeth you know."

Goo is attempting to climb out ...

And he is making some progress.

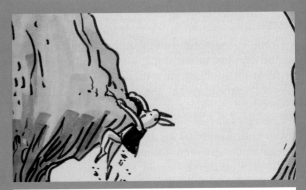

He pulls himself up to an overhang.

Clover climbs up the edge of her balcony.

She tests the bungee cord around her waist.

She looks down.

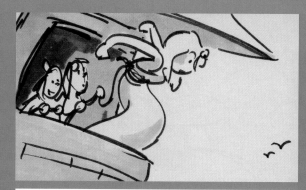

CLOVER: "For ..."

CLOVER: "Goooooooo"

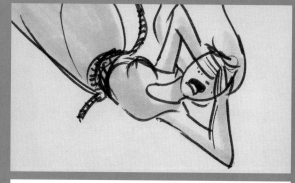

She shuts her eyes and falls.

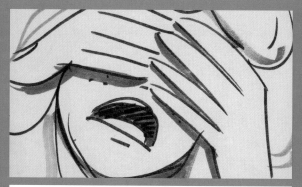

CLOVER: "ooooooooooooooooooo."

Meanwhile, Goo makes it over the ledge ...

To the top of the overhang just as Clover comes screaming down.

Goo looks up ...

And sees Clover coming right for him.

[Crash!]

Goo falls as Clover bounces back up.

DAISY: "Did you find him?" CLOVER: "I couldn't see anything."

WEED: "You want a flashlight?"

GOO: "Love can really knock the wind out of you."

The sultan is amused.

Scheherazade continues.

GOO [Voiceover]: "I've got to find a way back up."

GOO: "My true love waits for me."

Scheherazade grows weary.

She can barely hold up the drawings anymore.

The sultan takes notice and calls it a night.

SULTAN: "I wonder if Goo will ever get his true love?"

DUNAZADE: "You couldn't do it, could you?"

Scheherazade shakes her head.

So Scheherazade couldn't poison the sultan. What will she do next? Does she have a plan or is she making it up as she goes along? What will Goo do too?

Everything Speaks, If You Know the Code

Codes are like language, in the sense that we don't realize that we have learned them. They appear neutral. A code is a way to figure out what something means. Codes determine the genre of a film and gives you an overview of what you will be seeing. They provide a context to understand what happens. Actions in one genre may be totally out of place in another genre. What if a gun in a Western started acting like it belonged in a horror movie? The gun, quietly lying on the table, starts to aim at people, and the suspenseful music starts. It wouldn't be following the code of the Western genre.

What are codes? In order to demonstrate how codes let us understand the world, let's turn to two films that revel in codes: *The Matrix* and *The Golden Compass*.

In *The Matrix*, we are swimming in signs. The first five minutes reveal a plethora of signs determined by codes. The first scene opens with a flashing cursor. Instead of a current computer desktop, it is an old-style screen of text command lines and it is starting a trace. We hear voices over this image. The image transforms unlike any command line. Letters fall like a waterfall of data. The image morphs into an abstract space of data, then into a bright light that turns into a flashlight. Police, with guns out, raid into a room. A woman sits with her back to us, she doesn't move, and then she slowly raises her hands. We cut outside to a street filled with police cars as the agents arrive. We have seen this before—we know the code. The agents come and proclaim jurisdiction. The cops protest. We come to learn that these "agents" are not the typical FBI-type agents but are like super agents with unbelievable powers. We learn that the woman is Trinity who also has unnatural powers. The code here is that of superhero comics. Trinity wears a black leather outfit looking very much like a superhero, which her actions reinforce. The fact that she transforms in a phone booth supports that this is the correct code to read the action by. Remember Superman and his phone booth?

In the next scene Neo is introduced, his computer tells him to follow the white rabbit, a reference to the surreal world of *Alice in Wonderland*. Neo tries the escape key but there is no escape from the matrix. Then his computer displays "Knock, knock, Neo," and there is a knock at the door. The rules of reality are beginning to change before his and the audience's eyes. The people at the door have come for illicit computer disks, and it has all of the trappings of a drug deal. Even though *The Matrix* presents a totally metaphysically new world, it is couched in the codes we understand.

The Golden Compass has a different approach to codes. It is a fantasy genre and it begins with images of space and a narrator telling us about magical powers of dust. We also learn that this is a parallel universe, and in this world people's souls exist as animals outside of their bodies. That is cool so far, but the souls are called "demons." Why rename things that we already have connotations to? Dust is stuff to have to clean, and souls are supposed to be anything but demonlike.

The film has high production values but I felt oddly unemotional watching it. Everyone on screen seemed to think that things were extremely significant but the filmmakers didn't share that information with the audience, and that was the problem. I wanted to like the film but I didn't know their codes, and so, to me, dust was dust and I didn't care. I felt like I was watching a foreign film without subtitles.

There was one scene of striking visual power. A new teacher who has come to meet the little girl, Lyra Belacqua, is very nice to her, however, underneath the table we see her true intentions: Her demon is menacing the girl's soul. If we don't understand the code it is hard to care about the characters. In this scene, the codes were perfectly clear.

Sometimes codes can be used to deconstruct or critique a genre as with Clint Eastwood's *Unforgiven*. This film uses the code of Westerns to create a powerful film that deglamorizes the lure of the gunfighter. It shows gunfighting for what it really is—there is no glamor in real people dying from bullets.

Codes Specific to Film

In addition to our everyday codes and genre codes, there are codes specific to interpreting film. Cross-dissolves typically signify time passing. A split screen signifies two or more events happening simultaneously. Slow motion is for extreme actions such as falling or explosions. Slow motion can also signify danger, especially if children are around.

Semiotic Square

Semiotics, the world of clues, is a vast topic with many more areas of study. But in the limited space we have, I would like to present one more topic, the semiotic square invented by Algirdas Julien Greimas. Robert McKee, in his book *Story*,[12] utilizes the square as a tool for analyzing the thematic variations involved in a story. First we have a primary value. To this we add the opposite or contradictory value to create a binary pair. These are placed in opposite corners. Then to each of these we add their opposites to arrive at the square.

Positive value	Contrary
Negation of the negation	Negative value

Various scenes or characters can take on each quadrant of the square to present a filmic argument that explores all sides of an issue.

Semiotic Analysis of the Scheherazade and "Dumb Love" Stories

Let's look at how Scheherazade and her story, "Dumb Love," utilize semiotics or clues. In the opening scenes of the palace and in the town of "Dumb Love" it is raining. The palace is an elevated place not unlike the castle in "Dumb Love." The scale of the palace is a metaphor for the sultan's power. Setting the scenes at night is also a metaphor for the sultan's state of mind that casts a shadow over his kingdom. There is daytime where he lives, but by choosing not to show any scenes in the full light of day we immerse the audience in his world of madness along with Scheherazade.

Scheherazade has used repetition to make a comparison between the places. Rainy weather connotes gloom and uncomfortable conditions. Lightning suggests forces out of control. This comparison connects the two places without ever verbally stating so. This way it stays below the sultan's threshold of awareness. He is also unaware that by Scheherazade telling about a monster who can't love that she is saying that he is like the monster who has forgotten how to love.

Scheherazade's task is not easy. She is like the lovers in the prologue, who brave the elements and risk getting caught in the name of love. The shaky rope bridge, which connects the two sides of the town, is a metaphor for the obstacles to love. It will not be easy to "reach" the sultan. The palace itself also metonymically represents the sultan.

Scheherazade's charcoal is like one of Hitchcock's symbolic objects creating stains, meaning one thing and later taking on another significance. Scheherazade's playing with fire by going along with her curiosity. We could have put in a scene of her and her sister sneaking around thinking they are about to be caught, and then reveal it was only a curious cat. Scheherazade's ritual of lighting the candle now has new meaning—she is guilty of opening the forbidden door.

Adding Cupid and his arrows to "Dumb Love" was a fun afterthought. Cupid's arrows literalized the expression "love hurts." A quick, free association on the theme of Cupid reveals a baby is the result of love; wings suggest flying, a feeling associated with love; Cupid's nude, suggesting in love you are vulnerable; sometimes Cupid is blindfolded, suggesting love is blind; and his arrow tips are heart-shaped. Cupid's power was supposed to be even greater than Hades over the dead in the underworld. This alludes to love's power over Goo in the underworld. Love is what drives him to reach upward to return to Clover.

Semiotics covers everything in our world. Everything speaks and all speaking is unavoidably rhetorical. This speaking is different from everything calling attention to itself graphically where the images yell, "Look at me!" Here things are silent and have to be "read" for them to yield their meaning.

Watch *The Matrix* and *The Golden Compass* to study cinematic codes. Watch *The Straight Story*, *Fantasia 2000's Pomp and Circumstance*, *Pan's Labyrinth*, *The Orphanage*, and Hitchcock's films to study semiotic significance.

POINTS TO REMEMBER

- Explore all the ways images ask questions to get powerful narrative questions.
- Use semiotics to find ways to speak indirectly, thus engaging more participation from your audience.
- Stack your connotations so that if you present one aspect, it will trigger the whole thing in the minds of your audience.
- Everything speaks, it is impossible not to communicate. Remember, you have to teach your audience what the signs mean.
- Be sure to check out Daniel Chandler's book, *Semiotics: The Basics*, and his online seminar, "Semiotics for Beginners," at http://www.aber.ac.uk/media/Documents/S4B/semiotic.html.
- Film is created like a dream. Slowly let it evolve layering significances and associations until you have a rich tapestry of signs.

"For me? You shouldn't have."

References

1. Sharff, S. *The Art of Looking in Hitchcock's* Rear Window. Limelight Editions, 1997.
2. Truffaut F. *Hitchcock by Trauffaut*. New York: Simon & Schuster, 1967.
3. Zizek, S. *Everything You Always Wanted to Know about Lacan But Were Afraid to Ask Hitchcock*. Verso, 1992.
4. Lakoff, G. and M. Johnson. *Metaphors We Live By*. University of Chicago Press, Chicago, 1980.
5. Chandler, D. *Semiotics: The Basics*. London: Routledge, 2004.
6. Ibid.
7. Ibid.
8. Lakoff, G. and M. Johnson, *Metaphors We Live By*. Chicago: University of Chicago Press, 1980.
9. Chandler, D. *Semiotics: The Basics*. London: Routledge, 2004.
10. Ibid.
11. Ibid.
12. McKee, R. *Story*. Regan Books, 1997.

How to Convey and Suggest Meaning

Events of the story
Threshold of Awareness

WORK HERE: STRUCTURAL LEVEL

DIRECTORS DIRECT ATTENTION

DIRECTING THE EYES AND EARS

READING SIGNIFICANCE

CONSTRUCTING MEANING

The director captures the audience's attention through the presentation of clear images that help them construct the meaning of the story. Their minds are led to create expectations and rationalizations that hold the story together, based on clues and facts that have been provided or suggested.

In this chapter we are going to begin learning about how the mind puts ideas together to construct meaning. I would like to introduce you to cartoonist Rube Goldberg. He is remembered for a series of popular cartoons depicting "Rube Goldberg machines," complex devices that perform simple tasks in indirect, convoluted ways.[1]

His work has inspired many artists, cartoonists, and even engineers. Perdue University sponsors an annual Rube Goldberg contest, which might have started at Perdue because Rube created a cartoon demonstrating how a numbskull could become a Perdue engineer. "According to Goldberg: Seal balances ball and applauds self, causing string to start one-man band. Co-ed, hearing music, does Charleston, kicking over oil lamp and burning string, dropping basketball on switch, which starts atomic machine, lifting numbskull so he can crib answers and become a successful engineer."[2]

So why are we exploring Rube Goldberg machines? His machines have an anticipation factor, as the machines make slow but steady progress toward their goals. In other words, they tell a story.

Continuity and Causality: How We Put Juxtaposed Images Together

When new media are developed we generally treat them like the old media. So when faced with a computer screen for the first time, designers likened it to a desktop. We treat the unknown in terms of the known. The "virtual" desktop was based on the layout of an older "real" desk. Sometimes the same problems of the old media can invade the new media, for example, I have seen some pretty crowded and messy computer desktops.

Movies were born of many of the arts. Photography, painting, folktales, myths, literature, and especially theater arts all influence film art. So it wasn't unusual for the first films to simply record everyday actions, and not long before they recorded staged actions as if they were happening in the older media of theater.

The next stage of the new film media was to discover what was unique about it and unlike any of the other arts. What new possibilities could it offer? Film could record actions and then cut up the pieces and reassemble them together. This opened up new worlds and became the single most important aspect of film-making, the juxtaposition of a series of shots.

Rube Goldberg Meets the Movie Saw

Each year in my son's school the seventh graders have to create a Rube Goldberg machine for their science project. It has to have 15 steps, utilize several simple machines (levers, wheels, pulleys, etc.), fit in a prescribed space, and actually work. My son chose to make a machine based on the movie *Saw. Saw* is a gruesome film with a redeeming quality—its theme. The theme of the *Saw* series is that we have to appreciate our lives before they are taken from us. It teaches us that life is a gift, however, the method the film uses to teach this lesson leaves a lot to be desired. The main character has decided to play "God" and puts his victims in near-impossible

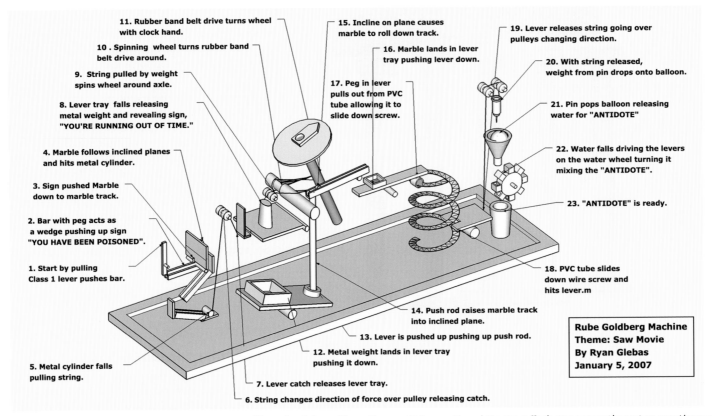

11. Rubber band belt drive turns wheel with clock hand.

10 . Spinning wheel turns rubber band belt drive around.

9. String pulled by weight spins wheel around axle.

8. Lever tray falls releasing metal weight and revealing sign, "YOU'RE RUNNING OUT OF TIME."

4. Marble follows inclined planes and hits metal cylinder.

3. Sign pushed Marble down to marble track.

2. Bar with peg acts as a wedge pushing up sign "YOU HAVE BEEN POISONED".

1. Start by pulling Class 1 lever pushes bar.

5. Metal cylinder falls pulling string.

15. Incline on plane causes marble to roll down track.

16. Marble lands in lever tray pushing lever down.

17. Peg in lever pulls out from PVC tube allowing it to slide down screw.

19. Lever releases string going over pulleys changing direction.

20. With string released, weight from pin drops onto balloon.

21. Pin pops balloon releasing water for "ANTIDOTE"

22. Water falls driving the levers on the water wheel turning it mixing the "ANTIDOTE".

23. "ANTIDOTE" is ready.

18. PVC tube slides down wire screw and hits lever.m

14. Push rod raises marble track into inclined plane.

13. Lever is pushed up pushing up push rod.

12. Metal weight lands in lever tray pushing it down.

7. Lever catch releases lever tray.

6. String changes direction of force over pulley releasing catch.

Rube Goldberg Machine Theme: Saw Movie By Ryan Glebas January 5, 2007

In stage one, if this was our master shot, with the camera locked in place, we would see the whole machine as it sequentially goes through its steps. Each step causes the next as a continuous movement. It would appear seamless because it is staged before us with no visible cuts in the action.

lethal situations that they have to try to escape from. In my son's version, when you start the machine, you learn you have been poisoned (pretending of course). The machine chugs along through its many steps, and after pointing out that time is running out, it pours you the antidote, and reminds you that life is good.

Seamless Continuity of Space and Time

Classical continuity is the technique of making films appear seamless. This simply means that we don't see any gaps in the filmic presentation of space or a break in the temporal flow. The art of editing is said to be an invisible art. This is another way of saying that it is below the viewer's threshold of awareness. If there are gaps in the presentation of the world then they catch the viewer's attention and destroy the illusion, kind of like a glitch. Our approach is that each area of the director's arts is meant to be invisible. That is why we have been working at structure to achieve our goal of providing the spectator with an emotionally satisfying experience.

Give the audience enough clues to construct the story, but you don't have to spell everything out. You are implicitly promising them that their questions will be answered. This gets them more involved because they are using their imagination. They will create their own story based on what they think it means. We construct our experience unconsciously from the many fragments that we receive from all our senses. The director has to guide the audience with a meaningful, logical, emotional sequence, giving the appearance of reality.

Cut Up and Put Back Together

In our second version of the *Saw* machine, we will break it down into a series of separate shots and then edit or connect them together. Film presents a complete seamless world, but this world is actually an illusion made up of many diverse parts. Editing is the process of deciding where to put all of the pieces and hook them up. With film, we weave together all parts into a story that the viewers complete as they perceive, read, and construct meaning from what they see, unlike with paintings, where the audience has time to look where they choose. The movie director must select precisely what the audience is allowed to see in each shot.

In stage two, we are also closer to the action. Every shot is a close-up of what you want the audience to see. This accomplishes three goals. First is that it directs our attention to just the part we want the audience to look at, and second, the closer view brings more emotional engagement. Finally, there is an aspect of surprise because we can't anticipate what is going to be shown next since we don't have the ability to look ahead and see where it is going.

Narrative questions are the drive that keeps us watching a movie—we want to know what will happen next. Causality, or causes and their effects, is the glue that weaves this world together. One event causes the next and so on. There are several types of causality. The first is physical causality. The *Saw* machine is an example of physical causality where one action leads to another based on physical forces. However, physical causality can become predictable because it runs just like a machine. What goes up will always come down, that is simply the way the physical world works. When we clearly know the rules like the law of gravity then we know what to expect and there are no surprises.

Creating or storyboarding a Rube Goldberg machine is a great way to learn to utilize continuity and causality to create a seamless flow. There are many Rube Goldberg machine movies available on the Web.

The laws of physics are unchanging and precise, the machines that we build are not. This is where Murphy's Law enters the picture. "The earliest known versions of Murphy's Law are in reference to stage magic.... It is an established fact that in nine cases out of ten whatever can go wrong in a magical performance will do so."[3] Thus, we have the expression, "If something can go wrong it will." Others have added, "… at the worst possible time."

The third objection is that the world is not a machine. Going back to the *Saw* example, human emotions are not predictable like machines are. My son added the human element when you learn that you have been poisoned. Having to wait for the machine to pour the antidote added and transformed a simple machine into a dramatic story.

When we watch movies we are trying to guess what will happen. We are attempting to guess what consequences an action will have. Narrative questions are just that. If these causes take place what will be their effect? What kind of causality will want to make us continue to pay attention to find out what will happen next?

The following images show stage two of the exact same event, this time it is cut up and edited together. In animation, this is worked out in the storyboard phase. When the actual film is shot we shoot more than we need to in each shot, overlapping the actions so we can make choices in editing where to put them together. In this version the camera also moves to track some of the actions. Look at it carefully to see if you can find any gaps in the temporal flow.

The machine lies in wait.

A hand pulls the lever, and the machine informs about the poisoning.

The marble falls down the track ...

And continues ...

It hits the weight, pulling the string.

The string releases the catch.

The lever falls, releasing the weight.

The string on the weight turns the clock.

The weight continues to fall ...

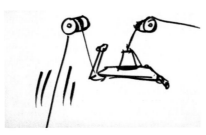

The weight tips the lever, pushing the rod up.

The rod tips the track, causing the marble to roll.

The catch releases, freeing the tube to slide down the spiral.

The hypo needle is released.

The needle pops the balloon ...

And the balloon releases the antidote into the cup.

Glitches or gaps are where the actions don't hook up correctly. There is a break in the action when the rod tips the track causing the marble to roll but there is no shot showing how the marble releases the tube to slide down the spiral. After that there is no shot showing how the needle is released. These gaps are breaks in the flow of time.

Multiple Types of Causality

Newton's laws of motion, inertia, force, and momentum are very useful in action sequences and especially comedy. Life being out of control is very funny, if it is happening to someone else.

Physical causality, however, is not the whole story. What else is there? After I ask this question in my story class, I ask a student to get up and turn on a light. He or she does. I say some words and the student acts. The class now gets the point about *linguistic causality*. In other words, when we speak we can create causes. For example, consider when I tell you, "Please continue reading." My words have caused you to continue reading and also to consider the cause of words creating effects.

Look how much more emotional this shot is when we add the character's reaction shot. We become much more emotionally involved. A simple look can be a cause in human actions. I am sure you have heard the expression "If looks could kill"? Emotions are a form of causality. If we feel something, if may cause us to take action. We may take action to change the situation, persuade others to change the situation, or try to put our heads in the sand and forget about the situation.

Emotional causality doesn't only react to our emotions. We act when other people have emotions. We try to make a loved one happy when they are sad.

Detection of a crime is said to be a matter of opportunity and motive. Motives are reasons based on causes for anyone to take action as an effect of those causes. In film, character motivations are one of the most important tools for bringing believable characters to life.

Emotional causality can become unsettling when one person blames his or her actions on another and vice versa. In this case each action creates a loop causing more and more reactions and the actions escalate. It is a variation of the kid's game, "He started it."

Human emotional actions are even more complicated because we are the only species who use signs. Lions don't write books or make movies in order to change a situation. They can't change their spots, if they had them. Our semiotic-based imagination allows us to create these conditional situations where we can imagine lions with spots that spot removers can't remove.

Semiotic causality exists because we respond to signs. We stop at red lights because it is a sign to stop. Number signs can be a cause for humans. We read the stock market quotes, the speedometers of our cars, and the thermostats in our refrigerators. The wrong number could have terrible consequences, like getting a speeding ticket or ice cream melting. In the beginning of our country a lantern was a big cause. "One light if by land and two if by sea" was a signal for the colonies as to how the British troops were approaching.

Structure affects how we interpret screen events. If we juxtapose two shots the audience will make a comparison between the two items perhaps attributing that the first shot caused the second shot. Press a button in shot one and a car explodes in shot two. Our minds make the connection that pressing the button caused the car to explode, even if we later learn it was just a doorbell.

Natural forces such as weather and geological forces follow the laws of physics. In film they don't have to. Welcome to the twilight zone of *supernatural causality* where things can happen for no explainable reason. Horror films exploit this all the time. In fact, horror films couldn't exist without it.

Inanimate objects can take on a malicious presence. Film can show ghosts and other things that aren't there. A character looks and sees something. Someone interrupts that character and he or she turns away. When the character looks back, the thing is gone. The supernatural quality is simply created in the minds of the viewers when they try to make sense of the edit.

Seeing the future is impossible although that doesn't stop many fortune-tellers from trying. In movies, predestination is achieved by simply showing a shot of the outcome of an event before it appears in the film. Later in the film when the event's full context is shown, it will feel like we have seen it before.

The television series *Wonderfalls* exploits strange sequences of causality when plastic animals tell a girl to perform random acts, like breaking a taillight. Events progress and the small action suggested by the plastic animal is revealed to be part of the catalyst of a grand plan that changes people's lives. The significance of the actions leaves the girl feeling crazy but suggests to us that the world is more complicated than we can ever imagine.

Movies Are a Signifying Systems Machine

In real life, every effect usually has multiple causes. In movies, we try to simplify the cause-and-effect chains so the audience can learn life lessons. Movies demonstrate that if you do this, then this will probably happen. That is what movies are—great chains of causes and effects structured within a hierarchy of narrative questions. Movies are interesting because they clearly depict the sequencing of many types of causalities involved in events, and in movies these chains of causalities are presented with signifiers and proceed to a prearranged conclusion.

Screen Geography: Letting the Audience Know Where They Are

Viewers must be oriented to where actions are taking place in space and time. They construct mental spaces based on the information given on the screen. Action in a movie is judged by how it appears on the screen, not how it is in real life. Action must appear to be going in a constant direction in consecutive shots. Contrasting directions may be used to show travel of going and coming back. Going west is going to the left according to our usual map reading.

Start with a stage view of the action. In this long view we can see where everything is in relation to everything else. If we run an imaginary line through the plan of the action, we must stay on one side of the line in order to avoid confusion.

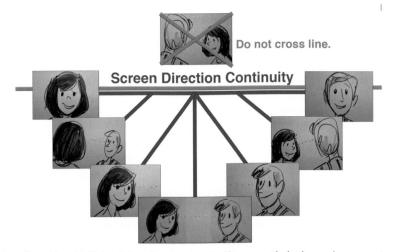

Let's go for a drive with Dick and Jane. As you can see by the arrows the background moves past them.

Conversations in vehicles cause the background to pan in opposite ways. (*Credit:* Art by Jessica Dru.)

(*Credit:* Art by Jessica Dru.)

The driver's direction should match the direction that the car is going. (*Credit:* Art by Jessica Dru.)

Consistent with driver. (*Credit:* Art by Jessica Dru.)

Crossing the line of action appears as if the car suddenly is going the wrong way. (*Credit:* Art by Jessica Dru.)

Entrances and exits through doors require careful analysis to maintain continuity and screen direction. They also call attention to themselves so time them carefully so as not to distract from some other important action.

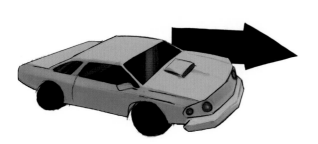
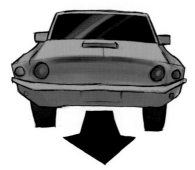
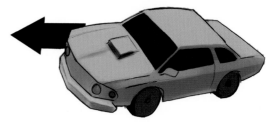

In order to change direction we can either insert a neutral shot of the car ...

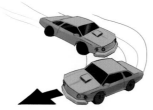

Or, we can show the audience the actual change of direction in a longer shot. (Credit: Art by Jessica Dru.)

Neutral shots are done with head-on camera axis. They can be used to distract the audience to cover a change of screen direction. They also add variety.

Reaction shots of a character viewing the action can also cover a change of direction.

Eyeline Matches

Characters of different heights looking at each other in separate shots must align their look in the frame to match. Characters in separate shots must appear aligned to appear as if they are looking at each other. Characters shown looking are generally followed by shots of what they see.

Time Continuity

Film always appears as if it is happening now. This is not to say that we can't suggest that an event happened in the past or will happen in the future or maybe didn't ever happen. They must be framed by context *as if it were happening in the past or future*. A simple framing device might be to narrate over a scene: "I remember back in 1971 ...." The audience will take this event as to have happened in 1971, but in order for them to do that, they would have to first experience

(Credit: Art by Jessica Dru.)

the scene in the present, just like in order to not think of a spotted elephant, you first have to think of a spotted elephant.

Film needs to present the illusion of a continually flowing present. We need time to focus on important moments, giving time for the audience to feel. If the film moves along at too fast a pace the audience will not be able to process information about the story and thus won't feel anything about it. They will not be able to process the narrative. If you gloss over key emotional moments that the characters are feeling, the audience will not be able to feel them either. We need to focus on those feelings as the audience "reads" the characters faces. Show the change of emotions. In live action let your actors do the work. In animation let your storyboards and voice talent inspire your animators.

Let's return to Scheherazade. She is fighting something that may feel familiar to you as a storyteller—writer's block!

Dunazade sleeps as papers fall to the floor.

One hits her and she awakens.

She inspects it.

She looks and sees …

A pile of crumpled papers at her sister's feet.

Scheherazade is looking at a wall full of drawings.

She throws her arms up …

And rips drawings off the wall.

She kneels amidst the rubble.

She pulls at her hair …

And begins to sob.

DUNAZADE [Offscreen]: "Scheherazade."

Scheherazade opens her eyes.

Scheherazade rips the puppet from her sister's hand.

She is frustrated.

She holds up a blank page.

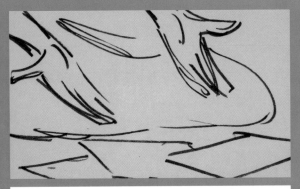

She shows her sister blank pages. She has run out of ideas.

DUNAZADE: "You'll come up with something."

Dunazade can see she is not getting through.

She thinks a bit.

DUNAZADE: "I know what could inspire you."

DUNAZADE: "The sultan's library."

DUNAZADE [Offscreen]: "I'm sure you can find something."

Scheherazade nods approval.

Will Scheherazade find inspiration in the library or through something else? As a storyteller you will often find you run out of ideas. When this happens, and it will, take a break, go for a walk. Go to the library or on the Web. Watch some movies. Sources of inspiration are everywhere. Creativity takes time, dedication, and hard work.

History of Film Editing

What do you see with the next two shots?

Most people see a fireman climbing to rescue a woman in a burning building. This appears obvious, but it may not be true. Suppose we framed the shots a little wider. Now what do you see?

Could the smoke have gotten in our eyes the first time? Now, the fireman, in New York, rescues the woman, in Paris? The images don't belong to the same sequence, yet our minds still try to make a connection between them. Our minds work by these associations not logic.

Filmmakers didn't always have the techniques that we now take for granted. The Lumiere brothers created the first film story in 1895 with *Watering the Gardener*. They set up a gag and captured it in front of the camera.

Techniques to capture the audience's interest and achieve dramatic goals evolved over time. George Melies went the next step beyond the gag to tell a complete story consisting of a collection of separate shots each telling a little story without any attempt at a continuity of action.

Edwin S. Porter achieved something more radical in 1903 when he cut together *The Life of an American Fireman*. He used preexisting footage from multiple sources and created a new story by juxtaposing images, one that never existed! "It implied that the meaning of a shot was not necessarily self-contained but could be modified by joining the shot to others."[4] The dramatic problem in the first shot was resolved by a shot from a totally separate event. By joining the significant shots together the viewers constructed the meaning in their own minds and saw a single event.

I have previously suggested that all shots are really close views of what you want the audience to pay attention to and the next great innovation was the close-up. Lacking a way to create dramatic emphasis with theatrical staging D. W. Griffith moved the camera. "At the moment when an actor's emotional reaction became the focal point of the scene, Griffith simply cut from the establishing shot to a closer view."[5]

D. W. Griffith capitalized upon one type of cut that Porter's fireman film included, the parallel cut. This type of cut suggests that two actions are happening simultaneously. The movie cliché of the cavalry saving the day in the knick of time uses this technique of cross-cutting. Besides implicitly comparing two actions, parallel cutting also functions as a story-delaying tactic. Cross-cutting creates the effect of dual delays with each one acting to delay the answering of the narrative question for the other, which raises the tension even more.

Action 1: Will the hero get there in time?

Action 2: Will help arrive too late?

The two actions about to meet.

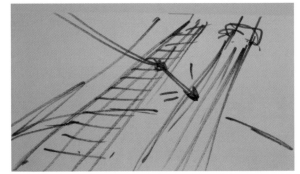

It was up to the Russian filmmakers to take editing to the next step. "Where Griffith staged scenes in long shot and used inserted close shots of details to heighten the drama, Pudovkin held that a more impressive continuity could be obtained by constructing a sequence purely from these significant details."[6] Vsevolo Pudovkin learned this from the experiments of Lev Kuleshov. "Kuleshov's experiments had revealed to him that the process of editing is more than a method for telling a continuous story. He found that by suitable juxtaposition, shots could be given meanings which they hitherto had not possessed."[7]

Pudovkin suggested that the order determines the meaning of the sequence. A shot of a smiling actor cut to a close shot of a revolver, and then another shot of the actor terrified, would lead the audience to read this to mean that the actor got scared when seeing the gun.

If the two shots of the actor were reversed, the audience would read it to mean that the actor saw the gun as a chance to master a scary situation. The same shots are used in the two cases, but a different emotional effect would be achieved because of the meaning suggested by their order.

In another experiment, within the context of a movie, Kuleshov took a shot of an actor with a neutral expression and juxtaposed it to a shot of soup, a shot of a dead woman lying in a coffin, and a shot of a girl playing with a toy.

The audience felt the pensive mood of him looking at the soup, were touched at the way he looked at the woman in the coffin, and liked the light smile he displayed watching the girl playing. *The audience didn't know all three shots of the actor were the same shot!* The whole was greater than the sum of the parts.

Scheherazade moves through the moonlight.

The door to the library opens …

And Scheherazade peeks in. She sees …

The sultan writing at this desk.

He gets up and turns to leave.

He heads toward Scheherazade.

He wipes past the camera.

The sultan leaves the library …

As Scheherazade secretly gains entry.

She hides until she hears the door shut.

Scheherazade opens the sultan's book.

It is his diary.

She reads the thoughts of the sultan.

What secrets does the diary reveal?

Time passes.

Scheherazade arrives.

She begins to draw.

Holding up the drawing for the sultan she shoots a smile to her sister.

Dunazade acknowledges.

There are strange goings on at the Catfield castle.

Electricity fills the air as an eerie experiment proceeds.

The experiment is a success. Clover has a new groom.

Meanwhile, a solitary figure scales the cliff.

Goo has finally made it to the top.

Goo now arrives at Sticks' window.

Sticks wakes, sensing something.

There at the foot of his bed is ...

MONSTER: "Why didn't you tell Goo to jump sooner?"

STICKS: "Ah. I wasn't expecting a rockgram!"

MONSTER: "He fell to the depths of hell because of you."

STICKS: "Please Mr. Monster, I didn't mean for him to fall."

GOO: "Sticks, it's me!"

Sticks reacts.

He climbs out of bed and …

Starts to strangle Goo. STICKS: "What are you trying to do, scare me to death?"

[Pow! Zap! Bam!]

258

Meanwhile at Clover's tower …

CLOVER'S FATHER: "Clover, I'd like you to meet …"

CLOVER'S FATHER: "Your new groom."

Clover looks.

She screams!

The fighting comes to an abrupt halt …

When Goo and Sticks hear the blood-curdling scream.

They don't have a clue what made the sound.

CLOVER'S FATHER: "You'll feel better at your wedding tomorrow morning. Take this, it will help you sleep."

Clover takes the sleeping potion . . .

And falls into the deepest sleep filled with dreams of Goo.

What did Scheherazade learn in the library? But more important, will Goo get to Clover before she gets married? Time is running out.

We fear that Scheherazade can't come up with more stories. She has writer's block and the pendulum swings toward fear. This causes her to take another forbidden action. She sneaks into the sultan's library. We again fear for her safety. Then she learns about the sultan's painful past. Understanding what he has gone through gives her insight as to what happened to him and her voice returns. We are left hopeful.

We have used temporal eclipses to condense parts of the Scheherazade story, otherwise this book would be over 1001 pages! Stories are never in real time—even the television series *24* has the boring parts cut out. We cut out passage work, the boring parts. If we know a character is going to travel from one place to another we don't need to see the whole journey. If we see the trajectory or passage that the character will travel, it is predictable. Predictable is equal to boring. A few highlights suggest the action and most of it can be cut away.

Why Do We Have to Tell Stories?

Everything in film is an illusion. Light on the screen, sound, and the audience are the only things that are present during the viewing. Film theorist Christian Metz called film an imaginary signifier.[8] It refers to a reality that is not present or maybe never existed. Our response to film is thus, "I know it's only a movie, yet all the same I lose my self in the story." We engage our imagination with a dream machine that evokes our own wishes, desires, guilt, and fears.

In cinema, stories are told through a sequence of images, words, and sounds. When we watch a film, I believe that we narrate it to ourselves with our own inner voice.

Retroactivity

There is a trick involved in how the audience then speaks this filmic sentence internally. Meanings swim around in the images. Is he guilty or is he innocent? Did it really happen? We think we know what happens but we are not always sure. The trick is in how we anchor meaning. In a chain of signifiers (a flow of words or a sequence of images) meaning is not a positive element that emerges like looking up a word in a dictionary. Rather, meaning emerges relationally in linear sequence, when the chain is anchored by the final punctuation. Let me translate. When we speak, meaning arises only at the end of the sentence.

I like pizza with lots of extra toppings like bananas, radishes and peanut butter, not!

The entire meaning can change, for example, just by putting "not" at the end of a sentence. Meaning is anchored retroactively by a sequence of images in film. Retroactively means after the fact. After we have watched the film and guessed what it means then meaning gets activated again.

So meaning is anchored retroactively. So what? How does this relate to us as filmmakers? Well, for starters, if film is narrated as we have suggested, then meaning only arises at the end of a scene and full meaning is delayed until the film is over. This example from one of Kermit the Frog's public appearances demonstrates retroactive reframing. When is an inchworm not an inchworm?

There is a scene in Mel Brooks's *Blazing Saddles* of Jim, "The Waco Kid," sitting on his horse facing a line of outlaws. He is not moving very fast for a legendary gunfighter; in fact, he doesn't move at all. Taggart, the lead outlaw, tells his gang to shoot. Suddenly the guns shoot out their hands one after the other. If "The Waco Kid" was really a fast gunfighter this could all be conceivable, that is, until the last shot gives meaning to the filmic statement. It gives meaning, but it also plays against our expectations. We expect to see him with smoking guns held high. But instead we cut back and he still hasn't moved! This unexpected shot means that he is even faster than we were led to believe and that is why it is funny.

There are instances where the ending of the film can change the meaning of everything that you think you have seen before. Often Sherlock Holmes and other detective stories and mysteries accomplish this trick by revealing unexpected information. The retroactive endings of *Sixth Sense*, *Fight Club*, and *The Village* radically change the meaning of what you think was happening while you watched the film. They answer narrative questions you didn't know to ask while watching: *Sixth Sense*: Who sees dead people?; *Fight Club*: Who are you fighting?; *The Village*: What time is it?; *The Shining*: Déjà vu, Jack?; *The Empire Strikes Back*: Who's your daddy?; *Badlands*: What if …?

The Film as Time Machine

Film can take us anywhere, anytime. Film is a time machine whereby we travel through the linear narrative. We can go to the past or present just as easily as our minds can imagine them. Instead of bothering to study history, Bill and Ted in *Bill and Ted's Excellent Adventure* go back in time and learn from the people who made history.

There are several types of time as it relates to film. There is chronological time, or the time it takes to actually show the film. There is the edited film's narration. This is the time of the story. This may cover hours or years. There is the viewer-constructed imaginary time of the story. This usually roughly corresponds to the narrated story time. Finally, there is emotional time of watching the film. This is how long a viewer feels the film is, after watching it.

Pacing: The Expansion and Contraction of Time

Time in film is not necessarily real or objectively measurable. Film can actually speed up or slow down the experience of time. Time is subjective, and just like real life, if the film is good, time flies by. If it is bad it, it feels like it goes on forever.

The director's job is to present one thing at a time just as if it were a sentence so that the audience can "follow along with the story." Too fast or too much information and they get confused. Too little significant information or too slow of a presentation and the audience gets bored.

Pacing is how we keep the audience's interest allowing them a chance to rest occasionally so they don't experience attention fatigue. We present cycles of rising action and tension. Punctuate intense action with periods of rest. Besides being a change in the pace or rate of information presented, pacing can vary the emotional tone, for example, going from happy to sad or funny to scary.

The pacing is balancing, between boredom and confusion, to maintain interest in the narrative generated by the narrative questions. We manipulate time for emotional dramatic purposes. We contract it to move the story along and expand it to heighten tension.

We must add extra time to allow the audience to read parts of the story that are complex. Highly dramatic moments require extra time and can be stretched out in time to allow the audience to become fully emotionally involved. Showing extra significant details helps "milk the moment" of dramatic intensity.

We can move the story along quicker through jump cuts. These gaps in time get hidden by the dramatic flow of the story. To make a cut feel seamless, we cut away to something else: start the action and cut away to another action and return with the first action further progressed. The audience doesn't feel like they missed anything. Dialogue and reactions can also distract from the fact that the cuts jump.

The ticking clock is a device used to heighten the experience of time whereby the film moves to a climax against a specific deadline. Almost all films employ implicit ticking clocks usually in the climax of the story. If an action doesn't happen before the clock counts down then there are terrible consequences. In *Goldfinger*, we literally see the clock on the bomb ticking away as James Bond tries to defeat Oddjob before he can disarm the bomb. If Cinderella doesn't leave the ball before the clock strikes midnight, she will turn back into the commoner. As we shall see in *Back to the Future*, the ticking clock doesn't exactly tell real chronological time. If your ticking clock is just telling chronological time, then your movie is the bomb.

What would you imagine would be the opening image of a film entitled *Back to the Future*? Clocks, yes, in fact, a whole wall full of them. When I show my students the opening sequence, I point out a very special clock that most of them never paid attention to before: the one with the actor, Harold Lloyd, who plays Doc, hanging onto the top of a clock shaped like a clock tower building. This functions as a tribute to this early silent film comedian but also it foreshadows the ending of the movie, where Doc hangs on the clock tower. This image also shows what the film is about thematically: our hanging on to time, literally and figuratively. This opening shot is also interesting in that it upsets our expectations: the clocks are all telling the wrong time, they are late.

Here is the timeline of *Back to the Future*:

Start in present, 1980	Travel to past, 1955	Go "Back to the Future," changed present, 1980	Go off to the future

This is what is narrated to the audience:

Marty's parents kiss at the dance leading to them having a family.
Marty grows up and meets Doc and learns that he built a time machine.

Marty goes back in time, unfortunately interrupting the fateful meeting of his parents.
Marty gives Doc the missing piece to complete his plans for a time machine.
Marty gets his parents to kiss, but not exactly how it originally happened.
Marty then tries to return to the future.

The chronological time of the film is 120 minutes. The story time of these events takes approximately 25 years. The first time that I watched it I was lost in the story and time disappeared.

This is the chronological timeline of *Back to the Future*. This is the story we construct in our heads to make sense of the events we are seeing.

Past, 1955	Present, 1980	Future

How long does it take a DeLorean to get from 0 to 88 miles per hour?

Let's look at how the "race with lightning" is structured. *Back to the Future* is smartly structured in that it gives the audience the necessary information about how the race with lightning will work well before the climax of the movie. Doc explains how it will work to Marty (and the audience) in his lab with a scale model of the scene. This is wonderfully demonstrated visually of how the plan is supposed to work, and additionally, because of the mishap during the simulation, we get to see what is at stake—the whole thing could go up in flames!

By the time we arrive at the climax of the movie, we already know that Marty has to accelerate the DeLorean to 88 mph and arrive at the wire where the lightning will strike at 10:04, generating the necessary gigawatts to send Marty back to the future. With the audience having this information, the filmmakers could dive right into the action.

There are ticking clocks in the scene, one in the car and another on the clock tower. This made it interesting to analyze because I could compare how the chronological time was different from the emotional time.

The overarching question in the narrative question hierarchy is, will the plan work and will Marty get back to the future? Within the main question are a series of smaller ones that delay the answering of the main one.

The sequence opens with a night shot of the clock tower. Doc walks up to the camera, looks at his watch, and asks the first narrative question for us, "Where is that kid?" A police officer asks Doc what he is doing. Will the officer stop the plan? Marty shows up and tries to warn Doc about the future. As they argue over the letter, time is ticking away. Marty has to leave or risk losing being stuck in the past.

Now to build maximum excitement, everything that can go wrong does go wrong. The DeLorean won't start and the cable plug pulls out. Now as the clock ticks we want to know will Marty be able to start the DeLorean and will Doc connect the cable? Marty starts the car and begins the race against time intercut with Doc struggling with the cable.

The story time, as related by Doc, tells us that the lightning will strike in 7 minutes and 22 seconds. From the start of the engine to the lightning bolt hit it takes 8 minutes and 9 seconds of chronological time measured with a stopwatch. This is a difference of 57 seconds longer than it should have taken! Does it feel like it? No, the story races along. In fact, it races along so fast that most people don't notice that there is one shot of the car supposedly going almost 88 miles per hour where it is not moving! The narrated emotional time was longer than clock time, yet it felt like it was shorter.

In analyzing *Back to the Future*, I discovered that it takes over 90 seconds for a DeLorean to accelerate to 88 miles per hour. What was really amazing was that it took almost 30 seconds to travel one block going 88 miles per hour. This was a great example of understanding the enemies of design. They cut out boring parts and slowed down time in the moment of greatest excitement so you could drink it all in and enjoy the moment—story-delaying at its finest.

The sequence concludes with a wonderful shot that acts as a bridge to the future. Doc cheers and looks up at the clock tower. We hear a helicopter approach and suddenly we are back in 1980. It is as if Doc had looked up to see the future.

How Time Is Manipulated

Filmmakers add extra little delays in presenting the narrative that suspend time. Remember the narrative has us speaking each of these ideas one at a time in an effort to find the answers to the expectations and questions that it sets up. This keeps us very busy. The secret to this magical transformation of time is that time changes occur in between cuts. That is why it is not obvious that it is happening. This is also why it can be so powerful. Cuts must match on actions so as to appear as one flowing action.

Animation is especially good at manipulating time. Tex Avery's cartoons, such as the "Droopy" series, seem to live in extremes, either painfully slow or hyper fast.

Why Cuts Work

The cut appears "natural" even when it is actually a "total and instantaneous displacement of one visual field with another."[9] According to Walter Murch, editor and author of *In the Blink of an Eye*, the ideal cut satisfies six criteria at once: emotion, story, rhythm, eye trace, two-dimensional plane of screen, and finally the three-dimensional space of the action. If the emotion is right and the story is advanced, the audience will be forgiving and unconcerned about the other four criteria that relate to chronological continuity. *The audience follows the story, NOT individual actions.*

Murch suggests cuts work because they resemble the way images are juxtaposed just like the way we think and dream. Film-cutting mirrors how our language works. Our language divides the world up into things. Those are the cuts in our "speaking metaphor," you are narrating one thing at a time, the ideas of your story.

Editing: Constructed Significance

As we watch and read a film we continually try to figure out what will happen and what it all means. In addition to being a ventriloquist, magician, hypnotist, art director, semiotician, writer, and cinematographer, the filmmaker should be an epistemologist, that is someone who studies how we know what we know.

The story is a signifying system that continually sets up expectancies and then validates or rejects them. Once the rules of the world are set up the story only has to follow its own internal logic. We know that driving 88 mph in a plutonium-powered DeLorean will get you a speeding ticket in the real world. We also know that in the movies it can cause you to travel in time.

Context allows the same action to take on different meanings at different times because the audience has different information each time. Context allows Charlie's ring to transform an object of affection to one of horror (see Chapter 9).

Notice how Scheherazade's storytelling ritual of lighting the lamp changes in tone each time, even though it is the same action repeated. The messy activity of drawing with charcoal will also undergo a transformation for Scheherazade.

The Rule of Threes

Why is there a rule of threes and not ones, twos, fours, etc.? The rule of threes has to do with pattern recognition and developing expectations based on a pattern. With one or two you cannot see a pattern emerge, but by using three you can. If we have four or more, we can establish patterns, but we run the chance of being repetitive, thus boring. Stylistically three gives us a nice model for real life.

A character attempts to achieve his goal and fails. The status quo doesn't want change. So, the character realizes that he has to try harder. The second attempt also meets with failure. We now have the beginnings of a pattern—we expect the character to fail again. The stakes are raised now because of the pattern. He has failed twice, how can he possibly make it this time? The character tries once more, but this time, having learned from the two previous attempts, he achieves the goal. This helps create surprise because we expected him to fail based on recognition of the pattern. The story teaches not to give up and accept what appears to be a pattern because our view was too narrow. The pattern didn't include that each failed attempt was a learning experience.

Comedy can play with this by providing two failed attempts, and thus contrary to expectation, a third failure but in a novel way. The coyote in "The Roadrunner" cartoons experiences one failure after another.

Cutting: What Part of the Action Do You Show?

- If you only show the anticipation of an action, the audience will wonder if the action happened or whether it will happen in the future.
- If you show just the aftermath of an action, you imply that the event already happened before we arrived to see it.

- If you show the lead up to the event then cut to after it, you imply that the event happened but while we were away from the scene.
- Whenever you don't show the event but imply that it happened, the audience will create it in their own minds.

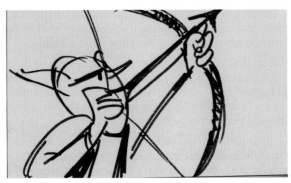

The anticipation of the action.

The action itself.

The aftermath of the action.

Each part suggests the whole in the minds of the audience. The more you allow the audience to participate in the construction of the story, the more they will make it their own. Thus, they will feel all the more because they are reacting to their own experience. This is using suggestion to its full potential.

Motivated Cuts: Cut for a Reason

In order for cuts to remain "invisible," they need to follow certain criteria. They must be motivated. The biggest motivation they can have is to move the story forward. There are other motivations to cut, most of which involve giving the audience information to follow the story. The following is a list of reasons to cut to a new shot:

- To delay the answer to a narrative question.
- To provide a new view for information by changing the position of the camera.

- To create rhythmic pacing.
- To provide contextual meaning by showing a wider view.
- To make connections for the audience by comparing two shots.
- To visually compare and contrast ideas.
- To recall a memory of an earlier scene for the audience.
- To show what a character is looking at.
- To point out something to the audience in detail.
- Cut away to compress time and cut out boring parts. The boring parts are those without narrative questions or are not relevant to the theme of the movie.

Why We Speak the Narration to Ourselves

Expectancy is what drives the narrative. Expectancy of what? Answers to the narrative questions, of course. The narrative sets up expectancies that we want narrative closure on. In other words, we want to know what it all means. Meaning is so important in human existence that psychologist Viktor Frankl believed that those who were able to survive the Nazi concentration camps did so because they were able to find some sort of meaning to deal with the overwhelming horror, which gave them a reason to live.

These expectancies in the narrative are related to desire:

- The desire to know: "What's happening, and what does it mean?"
- The desire for identity: "Who am I?"
- The desire to know wants: "What do you want?"

So what is the trick with expectancy? You have to wait until the story is narrated and until meaning is finally anchored by the ending. So, *storytelling is story delaying.*

POINTS TO REMEMBER

- Restructure to cut out boring passages and expand scenes to draw out dramatic moments.
- Tell the story through the juxtaposition of shots.
- Follow classical continuity editing—keep the structure invisible.
- Always cut for a reason.
- Utilize different types of causality and create story delays with Murphy's Law.
- Connect your shots logically as a sequence of causes and effects.
- Use storyboards to plan good continuity in space and time.
- Keep the pendulum swinging between hope and fear.
- Watch *Miracle on 34th Street* and *It's a Wonderful Life* to study uplifting supernatural causality. Watch *I Know What You Did Last Summer* to see the darker side of supernatural causality.
- Watch *Back to the Future* for its manipulation of time.
- Use Murphy's Law to create great obstacles.

References

1. Wikipedia entry on Rube Goldberg.
2. Perdue University, Rube Goldberg Contest Web page.
3. Wikipedia entry on Murphy's Law.
4. Reisz, K. and G. Millar. *The Technique of Film Editing.* Hastings House, 1968.
5. Ibid.
6. Ibid.
7. Ibid.
8. Metz C. *The Imaginary Signifier.* Indiana University Press, 1982.
9. Murch W. *In the Blink of an Eye.* Silman-James Press, 1995.

Dramatic Irony

Who Gets to Know What, When, Where, How, and Why (Including the Audience)

"Little did they know …." Narration is the control of the flow of information as to who gets to know what, when, where, how, and why. This includes the characters and the audience. Who gets to know first? Do the characters or the audience get the information first? Believe it or not it makes a big difference in how the scene plays emotionally. The pace at which the audience gets to know information speeds up, as they get more involved in the story.

This can work in three ways. First, the audience gets questions answered. Second, the characters get information that answers their questions. Third, the audience gets to see what happens as characters gain information that they didn't have before. The audience witnesses the process of discovery. The audience can be ahead of what the characters know, creating tension from watching characters do something that may not be the right choice for them. Characters have to act in ways that get themselves into trouble and then have to act to get themselves out of it. It is the director's job to orchestrate this flow of information, creating tension and fulfilling closure when withheld information is finally played out.

It is pleasurable to watch this from the perspective of having more information than the characters. We will root for them to do the right thing. For example, watching a character who we know is lying and knowing it would be better if he or she told the truth. It is suspenseful to watch a character who appears good, but we know that they are up to no good.

What is really important for the film audience's response is when they get to know something. Hitchcock points out that if the audience knows about the bomb under the table, the scene has much greater suspense no matter what is happening at the table.

Marc Forster's *Stranger Than Fiction* is an exposé on dramatic irony. Who is Harold Crick and what is so important about his watch? The narrator will tell us over the course of the story. This is normal so far. However, Harold Crick is an IRS auditor who discovers that his life is being narrated. And he can hear it. He alone can hear it, and us, the audience.

When the voice tells Harold that he is to die, he seeks help. His doctor is convinced that the voice he hears means that he is schizophrenic, and suggests a pharmaceutical solution. Harold opts for help from an English professor. Professor Jules Hilbert is unwilling to help until Harold mentions that the voice used the phrase "Little did he know …." Little did Harold know that Hilbert is an expert on dramatic irony who now offers to help.

This story uses parallel cutting to demonstrate for us the process of writing a story while at the same time entertaining us by being inside of a story. Normally the two worlds don't meet but that is exactly what happens in *Stranger Than Fiction*. Harold meets his creator, the writer Karen Eiffel. Karen is even more freaked out when she meets her fictional character in the flesh. Harold is exactly as she imagined him.

What is wonderful is how they gave the audience information without it feeling like an English lesson. You learn about comedy and tragedy viscerally. In tragedies, characters die. In comedies, they get hitched. Believe it or not, we have grown fond of an IRS auditor and so has his IRS case turned first love. We don't want Harold to die. Harold learns a wonderful lesson: to make your life as you always wanted. Even though the audience knows how it has to end, the film still manages to surprise you.

Let's go back and see if Scheherazade found inspiration in the library.

DUNAZADE: "I don't like this place. Why'd you bring me down here again?"

SCHEHERAZADE: "I went to the library like you suggested and you wouldn't believe what I found."

Dunazade listens.

DUNAZADE: "You can speak again."

DUNAZADE: "I'm so happy for you."

They hear a noise.

SCHEHERAZADE: "Shhh."

SCHEHERAZADE: "Come on, I'll tell you everything . . ."

SCHEHERAZADE: "And so the sultan's wife betrayed him."

SCHEHERAZADE: "He couldn't handle the grief so he kills each new bride so they couldn't betray him."

SCHEHERAZADE: "What I don't understand is that he wrote that his vizier told him to do it."

DUNAZADE: "So when are you going to tell the sultan you can speak?"

SCHEHERAZADE: "Soon, but it has to be the right time. Here he comes."

Scheherazade lights the lamp ...

And once more begins drawing.

Goo throws a lasso.

The rope flies out and catches ...

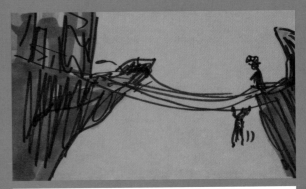

On the Catfield side of town. Sticks and Goo climb across.

270

They sneak to Clover's tower.

Goo begins to climb.

STICKS: "Goo."

GOO [Voiceover]: "What is it Sticks?"

STICKS: "I wanted to remind you. Don't look down."

Goo scrambles over the balcony wall.

Goo walks over to Clover.

Goo shakes her.

Goo doesn't realize Clover is lost in dreamtime.

GOO: "My true love is dead. What shall I do?"

[Creak!]

The door starts to open.

Clover's father looks around the room.

Goo hides under the balcony.

Meanwhile below, Clover's groom, the Jerk, shakes the trellis ladder.

The ladder falls.

This time Goo hangs on tight.

GOO: "You? You're gonna fight me?"

JERK: "You're right, I couldn't, but me and my clones can."

The Jerk jumps up and down and Goo slips.

GOO: "Ahhhhhhhhhhhhhhhhhhhhhhh! Not again."

Right onto the hermit.

Goo tells the hermit what has happened and he gets an idea.

Goo sends a note up with Pablo the parbit.

Up he flies.

Pablo the parbit delivers the message to Sticks.

Goo is back where he started from, only worse. He now believes that Clover is dead, but rather than seeking revenge he sends the parbit with a message of peace.

Why did Scheherazade wait to tell the sultan?

Can You Keep a Secret?

Disney's *Aladdin,* directed by John Musker and Ron Clements, is the story of a beggar, Aladdin, who with the help of a genie, pretends to be a prince in order to meet a princess who is pretending to be a commoner. The "Whole New World" sequence was one of the first storyboard projects I worked on that involved the

dramatic irony of information being withheld from the characters. This made the sequence more fun to storyboard.

Aladdin takes Princess Jasmine on a magic carpet ride. The ride concludes with them watching Chinese fireworks from the rooftop of a pagoda. Aladdin and Princess Jasmine talk about living in a palace. The irony comes from us knowing that he is dreaming and she actually lives in one. He knows that she is a princess and so does the audience.

Aladdin pretends to be the great Prince Ali in order to impress Princess Jasmine. The tension mounts because Prince Ali is afraid that he will be found out to be merely the beggar, Aladdin. The audience knows that Princess Jasmine is unimpressed with Prince Ali. In fact, Princess Jasmine only agreed to go with Prince Ali because she suspects that Prince Ali is really Aladdin, whom she has fallen for.

Princess Jasmine throws out openings allowing the opportunity for Aladdin to come clean. She guesses, "You are the boy from the market."

Aladdin is in the hot seat. He believes that if she knows the truth, then she won't like him. Instead of telling her the truth, he digs himself deeper into the deception saying that like her sometimes he pretends to be a commoner to escape the pressures of palace life. Because she has done this herself, she believes his story.

We know that if he tells the truth, she will still love him. Little does the audience know, however, that if Aladdin tells the truth then the story tension is over.

What is interesting about the scene is how the carpet and the genie, who also know the truth, react to Aladdin's deception. They are stand-ins for the audience, reacting as the audience does. They know Aladdin blew it. The situation gets worse. Before Aladdin can tell Princess Jasmine the truth, the tables are turned when Jafar, the villain, gets the magic lamp. This time Jafar knows the truth, but not Aladdin or Princess Jasmine. Whoever has knowledge also has power. These discrepancies of knowledge keep dramatic interests high.

Pendulum of Suspense

We have talked about keeping the audience swinging between hope and fear. It is like the Zen story from *Charlie Wilson's War*. An event may first appear good but over time it causes problems and appears bad. But with more time it appears to have been for good. But then again it turns out for the worse, and so on, and so on. We raise the stakes by giving the characters something to lose. We make it difficult for our characters by giving them obstacles and invoking Murphy's Law.

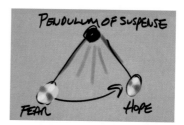

But what exactly is suspense, and how does it differ from surprise? Surprise is easy. Show something to the audience that they totally don't suspect. Monty Python's television skit, "It's Now Time for the Penguin on the Top of Your Telly to Explode," is a perfect example of surprise. When it actually explodes, it tops the gag.

Before we discuss what suspense is, let's look at how it can be generated with just the looks and gazes of the characters. This next example is a scene from Edgar Allan Poe's *The Purloined Letter* that tells the story of a queen who receives a compromising letter that must be hidden from the king.

The queen reads a compromising letter.

The king enters.

She is startled.

As the king hugs her, she places the letter on the table.

The minister arrives.

He greets them.

They grant him entrance.

He sees …

The letter on the table and …

The queen's reaction.

He quickly grasps the situation, and decides to use it for his own gain.

He presents papers and …

Places his own letter on the table.

The king signs the necessary documents and grants the minister leave.

The queen looks and notices …

Two letters.

The minister picks up …

The queen's letter.

She can only helplessly watch.

Acting like nothing is wrong …

The minister graciously leaves.

The queen can only watch.

She must hide her feelings …

From the unseeing king.

276

The Purloined Letter generates great suspense even though we don't know the contents of the letter. The king knows nothing. The queen knows that she has an incriminating letter that she has to hide but no time to hide it. The minister learns from the queen's behavior that he can use the letter to blackmail the queen. In this case, the audience knows all of the above. The queen can only helplessly watch as the minister steals the letter from under her nose. If she says anything, he could simply tell the king about the letter.

There are two forces at work for the audience. The first is *curiosity* or the desire to know. This is why narrative questions drive the story. In this case the audience doesn't know. The second force is *fear*. For the viewers to be held in suspense, they need to have enough information to anticipate what bad things might happen. In this case, the audience knows more than the characters. What is being suspended in suspense? Time is, or rather emotionally intense waiting for something terrible to possibly happen, or not. Give your audience time to imagine the worst.

"If a director wants to take advantage of suspense and draw the spectator into the film, the director must understand how to tell the story so that the spectator's desires will be activated. In one sense, the spectator is transformed into a major character of the film, into the 'peculiar character … who can see, hear, walk, fly, swim under water, jump from place to place, but, can not touch or move anything except his own body.'"[1] For films to create anxiety, they must first connect with our desires. We have to want something and then fear we may not get it. Spectators can respond with anxiety to things they might not even be aware of.

Altan Loker in his book *Film and Suspense* states to create suspenseful anxiety we need to activate cinematic wishes, experienced vicariously by the character, for sex, success, and spectacle or desire to see the fantastic or unknown.[2] Cinematic fears include fear of the unknown and the fear of punishment. Loker thought that guilt was key to understanding how to make good films. The movie *Nikita* incorporates this type of conflict, where instead of going to jail Nikita must accept becoming an assassin for a secret government agency. Loker redefines conflict as a condition that is caused by an impossible choice. *Sophie's Choice* presents the impossible forced choice of having to choose only one of your children to be spared from a concentration camp. Tension results from the waiting while the body is revved up and wants to go into flight or fight action.

Places for Dramatic Irony

Acting becomes much more interesting when characters can't come right out and say what is going on and how they feel. It is much more interesting for us to watch them dance around, implying, alluding, bluffing, and lying. We are watching carefully to see if the message leaks through.

Before a character takes action he or she often has to make impossible decisions or forced choices. Discoveries that a character makes that change the meaning about his or her situation can propel him or her into action.

An epiphany is the discovery of a profound truth that changes a character's view of life and his or her world. How does the character act different, once he or she has new knowledge? Do we show what the character has discovered, or do we make the audience wait? *The Simpson's Movie* makes a very big deal about Homer needing to have an epiphany and he just doesn't get it. It takes a full-blown song sequence for him to finally get it. This is a parody of plot development. The irony is that the characters are aware that they are in a scripted situation.

Dramatic irony in various genres often has the same effect. It makes the audience want to scream out, "Don't you get it?" In a comedy the response is, "Look out!" In a romance it is, "That is not going to work, tell them the truth." Thrillers have their spies, double agents, and triple agents, all of whom you have to watch out for—"Don't trust them." "Don't go in the basement" is the proper response to horror movies. The *Scream* movie series plays with characters pointing out the implicit rules of the horror genre only to fall prey to those same rules.

Here is a classic comedy/horror situation from *Abbott and Costello Meet Frankenstein*. Costello tries to warn Abbott that Dracula is behind him but he is so scared that he can't get the words out. Maybe this is unconsciously where I got the idea for Scheherazade to lose her voice.

The Dramatic Irony of Retroactive Reading

We watch stories forward but make sense of them backwards or retroactively. When we get new information, it can change the information that has been given before. There should be the sense that life flashes before our eyes, and now everything means something different.

Critique: What Does the Sultan Know?

Little did the sultan know that Scheherazade snuck into his library and read his diary. He also doesn't know that since she fully understands how his traumatic experience has led to his horrific behavior, her voice has returned. With the suspicious vizier watching her, the driving question now becomes, will she tell the sultan in time?

"Dumb Love" has a mirrored double dramatic irony. Miscommunications of this sort can often lead to double dramatic ironies. Clover doesn't know that Goo is alive and Goo doesn't know that Clover is not dead. The audience knows these things but they didn't expect the Jerk and his clones to attack Goo. This was a surprise for them.

POINTS TO REMEMBER

- Work out a chart of the key information. Map when different characters get to know this information and when the audience gets to know it.
- Use the chart for ironic commenting on the story.
- You, as director, control the flow of information about who gets to know what, when, where, how, and why. This applies to the characters and the audience.
- Give your characters impossible choices.
- Evoke desires and fears in order for your audience to fully invest themselves in the story.
- Watch *Stranger Than Fiction* and *Aladdin* and pay attention to how much more you know than the characters.
- Shakespeare also used dramatic irony in structuring his plays. Study them.

References

1. Derry, C. *The Suspense Thriller*. McFarland, Jefferson, NC, 1988.
2. Loker, A. *Film and Suspense*. Trafford, Victoria, Canada, 2005.

The BIG Picture: Story Structures

What is story structure? Structure is the relationship among the parts of something. Structure can also be the support for something. We have a skeleton of bones that support us and allow us to fight gravity. But muscles have to be connected to bones in certain ways for them to move properly. But muscles require blood flowing through the body to give them energy. Our bodies have a very complex structure.

We expect certain things to happen in a certain order. For example, the story of space flight requires several stages of its structure. First there is the preparation. Engineers need to check the rocket and its systems, and they need to fuel the rocket. Astronauts need to train for the mission. Summing up the rest of the parts, we have the blast off, exploration, return trip, landing, and celebration. Okay, that is obvious. How does knowing this help us make better movies? I was storyboarding on *Space Chimps* with our heroes returning from space. The script called for them to land on Earth. What is the problem? Well, since the audience already knows the structure, they already know what is going to happen. We know the heroes are not going to crash in the last scene.

The climactic end of a movie should not be predictable. It needs to be suspenseful and exciting. So my job

was to invent things to go wrong so viewers would worry whether the chimps would return safely. Out in space the chimp, Ham, destroys their spaceship and they need to make a new one. So I thought, what if they forgot to build landing gear? Now they have a real problem, and we have a great narrative question: How can they possibly land safely without landing gear?

To find answers to story problems always go back to what the story has been about. *Space Chimps* tells the story of Ham, grandson of the first chimp astronaut. Ham is a goof, but secretly he wishes he could live up to his grandfather's legacy. Ham works at the circus getting shot out of the cannon four times a day. He always misses the target truck. Within this story was an answer.

I chose to repeat a variation of the opening with Ham landing the spacecraft onto a moving truck and let the truck function as landing gear. This solution had several benefits. First, it provided an unexpected answer to the narrative question of how they will land. Second, it gave the chimps on the ground an active part: They had to steal a truck and drive it out on the runway! The third aspect that this solution provided was that it gave Ham a chance to prove himself worthy of his grandfather's legacy. Finally, it gave us a chance for cross-cutting between the chimps attempting to steal the truck and Ham trying to pilot the ship.

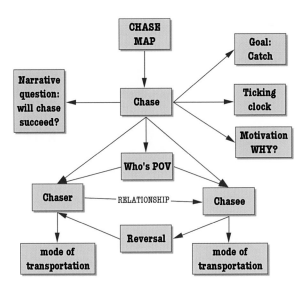

Primitive Filmic Structures and Propp's Story Functions

The earliest filmic structures used were the peep show and the chase. These two types can tell us something about story structure. The peep show is the unveiling of something hidden, surprising or desirable. The chase is an active conflict racing against time in the quest of something or the pursuit of someone. Other simple structures are metaphors of other activities such as the Jack-in-the-box, hunting, a tug of war, the roller coaster, and the rolling snowball.

Vladimir Propp was a Russian folklorist who analyzed thousands of folktales and discovered a common structure to them. He described them as having a fixed range of character types and the functions they perform. Functions were basically action verbs. Each function can be mapped out to show how a story event can be structured with its beginning, middle, and end. Mapping them out can also reveal many types of variations you can utilize to make the story function more interesting. The map gives an overview to show things you may not have thought of. Let's look at one of Propp's functions mapped out. I chose pursuit, also known as the chase.

The chase map is relatively simple. The next map, the theft map, also starts out simple. A thief takes something from someplace belonging to someone. Some maps can become parts of other maps. Once someone has taken something from someone that doesn't belong to them, they often get chased. The chase map becomes a subpart of the theft map.

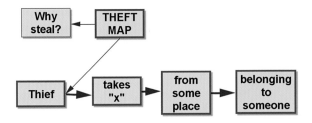

As I developed the chase map further, I discovered an answer to a question that had always puzzled me. How is film like a language if it can only show actions happening? Film includes spoken language and text, but I didn't want to have to resort to using words. We have seen this next drawing before. It says here is a person who appears to be about to take something. This pointing to the future is the narrative question. Will he take it?

But how do we know they are not taking something back, such as something that was stolen from them? We don't or can't know this unless we saw it earlier. Thus, context allows us to communicate more than what the image appears to say. Context provides what are known in language as qualifiers. This even allows us to get philosophical with our images. Thieves are thought of as on the wrong side of the law, but what if it is the U.S. president who has ordered the theft? What if the thief gives the booty to the poor? Our speaking metaphor is thereby enriched.

The next image shows additional aspects of the theft map. The entailments to the map can branch out further still. They can be great idea generators.

The Hero's Journey or the Neurotic's Road Trip

The hero's journey has spread through Hollywood faster than a Malibu wildfire. According to Christopher Volger, author of *The Writer's Journey*, the way that some Hollywood executives used to find stories was that they had to fit into one of two categories: either they were a fish-out-of-water tale or they were about an unholy alliance. If not, they went into the third category, the trash. The hero's journey gave executives an additional way of analyzing stories, one that seemed to encompass different types of stories that otherwise might have ended in the trash.

There was a good reason for it seeming to fit many types of stories—it was the paradigm for all stories. The hero's journey was originally described by mythology professor Joseph Campbell in his book, *The Hero with a Thousand Faces*, as a journey of self-discovery and self-transcendence. Having studied thousands of myths, fables, folktales, and stories from all over the world and all time periods he discovered that there was a common pattern or structure to the journey that each hero would take. Vogler's *The Writer's Journey* compares the process of writing to that of the hero, both going through facing fears of the unknown in analogous journeys.

What I would like to do is compare the hero's journey with two other types of analysis, Aristotle's plot curve and narration theory. Each approach has its own

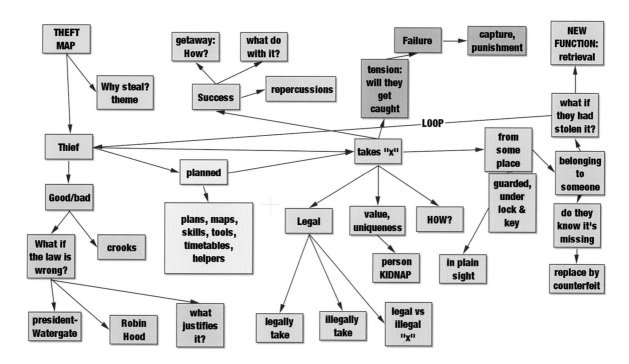

strengths and weaknesses. Aristotle was a Greek philosopher who wrote about the arts. Chap Freeman of Columbia College's screenwriting program took Aristotle's ideas about drama and mapped them onto a graph that charted the time along the horizontal axis and dramatic intensity along the vertical axis.

Aristotle's Plot Curve

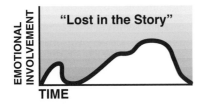

I like to think that the vertical axis is a measure of how much the audience is "lost" in the story. This curve is divided into three sections: the rising beginning, the middle climb to a crisis, and the climatic peak and descent. We are deeply "lost" in the story at the peak.

Timewise, the first section is approximately 30 minutes, the second 60 minutes, and the third another 30 minutes, for a total of 120 minutes, the length of a typical live-action movie. Animated films are somewhat shorter, around 75–90 minutes. I think that the vertical axis of the curve could also map the pace of the film. Things get more and more frantic as they build to the climax.

Narrative structure analyzes the two levels, the story events and how those events are presented through the structuring of the narrative questions and the delaying of the answers that tell the story. The chart that I present evolved out of this simple concept.

What Does the Hero's Journey Have to Offer?

The hero's journey addresses the mythic dimension, our stages of life and passages between them. What is it that starts the hero's cycle? The hero is psychologically stuck. Child psychologist Bruno Bettelheim, author of *Uses of Enchantment*, has observed that most fairytales are a metaphoric form about the transition through psychosexual developmental passages of childhood. This often happens at transition points in people's life stages. They don't yet know how to cope with the new demands placed upon them so they keep trying to use old ways that no longer are functional at this new level. The fairytale shows the child in a disguised form that helps the child overcome his or her obstacles.

A character may feel that something is missing from his or her life or that conflicts are overwhelming. This quest for self-discovery leads directly to the unknown. It is also the dwelling place of design's enemies, boredom and confusion.

It may appear desolate or like a sensory bombardment. The hero's journey is there to tell us what to do when everything goes wrong.

Classic Archetypal Structure or the Hero's Journey

When I was a sophomore attending Pratt Institute I completed a 22-minute animated film entitled *Guardian of the Grin*. My friends Bob Juneman and Rick and Bob Morrison performed the score. At the time, I had never heard of the hero's journey, but years later I looked at it through that lens. What I found amazing was that I had unconsciously structured my story to fit the archetypal pattern of stories.

The hero's journey is the story of human growth and change put into a dramatized form. Dramatic form is another way of saying the story is externalized in visible action. In addition to the hero's journey structure there are archetypal characters associated with the journey who are defined by the functions they serve in the story. These include:

- A mentor, who teaches the hero the perils of the journey.
- The trickster, a shape-shifting character who is often the catalyst for change. It is often hard to tell if the trickster is good or bad or maybe just necessary.
- Allies are the hero's helpers, such as Frodo's fellowship of the ring.
- The shadow forces are another—the dark forces that the hero has to fight. The shadow often is a part of ourselves that we don't want to recognize. Since we don't wish to acknowledge this part of ourselves we unconsciously use a process known as projection whereby these traits get projected onto other people. This is the same process that lies at the heart of storytelling. Internal conflicts are projected out into conflicts between characters who serve the various functions.

Are We There Yet? The Neurotic's Road Trip

The hero's journey has been told so many times that all the stages have been renamed. It is like the game of telephone where someone repeats a phrase to another who repeats the phrase to another, and so on. By the end the phrase is nothing like the original. The following is my version that I like to call the neurotic's road trip.

The neurotic's road trip starts with the would-be hero in her ordinary world. She gets a call to adventure. So what is the first thing she does? Hang up and go back to bed, of course. This is known as refusal of the call. Psychoanalysts call it resistance. Eventually, and it better be quick if you don't want to bore the audience, she takes the call: "You have just won an expense-paid vacation to the land of eternal darkness. Pack light."

So the would-be, clueless hero leaves home. Early along her journey she meets a mentor or guide. He may give her advice, maps, directions, training, or fortune cookies. Armed with this new knowledge, the hero travels on, possibly meeting other travelers along the way. Pay attention, you don't want to get lost.

Traveling along the neurotic's road, the hero meets an obstacle, known as the dreaded threshold guardian. It is his job to tell the hero, "You can't get there from here." It is the guardian's job to keep out posers and wannabes. So the first task of a hero is to get past the threshold guardian. Yes, these characters do take bribes.

Once the hero gets past the threshold guardians, she enters a new world unlike the one she is used to. It can be dark, chaotic, and threatening, filled with monsters both literal and metaphoric. It is here that the hero gets tested. The tests are part of the hero's training, after all, we learn from our mistakes.

This is all leading up to a supreme ordeal or a moment of the hero facing her worst fear. This feels like facing death and surviving. The hero has just killed her first dragon or maybe just overcame a fear of spiders. She made a big change in her life. You need to make the audience feel these fears viscerally and vicariously, so that they too may overcome their fears.

After accomplishing such an achievement, the hero gets a reward. The hero takes possession of what she has come for, whatever that may be. Once the hero has it there is a choice to be made. Does the hero stay or return home?

This section for me is a little confusing because now the hero has to rededicate herself to the quest. Didn't she already do the supreme ordeal thing? Actions have consequences that can bite back at us. Well, maybe the hero didn't finish the job. It is dark dramatic irony when we know that the villain is not fully dead. Sometimes what the hero has been fighting isn't fully dead and it is mad about it. So we cut to the chase.

It is at this point that the hero is resurrected. She has looked death in the face and is reborn. When someone is reborn there is a glow about her. She physically looks different, like someone in love. Finally, the hero returns home with the magical elixir, an object that motivated the entire quest.

The reason that I like to call it the neurotic's road trip is that it is really an emotional journey of dealing with fear that we all can relate to. It is the journey of the psychological process of change and growing up that we all go through. That is why we relate to it. It isn't in far away places that we become heroes but rather in our everyday lives of dealing with fears and injustice. It is just less boring to watch it in dramatic form.

What Is Wrong with the Hero's Journey?

Since the hero's journey functions as a road map and everyone has the same map, the stories created using that map might appear similar. When Wall Street demanded that Disney's corporate mandate create animated classic blockbusters once a year, the formula started to show. We know that when that happens, it bursts through the level of attention and the audience is taken out of the story.

Disney films would all begin with a character singing, "I want ...." Then the hero would always have a cute sidekick, one who would make great merchandise. Then there was the issue regarding disposal of the villain. It seemed that the hero couldn't actually kill the villain, rather the villain had to create his or her own demise. The hero being a good sport would allow the villain to live but behind the hero's back the villain would then attempt to kill the hero again, and somehow be responsible for his or her own fall to death. This tradition goes all the way back to the wicked queen in *Snow White and the Seven Dwarfs*. Repetition made the films predictable and predictable is boring. Surely there must be other ways to kill a villain. *Shrek* and *Hoodwinked* parodied the formula and were very fresh and fun in that way.

Sometimes I will turn on the television and something will capture my interest even though it has already started. Now, I don't know how far we are along in the hero's journey. Is this the ingoing threshold guard or the outgoing one? Is this a minor test or is it the supreme ordeal? I don't know, but I know that I am already "lost" in the story. Why is this so? Where else can we turn to find moviemaking guidance besides to a fish-out-of-water tale or unholy alliances?

Three Levels of Story Analysis

What I realized was that there are three interconnected levels of story analysis. The hero's journey and Aristotle's plot curve cover the macro level of story analysis, the structure of the story events. At the other extreme is *narration* or how the story is told through narrative questions. This level is why I could start watching in the middle of a television show and get sucked right into the story. It might take awhile to understand all that is going on but the narrative questions would drive me to do so. In between these two levels are Propp's functions and other story verbs and their entailing maps. This can tell us where the story is going in the short term.

Hero's Journey versus Aristotle

While the hero's journey is a great tool for giving structure to a film, when I compare it to Aristotle's plot curve, it appears that, one would think, that the supreme ordeal should be at the climax of the story in act three. However, in the hero's journey it appears in the middle of act two. The journey model doesn't seem to map cleanly to the dramatic curve in the temporal axis.

What gives the journey model its value is that there is room for suggestive interpretation. I think it is more valuable as inspiration rather than a specific plot formula.

Narration versus the Hero's Journey

In this corner we have Hollywood's powerhouse, the original trailblazer, just back from defeating the Minotaur in the labyrinth—the hero's journey! And in this corner we have a relative newcomer, often wearing a cloak of invisibility, pushing the spectator with pulverizing persuasiveness—the narrative process! Who would you bet on?

In the Warner Brothers's cartoon *Duck Amuck*, Daffy Duck shouts, "I demand to know who's responsible for this." We don't usually think to ask who is responsible, but Daffy does. After he is been beaten up for the entire cartoon the camera pulls back and reveals Bugs Bunny at the drawing board, who comments, "Ain't I a stinker?" There is a lot of truth in this scene. All stories are narrated, but we don't always get to see who is doing the narrating or we don't know what his or her agenda is. In reality, the narrator is director Chuck Jones, whose agenda is to entertain.

Both levels of events and structure are parts of the telling of a story. You can't have stories without either; they are interconnected like the two sides of a Möbius strip. This also means that stories can't be objective. They always have a point of view of an implied invisible teller, who has his or her own agenda.

Narration is continuously happening at every moment of a story, keeping us on the edge of our seats. The hero's journey doesn't provide this kind of analysis, which we have seen is the necessary motor that drives us through a story with its narrative questions, delay tactics, and final answers.

The Hero's Journey and Levels of Events and Structure

So the hero's journey is a way to structure the story events above the threshold of awareness. Meeting a mentor is a story event. Seizing the sword is a story event. How these are told is the narration structures of the events below the threshold of awareness. For example, seizing the sword might be presented in a metaphoric form of standing up to your parents.

By understanding each level of events and structure and how they interact we can structure stories on the macro and micro levels. By understanding how viewers construct a story out of our narration we can make stories that will touch our audience deeply.

So if the hero's journey is what gives structure to the plane of events, what does the narration do in terms of the story? The hero's journey gives us the macro structure. Narration gives us the micro structure. It helps us structure the movie shot by shot. Classical Hollywood shot structure sets up these narrative questions and statements.

Here is an experiment I would like you to try. Watch the first five or ten minutes of a movie and then put it on pause. Can you tell what happened? Of course you can. You can easily tell the story of the plot and the motivations of the characters. Now, can you answer the following questions?

- Did you hear the background music?
- Did you notice the shot sizes and framing?
- Did you notice the cutting up of time and space?
- Did you notice how much was deleted from actions?
- Did you notice the implied causality between events?
- Did you notice who knew what and when?
- Did you know when you got to know information?
- Did you notice whose view it was? What eye level was used?

Most likely you were too busy answering the first question: What is happening and what does it mean? You wanted to know the story. In fact you were creating the story. Your attention didn't go to the structural level: the framing, cutting, art direction, music. Narration is the control of the flow of information of the story, including images, spoken words, written words, sounds, and music.

Mentors

When I started storyboarding at Walt Disney Feature Animation, Ed Gombert was my mentor. In my quest to become a "heroic" storyboard artist, I would fumble trying to create exciting storyboards and Ed would look at them and suggest trying things differently. If I had questions, I would ask him and he would quickly do a drawing to solve the problem. I actually had many mentors at Disney and they each taught me different things. I am grateful to Walt Stanchfield, Vance Gerry, and Burny Mattinson who were all very generous with their time and knowledge. So who is the hero's mentor? It is someone who has already gone on his or her own hero's journey. Mentoring is about giving back and passing on knowledge in the cycle of life. We are all extras in everyone else's play. One hero can serve as a mentor for another hero on his or her journey.

Mentors come in all shapes and sizes and don't always look like the classical archetype of the wizard Merlin. Sometimes the mentor is also a trickster, who can trick you into learning without realizing it. In John Avildsen's *The Karate Kid*, retired karate master and handyman, Mr. Miyagi, agrees to teach karate to Daniel under the conditions that Daniel promises to learn karate and ask no questions. Mr. Miyagi then has Daniel paint his fence, sand his floor, and wax his car: "Wax on, wax off."

Daniel doesn't feel that the manual labor has anything to do with learning karate and is being used as Mr. Miyagi's personal slave. He gets mad and complains. His mentor tells him to "paint the fence," and throws a punch at Daniel. Daniel blocks it. In a rapid succession of paint the fence, sand the floor, and wax on, wax off, Daniel successfully blocks all of Mr. Miyagi's punches. Daniel was learning without knowing that he was learning.

Daniel still has much to learn about the spirit of karate. Daniel originally wanted to learn karate for revenge. He still needs to learn that karate is not for revenge but rather for self-defense and balance. Often the hero can think he is ready before he actually is. Daniel starts cockily dancing around and promptly gets flattened by Mr. Miyagi. Daniel learns balance through the pose of a crane. The tournament is his hero's test. He has to deal with fear. He has to build his confidence, his belief that he can do the impossible. In the end he has learned balance. The crane pose serves him well and the bully ends up respecting him.

In Taylor Hackford's *An Officer and a Gentleman*, the drill sergeant pushes Mayo to his limit wherein he comes to the realization that he has to become a navy pilot, he has nothing else. The military can offer strange places to find mentors. Colonel Kurtz in Francis Ford Coppola's *Apocalypse Now* might seem like an unlikely mentor for Captain Willard, the one who has been sent to terminate his command. Captain Willard can't decide if the army is crazy or Kurtz is, but he does profoundly learn from him.

Mentors don't even have to be people. In Disney's *The Lion King* the lion cub, Simba, has five mentors: Mufasa, Zazu, Timon, Puumba, and Scar. Some good, some negative. Uncle Remus, in Disney's *Song of the South,* teaches Johnny to deal with bullies by telling stories about Br'er Rabbit tricking Br'er Fox using reverse psychology. In this case, the mentor is a story. In Frank Capra's *It's a Wonderful Life*, George Bailey has an angel or hallucination for his mentor who teaches by showing George what the life of his town would be like without him.

For homework in Christopher Volger's story analysis class, I analyzed Terry Gilliam's *The Fisher King* in terms of the hero's journey. All four main characters went through their own hero's journey and were mentors for each other. In *The Fisher King*, the inmost cave was a video store, literally the place of dreams.

In Harold Ramis's *Groundhog Day* weatherman Phil Connors learns from his own mistakes as he has to repeat Groundhog Day over and over and over. *Groundhog Day* is similar to Charles Dickens's *A Christmas Carol* in that we learn from our own ghosts. Tony Robbins considers *A Christmas Carol* a perfect metaphor of the process of how we change. If you want to help someone change, you paint a picture for them of how their behavior has caused them pain in the past, what their present life style is costing them, and what pain it will cost in the future. Associations to pleasure and pain are what drives people. Here the mentor comes in the form of spirits of the person's own behavior, past, present, and future.

Paradigms of Changing the Impossible to the Possible

The hero's journey doesn't actually tell how the hero changes, it just shows the shape of the journey of change. So we still have the question of how does the hero's mentor help the hero to change especially when the hero doesn't want to change? What does the mentor actually do?

Sometimes the mentor simply tells it like it is. In Mel Brooks's *Blazing Saddles*, when Sheriff Black Bart has gotten the expected respect and gratitude for helping the townspeople but can't understand their reluctance to display it publicly, his mentor, "The Waco Kid," explains it for him: "These are simple people, salt of the earth, you know … morons."

Apprenticeship is a common form of mentoring, which can utilize many paradigms of change. Primitive magic, totems, and shamanism involve the stages of thinking we use as children.

Psychotherapies offer models of change, and although they are not as cinematically glamorous as say a medieval knighthood apprenticeship, they can still offer up great movies such as Robert Redford's *Ordinary People*. The Wikipedia entry on psychotherapies offers a hyperlinked list of over 100 different types of models of change. What do all these have in common? One thing is that they deal with fears. This makes them useful for us as filmmakers because we want our heroes to be afraid, and as success coach, Jack Canfield, would say, "Do it anyway." So why are we afraid? Fear usually arises because of what we believe. FEAR is an acronym that stands for a Fantasized Experience that Appears Real. In other words, we create our fears.

The hero's journey also mirrors the five stages of grief: denial, anger, bargaining, depression, and finally acceptance. This seems plausible because the hero's journey is really not a physical journey as much as an emotional one.

Now, you may be wondering why I am dwelling about the hero's mentor. Two reasons: The first is that you need to understand the journey your characters go through, and how they change in order to make it believable. If your audience doesn't believe that the hero has transformed then we have broken through their threshold of awareness and bounced them out of the story.

The second reason is that as filmmakers we go through the journey ourselves, and it is very scary and you will face many unknowns at every stage of the process from preproduction to distribution. In George Lukas's *Star Wars*, the classic example of the hero's journey, the impatient Jedi apprentice, Luke Skywalker, is overcome with fear, insecurity, and disbelief. "I can't," he tells Yoda. Yoda lifts Luke's fighter ship out of the swamp changing the impossible to possible. Luke says, "I can't believe it." To which Yoda replies, "That is why you failed." George Lukas's determination on his journey to make *Star Wars* changed the impossible to possible.

We need to deconstruct old beliefs about what is possible by questioning them and see if they are helping or hindering us. Stereograms are an optical illusion of depth created from information embedded in a flat two-dimensional image. At first you see just a flat image or graphic noise. Relaxing your vision, suddenly a different three-dimensional image pops out at you! You have just radically shifted your perception and thus your belief about the image. This is a great metaphor for the power of paradigm shifting!

Once again, it is time to return to the Scheherazade story.

Once again night falls upon the palace of the sultan.

Scheherazade is now truly inspired.

Her plan has a goal in sight.

She holds up the first drawing.

Clover's wedding day is a sad day for the Catfields …

For it is the day of Clover's funeral.

JERK: "I sure got rid of that pest Goo."

Clover wakes up.

She punches the Jerk out cold.

288

Meanwhile, up above, the McClods sneak into the palace preparing to attack. Sticks got the message WRONG!

The McClod bugler sounds the war cry.

Suddenly, war erupts.

Scheherazade continues drawing.

A great cloud of smoke rising up from the chasm.

The sultan perks up.

SULTAN: "Is the volcano erupting or did they awaken the dragon?"

Scheherazade goes back to drawing.

The sultan is really excited about the tale.

The vizier enters as once again the sultan notices …

And points to Scheherazade's face.

She is covered in charcoal dust again.

The vizier approaches the sultan.

He whispers in his ear.

The sultan is shocked.

SULTAN: "How dare you suggest …."

Scheherazade looks worried.

The vizier opens his robe and …

Pulls out the sultan's diary.

SULTAN [Offscreen]: "What are doing with …

SULTAN: "My diary?" The vizier opens the book …

And points to charcoal fingerprints.

The sultan is shocked.

SULTAN: "You, you read my diary?"

SULTAN: "How dare you!"

Scheherazade realizes her face is still covered with charcoal dust.

She tries to rub it away.

SULTAN: "You have betrayed me."

SULTAN: "The punishment is ...

SULTAN: "Death!"

The sultan's guards take Scheherazade away.

She turns to look at her sister.

DUNAZADE: "Noooo!"

Does this spell the end for Scheherazade?

Is it too late for Scheherazade?

Ending, Beginning, and Turning Points

When you have these you can begin. Believe it or not, I think you should start at the end. This way you know where you are going. I have seen so many movies where they start work on the first act and find problems and redo it. Then they do it again and again. Then when they finally get to act three they discover that act one again needs to be revised so that it properly sets up the ending.

The ending is what you want to prove by your story. The beginning is the ending asked in the form of a question. The middle is in the way of the beginning and the ending in the form of an obstacle.

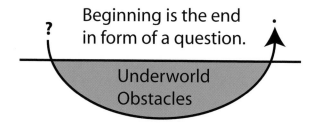

Turning points are moments in a story where the actions of heroes must take a new direction when they meet up with the consequences of their actions or obstacles presented by villains. Turning points define the transition into each new act. They offer a way to surprise the audience.

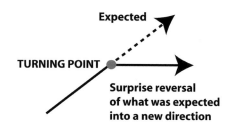

Types of Scenes

We expect every movie to have certain types of scenes, in fact, we are disappointed if they are missing. Each type of scene is there to give certain types of information to the audience and to help define the overall story arc. Their placement in the story is dependent upon each individual story.

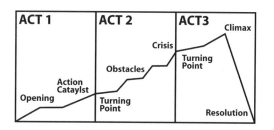

The Title

The title of a film itself gives the audience a great deal of information and creates expectations as to what they are about to see.

Once upon a time ...

The prologue is a quick setting up of the exposition. Exposition is a quick setting up of the background of a story so that the audience can follow it. It can be thought of as a frame for the story. When Scheherazade tells her tale to the sultan she tells the myth of the dragon's curse on the feuding towns.

Before It All Began

The backstory is all of the events that have taken place before the actual telling of the tale starts. It is usually limited to those events that have significance for where the characters are now. Backstories can be populated with ghosts or unfinished business that the characters will have to settle. These ghosts can haunt the hero until he or she puts them to rest by making changes.

This information from the past should be layered into the story in bits and pieces. This lets the audience participate by figuring it out for themselves how the characters were shaped by their pasts. Second, you want to keep the story in motion; too much backstory can slow it down.

Much of the *One Thousand and One Arabian Nights* backstory was given in the introductory chapter. I chose to keep Scheherazade in the dark about the fate of the sultan's brides so that she could learn about them during the course of the story.

Let's Get This Party Started

A turning point in the lives of the characters is a good place to start your story. The characters can't be passive; they need to be ready to dive into action. The opening scene often presents a metaphor for what is to come.

Start with a bang! Get the audience's attention right away. Then you can have a more relaxed opening. Scheherazade's story opens with families fleeing the kingdom. Scheherazade heads right into the mouth of hell.

Here Is What You Need to Know

Exposition sets up the rules of the world. The story should push the limits of plausibility, but not break those limits of believability. Once you create the rules you have to stick to them, or you are not playing fair and the audience will resent you.

Exposition informs the audience of the significance of what they see. Show the audience what they need to know in order to understand and thus care about the characters in the story. The key rule is to provide just enough information to let the audience follow the story. Never let your audience get confused. There may be things they don't yet understand, but they are still following you and asking the narrative questions you want them to be asking.

The exposition should always be dramatized or "acted out" in the story through actions or images. Characters who explain exposition stop the story; they bring the structure above the threshold of awareness. The best way to give information to the audience is when characters are on the run or during a fight.

In order to make a story world believable you need to layer in things that you will use later. If things are not set up properly then events can feel like they have come out of the blue and will thus break the story illusion. These planted items or bits of information let the audience know the significance of events when they happen. Payoffs are the rewards and punishments of what was planted earlier. My favorite item planted early in a story to be used later is from *Bill and Ted's Excellent Adventure*. They travel in time and hide a key. Later they meet themselves traveling in time and tell themselves about the key.

What Is at Stake

In order for the audience to become emotionally engaged in the story you have to show them what is at stake and it has to be big emotionally. You also need to let the audience know what is at stake early in the story. What is there to lose?

How do you signify that something will be lost? When Scheherazade sees the executioner it becomes real for her. This is dramatized by her losing her voice. Later when she discovers the catacomb tombs, we see what happened to the sultan's brides and what might happen to Scheherazade. We now fear for her life.

What Do You Want?

Knowing what characters want tells the audience where we are going. We should get to know what they want quickly. It may change over the course of the story when they learn that what they want is not the same as what they need. Knowing the characters' wants is a goal that functions as a focusing point for the story that helps to unify it. The goal also gives the story a direction. Each character in the story will have their own wants, some of which may conflict with the hero's wants.

Complications and obstacles prevent the characters from getting what they want and these should build in intensity. If the hero overcomes a major obstacle too early in the story, then other obstacles may seem insignificant. Obstacles come in many guises. The hero may overcome an initial physical obstacle only to face a more difficult emotional one. Obstacles are what make stories interesting. Be inventive with them.

There is an old Jewish proverb that states, "Be careful what you wish for. You may get it." Wishes often have a price. In the end the hero doesn't always get what they want but they do get what they need. That is more important.

"Of Course You Know, This Means War!"

Some event needs to get the story in motion. Some catalyst is needed to start the war. Bugs Bunny could only be pushed so far before he would retaliate.

Discovery of the Rosetta Stone

Characters often discover information that can illuminate everything and thus change their world. This information can turn apathy into passion and drive the characters into action.

Do I Have To?

Obligatory scenes are scenes that are created in the minds of the audience while they watch the film. They are based on what the audience expects. We expect that eventually we will get to know the answer: Will the characters get what they want? These expectations help the story feel like it is going somewhere. It is commonsense that you can't have a Western without a showdown. If you are not going to fire the gun sometime during the story, don't put it in.

As soon as Scheherazade reaches the palace, we know that at some point there will be a confrontation between her and the mad sultan. We also know that as soon as the vizier points out the forbidden door that Scheherazade and Dunazade have to go there.

We Can't Go Back Now

This is a moment when the hero has to face the fact that the chance of success for the quest is totally hopeless. The hero has set things in motion that can't be undone. Let him or her find something that renews hope.

The Calm Before the Storm

Before the climax of the film, it is a good idea to give the audience a chance to rest. It gives them time to think about what it all means and what is at stake. Let the characters convey their feelings about what is to come. It is a good opportunity to mislead your audience and surprise them.

Comic Relief

Comedy has the power to relieve unbearable tension. Remember attention has a fatigue factor. If you just keep the audience in intense tension too long, they might eventually saturate and tune out. Comic relief provides relief before the tension again ramps up. It also provides contrast that can make the tension feel all the greater.

A related concept is catharsis. This is the emotional relief and purging of the emotions from the buildup of tension. It is delivered to the audience with the answering of narrative questions.

Crisis

The crisis is a moment of truth for the hero. Does he or she have the right stuff? The hero decides to risk all and go after the goal. This major decision leads to the climax of the story. The hero has to decide to go for it. The main climax needs to occur near the end, not in the middle, because this is what everything has been leading up to.

Cut to the Chase

We definitely need scenes that explode into action. They provide a visceral release from the tensions and suspense created in the story.

Showdown with the Shadow

This is the moment we have all been waiting for. It is a climatic battle with winner takes all.

The Aftermath: Happy Trails

After the climax is over the story is over. But we should be allowed to hang out for a while with the winners, to share their success. We should see what it means to them, what they have learned, and where they will go now.

The aftermath also tells the audience what the journey was all about. The mysteries are revealed.

Epilogue

The epilogue is kind of like a P.S. that completes the emotional closure. Some films describe where its characters are today.

What Happens If You Move the Structure Around?

The ideal story shape is like a wave. It builds, rising up until it can't hold up anymore and comes crashing down. I offer here a new model of story structure combining Aristotle's plot curve, dramatic irony, and knowing that people love to see things blow up. The director controls the flow of information of who gets to know what, when, where, how, and why. Each section should have different amounts of information given to the audience.

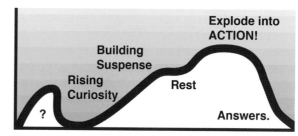

(*Credit:* Art by Joan LaPallo.)

Dive into the story quickly. Follow this with rising curiosity since at this point the audience doesn't know very much. Next, build suspense by letting the audience know enough to start to worry about the characters. At the peak, the wave explodes into ACTION! Finally, answers provide emotional closure, and the audience gets to understand what it is all about.

If you don't have a main question or if it is introduced too late, then the story will seem to be going nowhere. The audience won't know where they are going. Don't count on pretty scenery to carry the film. One way to solve the late introduction of the main question is through the introduction of a subplot with its own question needing an answer. This then can lead to the main question.

What happens if the story has the wrong shape? It can't be that bad, or can it? Let's see what can go wrong with the overall shape, even with great movies.

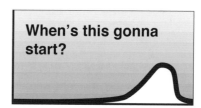

Disney's *The Jungle Book* starts off too slow. We don't know what the main character, Mogli, wants until he says he wants to stay in the jungle with Baloo, but that is not until the middle of the film.

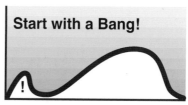

The James Bond movies address the slow start by starting with a bang! They open with a big action sequence that launches us right into the heart of the action. *Romancing the Stone*, *Star Wars*, and *The Matrix* all do this.

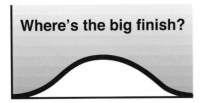

Some days the surf is flat. *The Remains of the Day* suffers from a lack of climax and even though there is tension, for me, it never felt like it went anywhere. The boy never goes after the girl.

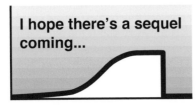

Some movies seem like they ran out of film. It feels like you got pushed off a cliff while leaving many questions unanswered. I felt that *No Country for Old Men, Zodiac, Match Point,* and the conclusion of *The Sopranos* suffered this fate.

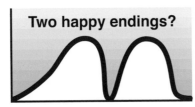

Disney used to be known as the happy-ever-after brand. *Ratatouille* had two happy endings. It felt like it ended in the middle because the narrative questions were answered. They had to start it up again, bringing in new questions.

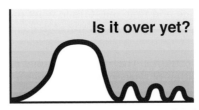

Sometimes there are many loose ends that need closure. *The Lord of the Rings, Return of the King* felt like it had about five or six endings. (*Credit:* Art by Joan LaPallo.)

POINTS TO REMEMBER

- Study your story in the script and storyboard stages, before you shoot.
- Chart out your stories as a mapmaker would. A director has to see the forest and the trees. Study your story with every kind of analysis: the hero's journey and the plot curve for the big picture, character emotions and plot functions for the mid-level, and narration and narrative questions for the micro level.
- Watch *The Fisher King, Starting Out in the Evening,* and *Groundhog Day* for their hero's journeys. Pay attention to the mentors in *Star Wars* and *The Karate Kid*.

Aiming for the Heart

13

Congratulations! If you have come this far, you have accomplished your quest. We have arrived at our goal, that of providing the audience with emotionally satisfying experiences. Once the audience decides what something means, they automatically feel emotions. This is an amazing aspect of how our minds work. They don't even have to think about it.

> **Meaning evokes emotion!**

Do We Really Identify with the Hero?

What does it actually mean to identify with the hero? What are we identifying with? How can we identify with someone who looks totally different than us? They may speak, dress, move, and act differently. They might even be younger or older or even the opposite sex from us. There are different types of identification.

The first kind of identifying that goes on in the movies is perceptual. We see things and identify what they are, and then we identify what they mean. With characters onscreen this goes a step further. We identify if we like them. Do we think they are good or bad? Are they like me, or not like me? What evidence do we use to judge that?

The Audience's Journey

Just as we learned that the writer goes on his or her own hero's journey, I believe that the audience does as well. What kind of journey is it? It is a very strange paradox: "This is about someone else," yet somehow I am watching me. The characters somehow stand in for the audience. But which character? If it is the hero we identify with, what happens when he or she is not in the scene? What happens if we watch a villain creating a plan to dispose of the hero? Why do we keep watching and do we stop identifying?

I have already suggested that when we watch movies we narrate them to ourselves. What are we doing when we do this? We are identifying things. But we do much more. We seek to understand and make sense of things; then we want to know if our guesses are correct. When it comes to characters, if we know more than they do, we wish to direct them: "Don't go in the basement"; "Look out behind you!"; "Go after her."

When a story is working the audience "loses" themselves in it. Earlier I suggested that we identify with the story. I believe we are identifying with the total emotional arc of the story. Emotions are what we share with the characters and their desires and fears. We identify with the questing hero as underdog, because we often feel like the underdog. The audience's journey is a journey where we traverse the dangerous underworld of our emotions.

Emotions must be believable to the circumstances that the characters find themselves in. As directors we need to show them the emotional triggers that cause a character to react. For example, what events must occur to allow cowardice to transform into courage? Why do the characters do what they do? Character motivation is the force that drives stories and the glue that holds them together. Motivated characters can be truly inspirational for us.

What Makes Us Root for the Hero and Hiss at the Villain?

When we root for the hero and boo the villain we are deeply "lost" in the story. What is it that we are so fired up about? Heroes are usually the ones who learn and change the most during a story. We identify with their struggles, including the courage to face fears, make sacrifices, and fight for what they believe in. Heroes must find out who they are and face up to these truths. They must become capable of love, yet able to let go. Movie heroes must be able show their feelings through their actions.

We like heroes because of these ideal qualities. Heroes don't have to be perfect, in fact, their imperfections can make them all the more loveable.

How does someone become a villain? Are they born bad? I can just see a want ad: "Villain wanted. Do you hurt people and enjoy it? Do you have special skills to make people feel bad? Do you have selfish fantasies of controlling the world? Have you accomplished a checklist of the seven deadly sins? Are you an expert at lying and cheating? Send resume of qualifications. Must be of evil bent." Villains can take on many disguises from the classic twirling-mustache type to environmental threats, monsters, criminals, corporations, family members, or bacteria.

What is the job description of villains? Basically, their job is to create conflict by making life impossible for the heroes and those they love. Conflicts come in all sorts of shapes and sizes. War is extreme conflict, but you better make it personal to the characters. What are your characters fighting for? Is it worth the sacrifice? Losses and gains drive many story conflicts like rags-to-riches stories. Mistakes can lead to conflicts. Love generates conflicts as well through jealousy, mistrust, or arguing over raising children. Love can even turn into its opposite, murderous passion.

Heroes take responsibility for their actions. Heroes are not passive. Your story must bring them to an emotional place where they have to decide and then take action. Heroes are heroic because they change and grow. Superman may be the exception. In contrast, villains are tragic because they don't change.

Fears, Flaws, Wants, and Needs

To develop full characters we need to understand what makes them tick. What is their true motivation? Why do they really do what they do? What do they really need? We need to know their fears, flaws, wants, and needs. Do they deal with their fear with anger, humor, or cowardice? Do they face their desires or run away from them? They better face them head on, or you don't have an active hero.

Character flaws provide a way to show the changes that heroes undergo. What are their limitations, vices, obsessions, inhibitions, or addictions? In other words, what inner demons must they overcome before they can deal with their external foes?

One way to develop characters who are internally consistent is to decide what rules govern their behavior. Arrange those rules in a hierarchy whereby certain rules are in operation most of the time, but under stress, the characters can act differently. Bugs Bunny, for instance, usually has a live-and-let-live attitude. But if he is pushed too far, watch out!

I would recommend taking a psychology class to understand what makes people tick. This is the heart of storytelling.

We are now going to look at four genres about specific emotions: love stories, tales of horror, comedies, and crime stories.

Love Stories: What Keeps Lovers Apart?

Imagine a love story where two lovers fall in love at first sight and get together. I bet you are waiting for something to happen. What makes love stories interesting is the obstacles that keep the lovers apart. In the beginning it is better to have "hate at first sight." This gives the story somewhere to go. The romantic chase is the interesting part.

The obstacles are what can make each love story unique. Parental objections are the defining obstacle of *Romeo and Juliet*. *Green Card* uses immigration as the obstacle. In "Dumb Love," our loveable monster, Goo, has to climb a volcano to get to Clover. Scheherazade must draw stories for the sultan and expose herself to danger for their love to come to pass.

Sometimes the obstacles can be internal such as fears of commitment or not wanting to get hurt again. As human beings, it is so easy to develop baggage that interferes with our relationships.

A love scene itself is difficult because being an end in itself, it stops the forward progress of the story. Interrupt the scene before you lose your audience. It is also difficult to sustain a sweetly touching moment. Cut it or throw a joke in before it gets too sappy.

In the classic Hollywood boy meets girl formula, infatuation runs high. It is the "rush" of being in love that accounts for the cliché "Love is blind." Psychologically, it is caused by an overvaluing of the love object because the lover projects his or her ideals onto the person he or she loves. The sultan sees the beauty and intellect of Scheherazade, and through her storytelling he falls for her.

In stage two, boy loses girl. Psychological disillusionment occurs when the love object no longer matches the ideal that is projected upon him or her. Now he or she is undervalued. Scheherazade has a mind of her own and betrays the sultan's trust. He loses interest in her and is ready to kill her like his other brides.

In stage three, boy gets girl back. Now if the parties involved are mature enough, real love can occur. This involves accepting the other's true nature even though it doesn't match the "fantasy." What will the sultan do now that he has learned that Scheherazade has betrayed him?

Why are so many movies about love? Love transforms people. Love is the source of great pleasure in people's lives, but it can also be the source of unbearable pain. We want to see what to do when things go wrong. We want models to live by.

So what can go wrong with love? It can easily become unbalanced and turn into an unequal relationship in the form of dominance and submission, dependency, or extracurricular affairs. Affairs create love triangles that are obstacles to love that offer a myriad of dramatic possibilities. Men and women think differently; play with the implications of this on how it affects relationships. Look for ways to break clichés.

Even if your story is not about love, you can still utilize love as a subplot to enliven any story.

What Is So Scary about Horror?

All stories have a fear factor. They are often set in a location that activates our basic childhood fears—it was a "dark and stormy night" for a reason. Most children and some adults fear being alone and in the dark. Good storytellers remember how scary it is being a child. I imagine the best storytellers are still in touch with the irrational fears of childhood and that is why they are good at it. Horror films focus on and exploit the monster's intent to cause us harm. They threaten us and exploit this through our vulnerability and fear of the unknown. Monsters are often scariest in the first act of a film when we know the least about them and we still don't know what they can really do.

Steven Spielberg's *Poltergeist*, directed by Tobe Hooper, created an incredible feeling of uncanniness in the beginning of the film. Act three felt like a letdown when they explained away all the horror and had skeletons attacking. Horror films are a special case whereby all of the narrative questions don't need to be answered. The not knowing contributes to their horrific effect. We need to see what happens to our questing heroes, not uncover mysteries of the universe.

Noel Carroll, in *Film, Emotion, and Genre,* suggests that horror breaches the normal distinction between inside and outside. Think about it: For most people if something punctures your skin and blood comes out, it is pretty horrible. The inside is supposed to stay inside. There is a quality of disgust that repels us. Monsters cross the boundary. Whether a monster rips limbs apart or acts internally like a virus, a boundary has been breached, and when the escape routes have been blocked it is all the more terrifying. What can be more terrifying than if the monster is already inside us? I am sure the surprise guest at the dinner scene from *Alien* made a few people jump.

Another boundary that horror films cross is that twilight area between life and death. I don't know what is worse, being a vampire that lives forever feeding on its mortal victims, or a zombie that lives but isn't alive. Frankenstein was created from dead body parts sewn back together and brought back to life. Similarly, the Mummy was also dead for a long time before coming back for a romp.

Things out of control can be used comedically or for horror. Things that aren't supposed to be alive but act that way and are also out of control are doubly frightening, such as the doll from the film *Chucky*. We all know that computers are out to get us, as demonstrated in the case of HAL from *2001*. The question of what if your dreams were out of control is answered in the *Nightmare on Elm Street* movie series.

A related theme to some power being out of control is someone having supernatural power. Pyrokinesis, or the ability to mentally start fires, can be cinematographically spectacular, like when it was used in *Firestarter* and *Carrie*.

Something about being watched without your knowing it is unnerving when you discover it. Most stalker films capitalize on this theme.

Good horror utilizes Scheherazade's secret—that storytelling is story-delaying. Make your audience wait for the scare. Horror should develop slowly. If you show the monster right away then where do you go? In *Alien* we watched the alien grow from a seed pod to a baby and finally to its most horrifying form as a teenager. Along with the characters, we had to learn about how deadly this thing was at each step of the way. The alien was probably on screen less than 5 percent of the film but it was one of the most terrifying monsters in horror movie history.

Provide the audience with a fake scare that reveals it to be something innocent, like a cat, and then while they are still feeling relief and their guard is down, provide the real scare. This structure works with comedy as well.

Find a new fear to utilize and you have got a new horror movie. Unknown stalkers, voodoo, superstitions, fairies, nymphs, gnomes, trolls, angered gods, demonic possession, claustrophobia, spiders, and snakes (but not on a plane) are some ideas filmmakers have used to create countless horror movies.

To learn more about how to construct horror films, watch the *Scream* movie series. The movies playfully examine the genre while at the same time provide some nice chills of their own. But the *Scream* series never mentions why it is usually a group of attractive teenagers that are the subject of horror movies. One reason could be that 14-year-old boys are the prime demographic target audience. However, on a deeper level, maybe monsters represent something the audience themselves are going through. Monster movies are a metaphor for the changes the body goes through in adolescent sexuality. The full moon comes out and the wolf boy starts a hairy transformation. Likewise, the full moon comes out and the vampire girl experiences blood. I will leave the details to your imagination.

The Rubberband Theory of Comedy: Aiming for the Backside of the Heart

As Monty Python would say, "And now here's something completely different." Comedy is like winding up a big spring. You have to tighten and tighten, building up expectancy and then you … make them (your characters and audience) wait some more … until … nothing. All that effort was for nothing. Then, boom! Time is compressed or expanded for the comedic effect. The thing you are winding up is the emotions of the characters—frustration, annoyance, anger, expectations, and high hopes. Then the rubberband comes undone.

The rational way to deal with something that doesn't work is to try a different solution until you find one that does. The comedic way of dealing with something that doesn't work fits the description of insanity, whereby if something

doesn't work you keep doing the same thing only harder. It is even more comedic if when something doesn't work, you take it personally, and put more and more effort into doing exactly the same thing until it explodes in your face! While dramatic characters must be driven but flexible, comedic characters must be blindly obsessed by their goals, like in *It's a Mad, Mad, Mad, Mad World* where the lure of buried treasure turns ordinary people into greedy maniacs.

The traditional approach to comedy is that the pompous must fall. It is those who think they are better than the rest of us that are the best targets for slippery bananas. In *The Dinner Game*, a pompous dinner group selects a person to make a fool of. The tables turn when the "fool," in trying to help, is such a bungler that he inadvertently gets revenge by making things terrible for his upper-crust host.

Misunderstanding is at the core of tragedy and comedy. In *The Inspector General* a beggar is accidentally mistaken for the inspector general of the town and treated royally. He must hide his old identity from those who knew him as the common beggar and pretend to know what he is doing as the inspector, which is fun to watch.

In "Dumb Love," Goo mistakenly thinks Clover is dead, just as Romeo thinks that Juliet is dead. One story ends tragically, while the other is upbeat. "Dumb Love" came about when I asked the question, what would happen if *Romeo and Juliet* ended happily?

Confusion also exists when someone dresses like the opposite sex. From *Some Like It Hot*, to *Tootsie*, to the TV show *Bosom Buddies*, cross-dressing is a great source of dramatic irony. Wikipedia lists over 50 films in their article on cross-dressing in film. Silent film stars Charlie Chaplin and Stan Laurel wore women's clothes in their films. Women also take part in dressing up like men, like in *Shakespeare in Love*. And even the cartoon character Bugs Bunny has been known to put on a dress from time to time.

In miscommunication there is a gap between what is expected and the actual result. In *The Russians Are Coming, the Russians Are Coming* a Russian submarine gets stuck on a sandbar. This one event leads to escalating rumors that drive the townspeople to hysteria when they mistakenly believe that a full-scale Russian invasion is attacking their little town.

Sometimes it is the situation itself that is the source of the comedy. In *What Did You Do during the War, Daddy?* we see a typical war scene of American soldiers sneaking up on a town. They enter a gate, suddenly a whistle blows, and a soccer ball lands on one of the soldier's bayonet. After some arguing the Italians will agree to surrender, but only after their festival. The festival leads to drunken revelry. When the Americans learn that air surveillance is on the way, they have to stage a phony battle to convince headquarters everything is under control, that is until the German army arrives. The situation is funny in itself, and the more the characters try to make things work, the worse it gets.

In suspense, we withhold information from the audience and our characters. We may foreshadow some threat. As directors we are in control of the flow of information. In comedy, we let the audience in on the joke, but not the characters. An important part of comedy is allowing the audience to feel superior.

Even clowns know the value of staging a gag clearly,[1] only they describe visual confusion as spaghetti. You have to let the audience in on the joke for them to get it. Telegraph your intentions to your audience.

In comedy, rules are made to be broken. Nonsense is not a random affair. It can only exist in rebellion to rules.[2] This is one case where you can even cross the threshold of awareness without destroying the story. A comic character can step out of the story and speak directly to the camera. This is known as breaking the fourth wall and is used frequently in theater.

Comedy is close to pain but doesn't cross the line. If it feels like it hurts, it is not funny. Humor frees us from psychic pain, if only for a moment. Comedy reveals ourselves as we really are, even if we choose not to see or hear it. If we laugh then we have probably recognized its truth.

Don't forget toppers—just when you though it was over ... it is time to laugh again. Why did the mathematician cross the Möbius strip?*

So Many Crime Shows

Movies can fulfill our powerful sense of justice: that goodness is rewarded and evil punished. The *Punisher, Death Wish, Lethal Weapon, Dirty Harry, V for Vendetta*, and *Robin Hood* are all great examples of justice that goes beyond the letter of the law. It is very important that your audience must be shown why the villains should be punished. What were their crimes? Do you choose to show the crime or just the aftermath?

On the surface, cop and criminal shows involve action with gunplay. I think people want to see crimes committed without having to deal with the consequences. I mean, wouldn't it be nice to get rich quick and get away with things? But just as strongly, they also want justice and crimes to be punished. With crime stories they can have it both ways. Your audience wants to witness crime and punishment.

The great thing about movies is that we can identify with the hero doing heroic stuff but also unconsciously identify with the bad guy. Why? Villains have all the fun. They get to do things that we are not allowed to do. We are guilty of wanting to see them get away with it. But we also get the satisfaction of seeing them get what they deserve.

Mankind is a flawed species prone to all kinds of sins, but we are also capable of redemption, transformation, truth, honor, and grace.

Let's return to the palace and see if it is too late.

---

*   To get to the same side.

DUNAZADE: "Your Majesty …

DUNAZADE: "My sister wanted you to …

DUNAZADE: "Have these."

The sultan takes the package.

SULTAN: "What is it?"

DUNAZADE: "When she read your diary …

DUNAZADE: "She fell in love with you and finished the story for you."

The sultan looks at the drawings.

Smoke rises.

304

And out of the smoke rises the dragon.

The crowd gasps.

DRAGON: "Have you not been warned? Yet you dare to disturb my slumber?"

DRAGON: "If you continue to fight …

The crowd lays down their weapons.

DRAGON: "I will destroy you all."

Behind the crowd comes the Jerk.

He looks up and sees …

Goo with a megaphone, in a hot air balloon that looks like a dragon.

The Jerk climbs one of the ropes caught on the dragon.

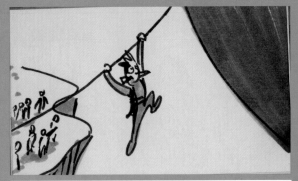

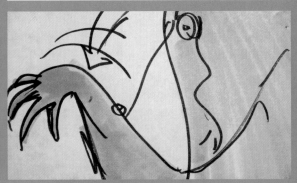

He attacks Goo.

Goo defends himself.

The Jerk slices through the rope.

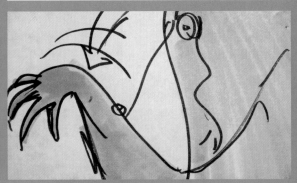

The dragon's arm falls downward . . .

Hitting Clover over the edge.

She falls.

Goo has to save her.

Goo jumps.

Clover is hanging on to one of the ropes.

Goo climbs down.

Goo reaches for Clover.

Clover reaches up, looking for help.

Clover dissolves into Scheherazade.

Tears well up in the sultan's eyes.

The drawings fall from his hands....

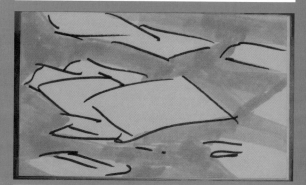

Scattering on the floor.

SULTAN: "What have I done?"

Suddenly, the sultan is cast in shadow.

He turns to look.

The vizier has transformed into …

A fire-breathing dragon.

DRAGON: "I told you she couldn't be trusted."

SULTAN: "You. It was you who made me kill all of those …

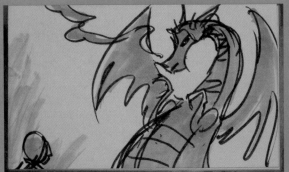

SULTAN [Offscreen]: "Innocents."

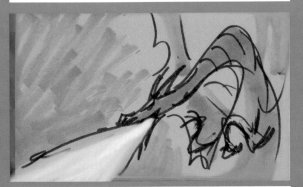

The dragon shoots fire at the sultan.

The sultan jumps out of the way.

Goo climbs down toward Clover.

He struggles to reach her.

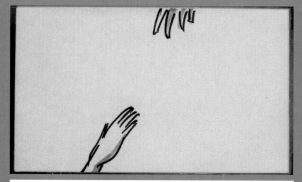

Clover reaches up.

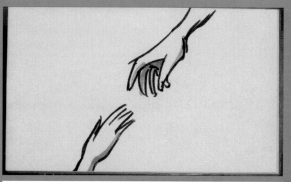

GOO: "Grab hold of my hand."

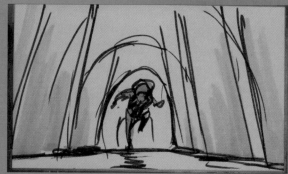

The sultan races down the hall.

The dragon is right behind.

The dragon's flames fill the hall.

GOO: "I can't reach her."

The crowd doesn't know what to do.

The sultan hides.

The dragon searches for him.

He makes a run for it.

The dragon bursts through the columns.

The sultan races away.

The flames graze him.

The townspeople go to help.

For the first time since the curse, the Catfields work beside the McClods in teamwork.

Ropes fly everywhere.

They create a monster chain working together.

Madame Knowitallish, Daisy, and Weed watch with baited breath.

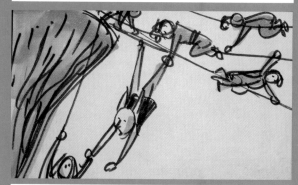

They suspend Goo upside down.

They lower him down.

Getting closer.

Goo reaches further ...

The dragon attacks with more fire.

It nearly misses the sultan.

The palace crumbles around the sultan.

He races down the halls.

Goo is lowered.

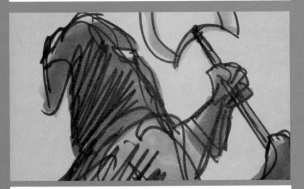

Meanwhile the executioner readies his axe.

Clover reaches upward.

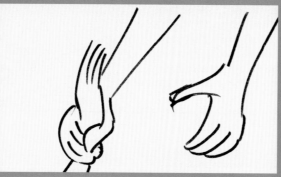

Goo grabs her hand.

The sultan makes it to the courtyard.

The executioner begins his morbid task.

He draws his axe.

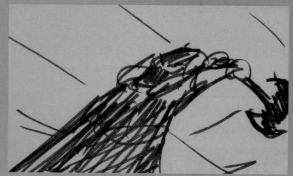

Dunazade gives her sister's gift—the conclusion of her story—to the sultan. The audience would have felt cheated if we didn't show the ending to "Dumb Love," so I tried an experiment, and let the story appear to tell itself. This functions dramatically to create dual storytelling delays, by cross-cutting between Goo's rescue of Clover and the sultan's rescue of Scheherazade. This also highlights the parallels between the stories. All this may not matter because it might already be too late for Scheherazade. Stay tuned!

Emotional Truth

The goal of filmmaking is to have the maximum impact upon the audience emotionally while challenging them intellectually. Film is about emotional truth, not logic. Luckily, I didn't go the logically accurate way when I directed *Fantasia 2000*'s *Pomp and Circumstance* sequence. Instead, I cheated in the greater service of emotional truth.

Donald and Daisy Duck both believe that they have lost each other to the great storm. When the flood subsides, the ark settles and the animals depart. Once again, Donald does not see Daisy leave. During the march of the animals off the ark, Daisy realizes that she has lost her locket and looks around for it.

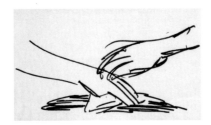

Into the frame comes a hand settling on his.

(*Credit:* Art by Aernout Van Pallandt.)

Donald looks up and sees Daisy. (*Credit:* Art by Aernout Van Pallandt.)

They look into each other's eyes. Then, after a beat, they are thrilled that each other is alive! Movie magic! The shot of the hands touching is very powerful. It is an iconic sign of their love and finding each other again. There actually is a problem with the shot—it is a total film cheat. In reality, or logical truth, they would have seen each other from 50 yards away, certainly way before they got so close as to touch hands.

If we chose the logical approach it might have looked like this next image.

Is this shot as powerful as the other sequence? No, it doesn't have any of the emotional intensity because we are so far away from them. Emotions are more powerful than logic. Logic works for Rube Goldberg machines, not for people. If we had stuck with logical truth, there would have been no magic! This is film magic at its best. The audience was "lost" in the story, and the fact that they would have seen each other before they touched was below the audience's

(*Credit:* Art by Aernout Van Pallandt.)

Donald is left behind to clean up the mess. Something in the dust catches his eye. The little sparkle shining through the dust is an indexical sign of hope. (*Credit:* Art by Aernout Van Pallandt.)

(*Credit:* Art by Aernout Van Pallandt.)

He reaches into the dust pile to pick it up. (*Credit:* Art by Aernout Van Pallandt.)

threshold of awareness. If we hadn't orchestrated it just right, they might have thought this and thus been bumped out of the story.

Then we ended the sequence with some more magic—the symbolic rainbow ending.

Emotions are more powerful than logic!

Music and Color: Not Meaning, but Meaningful

Pictures tell us what is happening in a story. Film, however, was never truly silent. Filmmakers knew to have piano players add accompaniment. It is the role of music and color to tell us how to feel in a film. "We human beings rely so much on visual cues that we often don't realize how much we really do relay on sound cues, and to what extent our mind takes those sounds seriously."[3] Music takes us over. When the beat starts sometimes without even realizing it we find ourselves moving to it, tapping our feet, and swaying our bodies.

Sound designer David Sonnenschein suggests that music has a narrative aspect in that we are guessing to see where the music is going to go.[4] Composer Carl Stalling created wonderfully inventive scores for the Warner Brothers' cartoons full of rising and falling melodies that build tensions that play with the listener's expectations. Big expectations sometimes get a little bang! Other times surprise comes from unexpected big bangs! They work like punctuation in speech. There are lots of exclamation points, long pauses for commas, and rising lingering ones for questions. Stalling achieves this from the scales, timing, and percussive quality of music, and a liberal use of sound effects.

Composer Aaron Copeland in a *New York Times* article dated 11/6/1949 gives the following observations about the use of music in film[5]:

- Music can create a more convincing atmosphere of time and place.
- Music can be used to underline or create psychological refinements—the unspoken thoughts of a character or the unseen implications of a situation.

- Music can serve as a neutral background filler.
- Music can build a sense of continuity in a film.
- Music can provide the underpinning for the theatrical buildup of a scene and then round it off with a sense of finality.

"Film music is coloristic in its effects…. Color is associative—bagpipes call up images of Scotland, the oboe easily suggests a pastoral scene, muted brass suggests something sinister, rock music may imply a youthful theme and so on. Also, color is not intrusive; it does not compete with the dramatic action. This is especially important for film music. The effect of color, moreover, is immediate, unlike musical thematic development, which takes time."[6]

"Music has a way of bypassing the human's normal, rational defense mechanisms. When used properly, music can build the drama in a scene to a far greater degree of intensity than any of the other cinematic arts. It is little significance whether the scene involves an intimate love relationship or a violent fight; music evokes a gut reaction unobtainable in any other way."[7]

Music can play upon emotions without resorting to words. Film composer Max Steiner insisted that every character should have his or her own musical theme. Variations in the theme's tone can imply the characters' state of mind. It also allows the filmmaker to refer to characters even when they are not presently onscreen (think of when you hear Darth Vader's marching theme).

Music helps defend the threshold of attention. By subtly smoothing over gaps in dialogue or just keeping a pulse going it keeps the audience's attention on the story. As we have seen, film is made from fragments. Music can serve as the glue that holds it all together. Each space has its own ambience, the little sounds that define the space acoustically, and this also serves to hold the pictures together.

Color may be silent but just as powerful emotionally. Each character can also have his or her own color theme that signals his or her presence. Color gives film a sense of temperature of warm and coolness. It achieves this power from contrast. If you start a scene all in dark greens and suddenly cut to a screen filled with bright red you will see its silent screaming power.

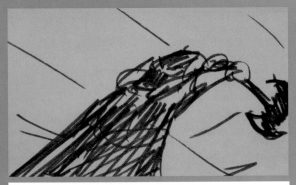

The executioner takes aim …

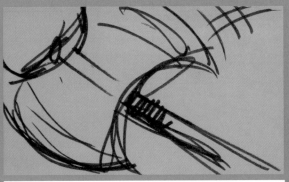

The axe begins to swing …

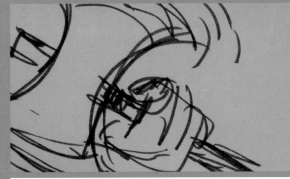

At the last second, a hand grabs it.

The executioner is shocked.

The sultan grabs the axe.

The executioner bows before the sultan. The sultan turns.

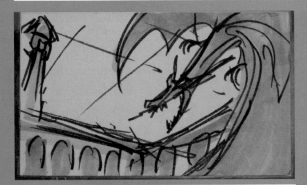

The dragon approaches.

The dragon strikes.

The sultan brings down the axe, cutting off the dragon's head.

Something begins to happen.

The dragon begins to vanish.

It is gone.

Clover is safe as they pull *Goo* up.

SULTAN [Voiceover]: "Scheherazade, I was out of my mind with jealousy. It made me crazy."

SULTAN: "I imagined I had a trusted vizier who told me to never trust anyone again and he, no, I did terrible things."

SULTAN: "Your stories have saved me and my kingdom, and I offer it to you."

SULTAN: "Scheherazade, will you marry me?"

JERK: "You can't have her. I was made for her, she's mine!"

Goo and Clover are startled.

Without warning the Jerk flies up . . .

And is carried off by a myth that has turned real.

Goo and Clover watch as it flies away.

Sticks now has two new girlfriends, Daisy and Weed.

MADAME KNOWITALLISH: "Herman, it's you!"

MADAME KNOWITALLISH: "After all these years. I thought you died when you fell into the chasm."

GOO: "Madame Knowitallish, it was you who put the curse on the town."

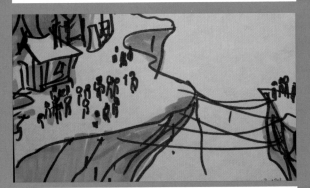

MADAME [Voiceover]: "Yes, but now I forgive all." [Everyone cheers!]

The rope bridge continued to be built up until ...

There was no chasm dividing the two sides. The sun sets under a rainbow.

Dawn arrives at the palace; big plans are under way.

What Is It All About?

Theme is the underlying message that unifies a film about what you believe about how the world works causally in relation to desire and fear. Physical causality is easy to understand. It is our emotional world of social relationships that doesn't make sense. What truly motivates people to do what they do?

Why should theme be so important? Like the function of music in a film, theme unifies and helps hold a whole film together. Second, it functions as a kind of metaphoric truth for us. Linguist George Lakoff believes that metaphors have the power to create reality for us. "Since most of our social reality is understood in metaphorical terms and since our conception of the physical world is partly metaphorical, metaphor plays a very significant role in determining what is real for us."[8]

We experiece film as a real event- our pulse races, we sweat and we experience real emotions from the illusions on the screen. Rather than identifying with the hero, the audience is being moved by how the hero's actions and the consequences of those actions trigger their own experiences. Film taps into their own desires, guilts, and anxieties. We don't have to suspend our disbelief because belief is automatic. Stories work on us automatically as long as we don't create holes in the story that distract the viewers. We need to keep engaging the emotions of the viewers by making them wish along with the heros or fear along with them.

Happy Ever After

Psychologist Bruno Bettelheim suggests that fairytales mirror the stages of a child's psychosexual development.[9] Fairytales present a solution in symbolic form that a child can utilize to help him or her grow.

Peter Pan addresses resistance to growing up. *Cinderella* addresses sibling rivalries. *Aladdin and the Magic Lamp* deals with wishful thinking. *Pinocchio* deals with the developing conscience. *Hansel & Gretel* deals with the oral stage. *Snow White and the Seven Dwarfs* deals with oedipal conflicts and the anxiety of separating from one's parents. Lewis Carroll's *Through the Looking Glass* deals with the mirror phase, when a child learns to identify himself or herself as autonomous and learn language in metaphorical mirroring.

Fairytales were mined like a gold rush of ideas for the Walt Disney Company. They reformed even the darkest of them into their trademark brand of "and they lived happily ever after." They needed to be careful because some stages are better suited to a dramatic presentation than others, for example, *Sleeping Beauty* deals with the latency stage, the short hibernation period between childhood and adolescence. The problem here is that the heroine sleeps through most of the story—not very dramatic.

Piglet's Big Compilation

Themes don't always show up on time. You need to search for them, nurture them, and let them evolve over time. Choose one theme and let it be your guide. Sure, you can have other themes, but they should all be subordinate to the master theme. Sharon Morill, president of Disneytoon Studios, asked me to direct a movie called *The Milne Stories*. It was a compilation of five of Milne's original Winnie-the-Pooh stories loosely held together with a frame story involving Rabbit looking for Small. After reading the script my first instinct was that it needed to be reshaped into a perfect wave, rather than a series of little hills.

A second problem was one that our characters inadvertently told us about. Rabbit comes running up informing Tigger and Pooh that Small is missing. Pooh

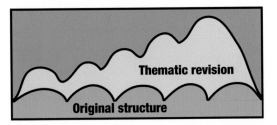

replies, "Who?" and Tigger inquires, "What do you want him for?" You see Small is a small beetle who is a "friend and relation" of Rabbit. The problem was that the audience might not know who Small is, and secondly, why should they care? We thought about what other characters could be missing and thought, "What if Piglet were missing?" Now our audience would care deeply.

We still had five separate stories with no unifying structure. The approach we took was to modify each of the stories to be about how, each time, Piglet had actually been the one to save the day, but nobody noticed. Our theme evolved into *even if you are small, you can do big things*—perfect for our young audience.

We still needed to shape it into a perfect wave. We chose to create Piglet's scrapbook to guide our characters on their journey. As Pooh stated, "It's Piglet's book of memories. I bet it remembers where Piglet is." And off they go.

With writer Brian Hohlfeld and the story crew we led our characters deep into despair as night arrived with a brewing storm. They argue and lose the book off a waterfall. The climax was that they had to climb a fallen tree over the waterfall to retrieve the book. Pooh gets in trouble and once again Piglet saves the day. Our theme unified the story and our climax gave us the perfect wave shape.

Since the film included several flashbacks, I worked with composer Carl Johnson to allow the score to tie the sections together. If we had strong musical closure after each story it would have felt like separate endings.

I felt like we had achieved our goal of giving our audience strong emotions when at the premiere screening a four-year-old boy got out of his seat and began calling out, "Piglet!" in an effort to try and help the characters find their friend. Theme is what ties it all together.

Theme also determines whether you like a movie. If you like the theme chances are you will like the movie; if you don't agree with the theme, it is possible you won't like the movie either.

Why We Watch Movies, Revisited

We started this journey in Chapter 1 with the question, "Why do we watch movies?" Our answer was to have emotionally satisfying experiences. True, there is usually a big emotional kick at the culminating climax and resolution of a story,

but the audience has emotional experiences happening all along the journey, not just at the end of a film. The cinematography might be beautiful, we may be attracted to the stars, we might laugh at a joke. The following is a list of some of the reasons we watch movies and what we experience along the journey:

- Narrative questions—puzzle solving.
- Narrative closure—relief from tension and questions answered.
- Sharing emotions—vicarious experiences.
- Magic and miracles—faith and belief.
- To feel safe from terror—mastery.
- Comedy—laughter.
- Voyeurism—spectacles, seeing secrets, and beauty.
- Learning about how the world works—a desire to understand.
- Escape confusion and boredom—excitement.
- Omniscient Point of view (POV)—dramatic irony, knowing more than people in real life.
- Punishment of evil—sense of justice.
- Magic, riches, flying, invisible—fantasies fulfilled.
- Musical support, harmonic tension, and closure, beat drive.
- Watching things blow up!
- Chases and violence—adrenaline rushes of the rollercoaster effect.
- Role models to internalize—underdog becomes hero.
- Characters they can relate to and understand—empathy.
- Expectations met but in unexpected ways—surprising twists, turns, and reversals.
- To learn how to overcome obstacles to your desires
- To participate in rituals in community with others.

The Story Knot and the Formula for Fantasy

So what drives us? Fear and pleasure drive us. Human beings like to imagine that we can reach a state that is conflict free and become whole. If this were true we wouldn't need movies and Hollywood would go broke. Obviously, this isn't going to happen anytime soon. Humans are inherently structured with impossibilities and paradoxes. "Fantasy is the primordial form of narrative, which serves to occult some original deadlock.... Lacan's thesis is much stronger: the answer to the question 'Why do we tell stories?' is that narrative as such emerges in order to resolve some fundamental antagonism by rearranging its terms into a temporal succession."[10] These internal knots are the source of our age-old original myths. They address the big unanswerable questions, like "Who are we?"; "Where did we come from?"; and "Why are we here?"

Why do we say that we have to tie up the loose ends at the end of a story? We follow the threads of a story that is woven together in a hierarchy of narrative questions and answers. Why the string metaphor? If these internal knots are so enigmatic and paradoxical to us, how can we learn about them? In stories these knotted threads are unraveled and mapped onto opposing characters in conflict, laid out in a linear sequence in order that we may try to make sense of our experiences and share them with others.

We all know that stories have to be about characters wanting something. But what is it in the nature of desire that we can never really get what we want? What motivates us? We are driven to desire things in spite of ourselves, sometimes when they are not even good for us. Desire is what motivates us but desire is meant to keep us in motion, desiring more. When we get what we think we want, it is momentary. It is then displaced by something else. We are off to the next goal. Desire drives us on a quest to seek answers. The desiring quest itself is the goal.

The answer to these questions comes in the form of fantasy, the imaginary, yet meaningful, solutions to the great questions of life. Film offers hope providing whole worlds where there are answers to the enigmas of life. As a child I loved Dr. Suess's *McGillicot's Pool*, that tiny little fishing pond that allows for the biggest of catches. It is a space for fantasy where dreams can come true.

Emotional Engagement of a Story

When a story isn't working, the emotional engagement stops (see Table 13.1).

Table 13.1

Engaging	Disengaging
Clarity, easy to follow	Confusing, hard to understand
Surprising	Boring, predictable
High stakes	Nothing at risk
Driven toward goal	Going nowhere
Emotional	Too much explaining
Action gets to the point	Tangents, unfocused
Appealing characters	Unappealing
Shows how it feels	Holes in causality and motivation

POINTS TO REMEMBER

- Find your theme and use it as your compass.
- Discover what fantasy you are trying to fill for your audience.
- We watch movies for many reasons but mostly to have emotionally satisfying experiences. This is your target as a filmmaker.
- Work at structure and keep it invisible by giving the audience reasons to love and root for heroes and reasons to hate villains.
- Engage your audience with close-ups; put them in the heart of the action.
- Make your audience wish for things to happen and let them imagine how events might have occurred. This makes them guilty participants of their own pleasures.
- Present your audience with moral choices.
- Watch *The Man in the Chair* for how it develops its theme.
- Pay attention to how the music and color in films affect you.

References

1. Grahmn, J. B. Ringling Clowns lecture at Walt Disney Feature Animation, 1992.
2. Stewart, S. *Nonsense.* Baltimore: John Hopkins University Press, 1989.
3. Schiffman, N. *Abracadabra.* Prometheus Books, 1997.
4. Sonnenschein, D. *Sound Design.* Michael Wiese, 2001.
5. Prendergast, R. M. *Film Music: A Neglected Art.* Norton, 1992.
6. Ibid.
7. Ibid.
8. Lakoff, G., and M. Johnson. *Metaphors We Live By.* Chicago: Chicago University Press, 1980.
9. Bettelheim, B. *The Uses of Enchantment: The Meaning and Importance of Fairy Tales.* New York: Knopf, 1976.
10. Zizek, S. *The Plague of Fantasies.* Verso, 1997.

Summary:
Recapitulation of All Concepts

14

Goal: Why do we watch movies?

Events of the Story	You want your audience "lost" in the story. You want them at the edge of their seats, emotionally involved about what is going to happen next.
Threshold of Awareness	The way in which the story is told should not enter the viewer's awareness. It should not cross this threshold or you put a hole in the illusion of the story.
Work Here: Structural Level	Structure is how the story is put together and how it is told, which must be a *clear* and *dramatic* presentation of an imaginary world of illusion.
Directors Direct Attention	The director directs the audience's attention to narrative questions that drive the story forward.

(*Continued*)

Goal: Why do we watch movies?

	Use the speaking metaphor to clearly present one idea at a time.
	Use magic, misdirection, hypnosis, and gestalt organization.
Directing the Eyes and Ears	Direct the viewers' eyes and ears with design and composition to lead the eyes where you want them to look. Ask, what am I looking at, and what is it the spectator wants to know? Utilize composition, design, perspective, and the camera.
Reading Significance	Learn how signs signify meanings and create associations. What does it say to me? What does this signify? What does it imply?
	Study semiotics and codes and learn to be a detective.
Constructing Meaning	You have to present the illusion of a seamless world of causality. What does it mean? Study your film from every level from the macro level of the hero's road trip to the micro level of narrative questions.
	Learn how to edit causality and continuity to construct meaning.
Aim Here: Emotional Responses	Emotions are the goal. Meaning evokes emotions automatically. How do I feel? Do I like it? Is it true?
	Learn thematic analysis. Study psychology.

Our goal has been to learn all of the techniques listed in the table and then forget them and start working intuitively. Then after a first pass at your film, use these tools to analyze and critique your work-in-progress in order to make it better. Remember to keep your audience "lost" in the story. Anything that is out of place on the structural level will attract their attention and they will be distracted from the story by being focused on the structure. Work to distract them with the story itself.

Scheherazade still has a few loose ends to wrap up. Join us as we say good-bye to her and the rest of the characters.

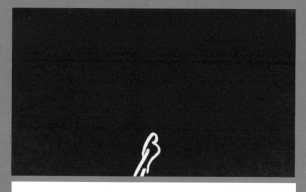

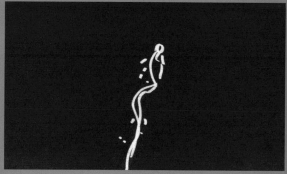

Fireworks light up the sky.

The palace is alive once more. The whole kingdom celebrates the marriage of the sultan to Scheherazade.

SULTAN: "Thank you. I owe you my life."

Scheherazade smiles.

They kiss and …

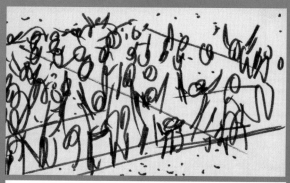

The crowd cheers.

325

Dunazade gets choked up.

She offers her gift to them.

It is a book …

Of Scheherazade's drawings from her many nights with the king.

Scheherazade hugs her sister.

The sultan and Scheherazade, hand in hand, descend …

The palace steps.

The girl who Scheherazade smiled at the day she went to the palace offers her a flower. Scheherazade has saved her life.

Scheherazade has saved the whole kingdom.

SMALL BOY: "Look everyone!"

Scheherazade and the sultan fly across the sky.

The End.

Fulfilling her quest, Scheherazade has truly earned her name, which means "savior of the city."

Asking Questions and Getting Answers

Writing is asking questions and getting answers. When a question is asked your brain starts searching to make sense of the question and find answers that give it meaning. The cortex of the brain has the job of generating possibilities.[1] They are not realities, but rather permutations of relationships in the mind. When you ask, "What if … ?" the cortex will literally generate all kinds of possibilities. These are the answers that we need for our stories.

The cortex generates answers even if the questions don't make sense. If we ask ourselves, "Why is the moon made of cheese?" our brains will find an answer. Solutions may appear as unformed wild fantasies. The problem is that we may censor many of our ideas. Censoring too soon destroys the process of creating chains of associations. We may censor ideas because they appear nonsensical or threatening. The director must have the courage to ask the questions and allow a holding space for the answers to emerge. It is similar to free association, where one says whatever comes to one's mind.

The writer can consciously apply these permutations. Comedy writing does this. It tries turning things inside out and upside down. First, the process starts with a great deal of randomness. Second (intuition plays a part here), we unconsciously pick out a vague pattern in the randomness. Each progressive selection process will lead to ideas that begin to fit the needs of our story. When there is a best fit, we will have an "A-ha!" experience. The story will evolve out of the chaos by the question-and-answer process.

Reference

1. Mauer R. "The Psychology of Storytelling." UCLA Workshop, Los Angeles, 1991.

15

Analysis and Evolution of the Scheherazade Project

Story Evolution: Making It Clearer and More Dramatic

Originally this book was conceived like any other film book. Each time I wanted to demonstrate a concept I had to make up some idea, and they all felt generic and uninspired. Scheherazade's story was dear to my heart, and could demonstrate all of the principles and techniques I needed. I chose to tell her story.

I had Scheherazade telling an invented story about Sinbad, only this story felt contrived and episodic. I remembered that I had created beat boards of another story that I had written. A beat board precedes a storyboard by only illustrating the key dramatic moments without regard for continuity. It allows you to critique the overall structure of the story.

This story was called "Dumb Love," an imaginative tale about two monsters from warring clans who, despite impossible obstacles, fall in love and heal their kingdom. This would be a perfect story to tell the sultan king because his problem was that he could no longer trust any woman enough to fall in love with her.

"Dumb Love" was also perfect because it was conceived as a silent film, perfect for demonstrating the art of visual storytelling.

Thematic Analysis and Dramatic Structures

Scheherazade's theme is the transformative power of stories. The theme of "Dumb Love" is that true love is unstoppable.

The story of Scheherazade in *One Thousand and One Arabian Nights* really didn't have a cinematic dramatic structure. The story's function was to provide a framework to hold a collection of tales of adventure and morals. I chose to use the Scheherazade story because it can illustrate so many of the principles of making movies. In order to make it more cinematic I had to give it an Aristotelian plot curve adding incidents and conflicts that were not in the original movie in order to allow the story to build in conflict to crisis and climax. In addition, "Dumb Love" also has a larger dramatic structure itself that at times mirrors the sultan's journey of transformation.

I like to proceed from broad strokes to specifics. If an idea comes I will write it down. The biggest twist for an ending would be to answer the narrative question, "What if Scheherazade failed?" The sultan condemning Scheherazade would provide an exciting climax. In order to reach this climax, I would have had to have her do something to lose the sultan's trust. It also had to be something that she did out of the goodness of her heart. Out of this need I created the forbidden door and the sultan's diary.

In order to explode act three into action I needed chases, obstacles, and turnarounds. The sultan's imaginary vizier who turns into the dragon created an unexpected turn just at the time I needed an obstacle. My problem was how to effectively visualize this idea. I think that I could have had more of it layered in earlier. The sultan learns that he has made a mistake and must race to save Scheherazade. Cross-cutting to the climax of "Dumb Love" even ramped up the suspense more. I tried to have both the Scheherazade and "Dumb Love" stories wrap up their closure at the same time to prevent an anticlimax or feeling of multiple endings. This was a challenge.

Story Parallels and Repetitions

Themes develop from making all a story's pieces fit together. Scheherazade used story parallels as an attempt to reach the sultan outside of his conscious awareness. I added other parallels to compare and contrast the two stories:

- The sultan is a monster who doesn't know how to love just like Goo.
- Falling papers. Clover's drawing ripped up leads the camera down to Goo in the chasm. Scheherazade rips the drawings when she can't come up with new ideas. The third time papers fall is when the sultan drops the drawings of story's ending.
- There are parallel chases in the end to rescue Clover and Scheherazade.
- Clover and Scheherazade both have balconies.
- There are parallel attempted executions.

Each time an action is repeated it can have a new meaning because it is taking place in a new context. The first time Scheherazade lights the lantern, it signifies we are going to a new place through her storytelling. Thereafter, it signifies a return to the ritual of storytelling. Scheherazade burns the drawing showing she wishes revenge against the sultan. Later when she burns her finger it signifies her guilt, anger, and fear at learning of the results of the sultan's insanity.

Hierarchy of Narrative Questions of the Scheherazade Story

Following is an analysis of the hierarchy of narrative questions in the Scheherazade story. The main questions contain a series of subquestions that must be answered before the main ones are answered:

Will Scheherazade heal the sultan or die trying?
How will she tell a story when she has lost her voice?
    She draws.
Will she fall in love with the sultan?
    She begins to want to understand him.
Will she open the forbidden door?

What will she find?
    She finds tombs.
How will she react?
    She wants to kill the sultan.
Will she? And so on.
    No, she falls in love. She heals the sultan. End of story.

Here it is in full detail:

- **Will Scheherazade be able to stop the sultan or will she become his next victim?** This is the main question of the story and overrides all others. This is the top question of the hierarchy.
- On the way to the palace, will her sister or the warnings of the beggar deter her?
- Realizing the consequences of what she is attempting to do, she loses her voice. How can she execute her plan when she has lost her voice?
- Once Scheherazade meets the sultan, new questions arise. Will the sultan grant Dunazade permission to hear her sister's story? Will the vizier stop her? Why?
- Scheherazade starts to storyboard for her sister. Will the sultan engage with the story or will they not survive the night?
- He stops the storytelling—is something wrong? He can't see the drawings. What will she do? Dunazade gives her sister the charcoal. This answers the question. The charcoal can draw bold but is messy. Notice how this action layers in crucial information that will payoff later, yet it feels natural to the story.
- The plan works for the first night. Will it continue to work? In addition to the Scheherazade story the viewer will also want the narrative questions in "Dumb Love" answered.
- Is the sultan falling for Scheherazade and what will she do? Is she falling in love back?
- The interest from the sultan leads Scheherazade to want to know more about him. What will she do?
- Will they try to enter the forbidden door? Did someone hear them? Will they get caught? Can they get back in time?
- What will they find behind the door? What they find changes their feelings from curiosity to hatred. Will Scheherazade try to get revenge?
- Will she follow through on her threat? Did she poison the wine? What will the vizier do?
- Scheherazade couldn't kill the sultan. Can she keep up the nights of storytelling? Is she running out of ideas?
- Scheherazade tries to find inspiration in the library. Will the sultan catch her? What does she find in his diary?
- Scheherazade's voice comes back. When will she tell the sultan?
- Before Scheherazade can tell the sultan, the vizier interrupts, whispering to the sultan. Does he believe him? The evidence presented doesn't lie.

- Will the sultan execute Scheherazade? Dunazade presents the gift of the story. Will the sultan read it? And will it make a difference?
- The sultan realizes he has made a mistake, but is he too late? Can he get to Scheherazade in time?
- Will the vizier stop him? Will the sultan be able to defeat the dragon?

At this point "Dumb Love" continues as if it is telling itself. This provides great cross-cutting between the two story climaxes.

The sultan prevails but now has to fully come to terms with what he has done. The vizier was a split-off part of the sultan so that he wouldn't have to feel the guilt for his crazy way of trying to assure himself that he would never be betrayed again. The sultan and Scheherazade wed and the main story question is answered.

This chart was made to track the progress and turning points in Scheherazade's and the Dumb Love Story. Scheherazade's story follows the lower curve and is intercut with the Dumb Love upper curve.

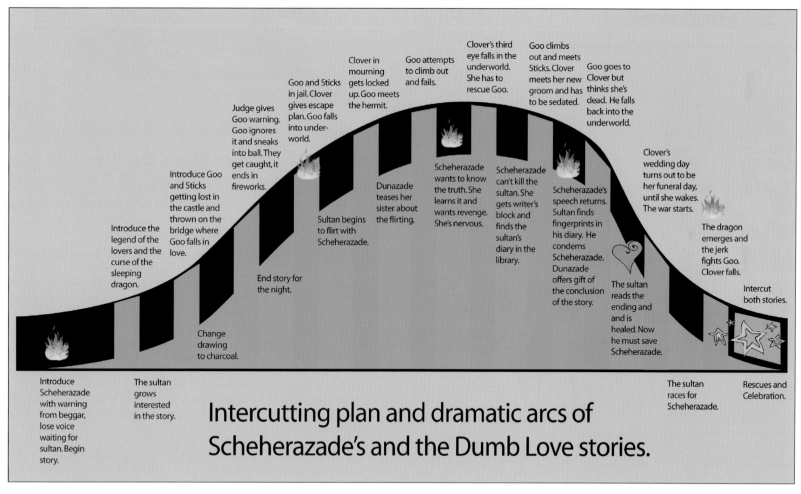

Intercutting plan and dramatic arcs of Scheherazade's and the Dumb Love stories.

This chart was made to track the progress and turning points in Scheherazade's and Sinbad's stories. Scheherazade's story follows the lower curve, her stories of Sinbad track the upper curve with vertical arrows showing when she goes into the story and when the story concludes. Later the Sinbad story was dropped and "Dumb Love" replaced it.

This was one of the first character sketches that I felt was headed in the right direction.

This is the Super Sculpey® model of the town for "Dumb Love."

Here is another exploration sketch of the characters.

Cuts for Length or to Make the Story Move Quicker

In the context of a book like this it is difficult to fully develop the characters without it requiring twice as many drawings and more dialogue. Here are some ideas that were cut in order to make the project manageable:

- The hermit originally had amnesia and couldn't remember anything, so he wrote everything down on scraps of paper. The idea was that if he couldn't think of what to say, he would reach in his pocket and read a scrap. The quote might be off the wall, like a fortune cookie, but it would somehow illuminate Goo's situation.
- Goo also was to get amnesia when he fell. He was driven to the light above without knowing why. When Clover crashes into him, his memory returns, and he has to find a way to reach her.
- Originally the parbit had a much bigger part. It was to be a companion sidekick to Goo and it didn't like Sticks.
- There was also to be wood sprites in the woods that attack Goo and Sticks.
- Goo's ex-girlfriends also were to have a bigger part to help show Goo's character development.

Changes Made to Make the Story More Dramatic or Resonant

- Delaying the reveal of the sultan makes him more mysterious.
- Creating a big reveal of the palace and interrupting it with the surprise foreshadowing of the blind beggar.
- Scheherazade going against the crowd as they are fleeing with their daughters shows her determination.
- The sultan is split in two, himself and the evil vizier. This creates retroactive reframe for the story.
- Putting the girl from the opening scene into the ending scene for closure. We see the personal benefits Scheherazade's quest has served.
- Dunazade's puppets were added after the story was developed.
- Adding Cupid to make "Dumb Love" more cartoonlike and humorous. It highlights the idea of love at first sight, and he won't leave Goo alone.

This last image is an original beat board of "Dumb Love." These were drawn on 3 × 5 self-stick notes with a Pentel Color Pen Fine Point #S360 Black. They were stuck onto 2 × 3-foot foam core boards. This allowed for easy reorganization of the drawings.

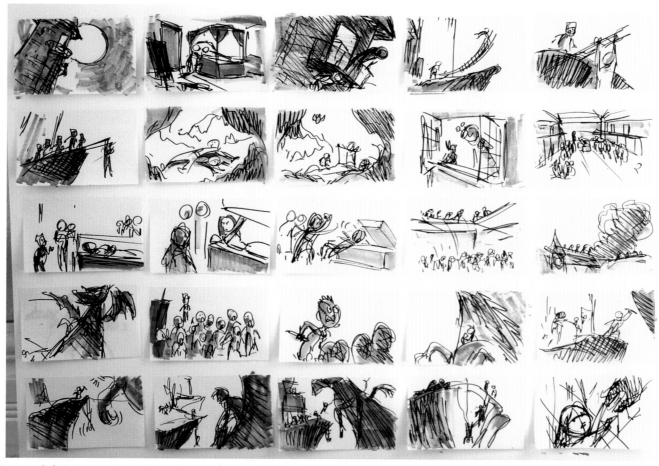

There is always more that you can do, but at some point you have to let go and release your creation to the world.

16

Conclusion: Now We Must Say Good-bye

What They Don't Tell You

I was filled with excitement and high expectations the day I learned that Walt Disney Studios wanted me to work for them. I was also filled with high doubts about my abilities. I came expecting to learn the great secrets of filmmaking from the masters at Disney. But, alas, the techniques that I have shared with you weren't taught in film school or when I first started at Disney. Nobody tells you that you will pour your heart into you work and then after a review it will be in tattered pieces on the floor. Nobody told me it is an emotional roller coaster. When the call to adventure rings, sometimes I hang up.

Filmmaking is a collaborative process and you need to learn to put your ego on the shelf. Even if you are the director, you can catch more ideas with honey than you can with vinegar. Build morale for the team. The reality is that it is hard work with very few actual guiding principles to help a beginner find his or her way.

Tips for Keeping Your Dream Alive

- Keep two books with you: one for networking and the other for ideas.
- Make sure you see the forest and the trees. Finely craft the details but don't forget to see the big picture.
- Hammer away, distilling the story, boiling it down to its essence. Don't be afraid to cut material.
- When you are stuck with a blank page, do something different.
- Keep your contacts and portfolio up to date.
- Create your own opportunities, and find niches that you do best.
- When you don't have work, your job is to look for work 40 hours a week.
- Save for a rainy day. Yes, even in Hollywood it rains.
- Push yourself. Thumbnail fast. Try alternate versions.
- Try a variety of compositions. See how each one tells the story differently.
- Create interesting characters and cast them visually.
- Create a website for yourself.
- Promote yourself.

- Don't make enemies or speak badly of others—it is a small world.
- Take classes in improvisation, selling, drawing, psychology, and business.
- Create a clip art file of ideas, tutorials, and inspirational images.
- Gain experience by experimenting using trial and error.
- Find a good mentor to guide you.
- Listen carefully to what directors want.
- Download SketchUp™, the free three-dimensional model creation program.
- Download Celtx®, the free scriptwriting program, and write.
- Don't just watch movies; study them until they yield you their secrets.
- Don't be afraid of making changes, and learn to be objective about your work.
- Remember that YOU are on your hero's journey, and it never ends.

Things Are Not Always What They Seem

I would like to leave you with a story that demonstrates the power of structured communication. The behavior of schizophrenics appeared crazy until Gregory Bateson, a British anthropologist, and his researchers discovered a family communication pattern that appeared to be of the type "damned if you do and damned if you don't." It is a paradox, like "Disobey all rules, including this one."

The result they found was that this behavior was an attempt at communication in a crazy situation.

The reason that I am sharing this story with you is that the result didn't have to be craziness. This double-bind structure had far-reaching therapeutic implications. Bateson's group also studied dolphins and observed how they could teach dolphins to do tricks by giving them a reward of fish. They then tried a new experiment: They would give the dolphins a fish reward *only* if they did a new behavior. Well, nobody told the dolphins about the change in the rules. So a dolphin came out and started doing tricks expecting to get fish and … no fish. "What is going on? What happened to the fish?" So at first the dolphin gets angry. Then the dolphin does a new behavior and gets rewarded. Suddenly a lightbulb goes on and the dolphin does 15 new behaviors that no one has ever seen dolphins do before.

I wish you well on your journey. If you are ever stuck with a story or fearful of having to pitch one, just remember Scheherazade. If you fail in your storytelling, you won't die; it just might feel that way. Use those feelings to make your next story better. Who knows, you might create 15 new stories.

Bibliography

Affron, C. *Cinema and Sentiment*. Chicago: University of Chicago Press, 1982.

Andrew, D. *Concepts in Film Theory*. New York: Oxford University Press, 1984.

Arnheim, R. *The Power of the Center*. Berkeley: University of California Press, 1998.

Arnheim, R. *Art and Visual Perception*. Berkeley: University of California Press, 2004.

Aumont, J., A. Bergala, M. Marie, and M. Vernet. *Aesthetics of Film*. University of Texas, 1992.

Bandler, R. *Time for a Change*. Cupertino, CA: Meta Publications, 1993.

Bang, M. *Picture This: Perception and Composition*. Boston: Bulfinch Press, 1991.

Baker, S. *Visual Persuasion*. New York: McGraw-Hill, 1961.

Bateson, G. *Steps to an Ecology of Mind*. New York: Ballantine Books, 1972.

Bateson, G. *Mind and Nature*. Cresskill, NJ: Hampton Press, 1979.

Beiman, N. *Prepare to Board*. Boston: Focal Press, 2007.

Benjamin, J. *The Bonds of Love*. New York: Pantheon, 1988.

Bettelheim, B. *The Uses of Enchantment*. New York: Knopf, 1975.

Block, B. *The Visual Story*. Boston: Focal Press, 2001.

Boorstin, J. *The Hollywood Eye*. New York: HarperCollins, 1992.

Bordwell, D. *Narration in the Fiction Film*. Bloomington: Wisconsin, University of Wisconsin Press, 1987.

Bothwell, D., and M. Mayfield. *Notan*. Mineola, NY: Dover Publications, 1968.

Branigan, E. *Narrative Comprehension and Film*. London: Routledge, 1992.

Brooks, P. *Reading for the Plot*. Cambridge, MA: Harvard University Press, 1984.

Brown, M. H. *Bodyworks*. Cincinnati, OH: North Light Books, 1990.

Campbell, J. *The Hero with a Thousand Faces*. Princeton: Princeton Universtiy Press, 1973.

Canemaker, J. *Paper Dreams*. New York: Hyperion, 1999.

Chandler, D. *Semiotics: The Basics*. London: Routledge, 2004.

Chatman, S. *Story and Discourse*. Ithaca, NY: Cornell University Press, 1980.

Clifton, N. *The Figure in Film*. Wilmington: University of Delaware Press, 1983.

Cobley, P., and L. Jansz. *Introducing Semiotics*. Lanham, MD: Totem Books, 1997.

Couch, T. *Watercolor: You Can Do It*. Cincinnati, OH: North Light Books, 1987.

Dancyger, K. *The Techniques of Film and Video Editing*. Boston: Focal Press, 2002.

Derry, C. *The Suspense Thriller*. Jefferson, NC: McFarland, 1988.

Dryden, G., and J. Vos. *The Learning Revolution*. Rolling Hills Estates, CA: Jalmar Press, 1999.

Dunn, C. *Conversations in Paint*. New york: Workman Publishing, 1995.

Egri, L. *The Art of Dramatic Writing*. New York: Simon and Schuster, 1960.

Eidsvik, C. *Cineliteracy*. New York: Horizon Press, 1978.

Elkins, J. *The Object Stares Back*. New York: Simon and Schuster, 1996.

Erikson, M. *Hypnotic Realities*. New York: Irvington Publishers, 1976.

Fabri, R. *Artist's Guide to Composition*. New York: Watson Guptill, 1986.

Field, S. *Screenplay*. New York: Dell Publishing Co., 1979.

Foss, B. *Filmmaking Narrative and Structural Techniques*. Los Angeles: Silman-James Press.

Freud, S. *The Interpretation of Dreams*. New York: Macmillan, 1911.

Hall, L. M. *The Secrets of Magic*. Carmathen, UK: Crown House Publishing, 1998.

Hauge, M. *Writing Screenplays That Sell*. New York: Harper Perennial, 1980.

Hill, J., and P. Gibson. *Film Studies*. New York: Oxford University Press, 2000.

Horn, R. E. *Visual Language*. Brainbridge, WA: Macro VU Press, 1998.

Indick, W. *Psychology for Screenwriters*. Studio City, CA: Michael Wiese Productions, 2004.

Innis, H. *The Bias of Communication*. Toronto: University of Toronto Press, 1999.

Itsuki, M. *Shoujo Manga Techniques Writing Stories*. New York: Digital Manga Publications, distributed by Watson-Guptill, 2001.

Johnson, B. *A Story Is a Promise*. Portland, OR: Blue Heron Publishing, 2000.

Johnstone, K. *Impro for Storytellers*. London: Routledge, 1999.

Katz, S. *Film Directing Shot by Shot*. Studio City, CA: Michael Wiese Productions, 1991.

Kilbourne, J. *Deadly Persuasion*. New York: Free Press, 1999.

King, V. *How to Write a Movie in 21 Days*. New York: Quill, 1993.

Lakoff, G., and M. Johnson. *Metaphors We Live By*. Chicago: University of Chicago Press, 1980.

Loker, A. *Film and Suspense*. Victoria, Canada: Trafford, 2005.

Mackendrick, A. *On Filmmaking*. New York: Farber and Farber, Inc., 2005.

Mamet, D. *On Directing Film*. New York: Penguin Books, 1992.

Martin, W. *Recent Theories of Narrative*. Ithaca, NY: Cornell University Press, 1986.

Mascelli, J. V. *The Five C's of Cinematography*. Los Angeles: Silman-James Press, 1998.

McAdams, D. *The Stories We Live By*. New York: Guilford Press, 1997.

McConnell, F. D. *The Spoken Seen*. Baltimore: Johns Hopkins University Press, 1975.

McGowan, T. *The Impossible David Lynch*. New York: Columbia University Press, 2007.

McKee, R. *Story*. New York: HarperCollins, 1997.

Meadows, M. S. *Pause and Effect*. Indianapolis, IN: New Riders, 2003.

Meredith, R., and J. Fitzgerald. *The Professional Story Writer and His Art*. New York: Apollo Editions, 1963.

Metz, C. *The Imaginary Signifier*. Bloomington, IN: Indiana University Press, 1982.

Murch, W. *In the Blink of an Eye*. Los Angeles: Silman-James Press, 2001.

Nichols, B. *Ideology and the Image*. Bloomington, IN: Indiana University Press, 1981.

Parramon, J. M. *Composition*. Tuscon, AZ: HP Books, 1987.

Peet, B. *Children's Books Series*. Boston: Sandpiper Houghton Mifflin Books, 1959–1977.

Pepperman, R. D. *The Eye Is Quicker*. Studio City, CA: Michael Wiese Productions, 2004.

Perry, J. *Encyclopedia of Acting Techniques*. Cincinnati, OH: Better Way Books, 1997.

Person, E. *Dreams of Love and Fateful Encounters*. New York: Norton, 1988.

Phillips, P. *Understanding Film Texts*. London: British Film Institute Publishing, 2000.

Plantinga, C., and G. M. Smith, Eds. *Passionate Views*. Baltimore: Johns Hopkins University Press, 1999.

Pratkanis, A., and E. Aronson. *Age of Propaganda*. New York: Owl Books, 2002.

Prendergast, R. M. *Film Music: A Neglected Art*. New York: Norton, 1992.

Rabiger, M. *Directing: Film Technique and Aesthetics*. Boston: Focal Press, 2003.

Ranson, R. *Learn Watercolor the Edgar Whitney Way*. Cincinnati, OH: North Light, 1994.

Reisz, K., and G. Millar. *The Technique of Film Editing*. New York: Hastings House, 1968.

Rothman, W. *Hitchcock: The Murderous Gaze*. Cambridge, MA: Harvard University Press, 1982.

Scheridan, S. *Developing Digital Short Films*. Berkeley, CA: New Riders, 2004.

Schwartz, M. E. *How to Write: A Screenplay*. New York: Continuum Books, 2007.

Sharff, S. *The Art of Looking in Hitchcock's Rear Window*. New York: Limelight, 1997.

Skinner, F. *Underscore*. New York: Criterion, 1960.

Sonnenschein, D. *Sound Design*. Studio City, CA: Michael Wiese Productions, 2001.

Stam, R., R. Burgoyne, and S. Flitterman-Lewis. *New Vocabularies in Film Semiotics*. London: Routledge, 1992.

Stefanik, R. M. *The Megahit Movies*. Beverly Hills, CA: RMS Productions, 2004.

Stewart, S. *Nonsense*. Baltimore: Johns Hopkins University Press, 1989.

Thomas, F., and O. Johnson. *Too Funny for Words*. New York: Abbeville Press, 1990.

Thomas, F. and O. Johnson. *Illusion of Life*. New York: Abbeville Press, 1995.

Toth, A. *Alex Toth by Design*. Gold Medal Productions, 1996.

Turner, M. *The Literary Mind*. New York: Oxford University Press, 1996.

Volger, C. *The Writer's Journey*. Studio City, CA: Michael Wiese Productions, 2007.

Vorhaus, H. *The Comic Toolbox*. Los Angeles: Silman-James Press, 1994.

Wagner, J., and T. Van Hasselt. *The Watercolor Fix-It Book*. Cincinnati, OH: North Light, 1992.

Index